THE LATE
WILL AND TESTAMENT
OF THE
DOCTORS COMMONS.

66g. f. 4.
30

Shewing how he hath difpofed of his Commiffioners, Doctors, Proctors, Surrogates,
Meffengers, Examinors, Parators and Promootors, and the reft of his Attendants,
With a fhort deportment of his Legacies, and how he hath
bequeathed them.

I Doctors Commons, in the Parifh of S. *Benedicts* Pauls-Wharf, being very aged, and finding by generall Com-
putation, that my time drawes to an end, and likewife much fhaken both in Body and mind with a *Weftminfter* ague, yet
of perfect mind and memory, to avoid all fuits and controverfies that hereafter may arife concerning my eftate, or any
part or parcell thereof, and to the intent and purpofe that my contentious days may be confummated and ended in Peace,
Doe conftitute, ordaine, declare and make this my laft will and Teftament in manner and forme following, That is to fay,
Imprimis, for my foele, I bequeath it to Gun-powder Makers, to be made into Gun-powder, which fhall be employed only for the difcharge of the new Canons : *Item*, I bequeath my body to the earth, from whence it came, decently to be buried, but not fumptuoufly, in the Convocation houfe, in the Cathedrall Church of S. *Pauls*, London, aforefaid, according
to the difcretion of my Executors hereafter named. *Item*, for my perfonall eftate (having never bin poffeffed of any lands,
I willingly bequeath the reverend Judges, Vicars-Generals, Chancellors, Commiffaries, Arch-Deacons, Deanes and Chapters; and their furrogates, and alfo all high Commiffioners, Judges, Delegats, Advocates, and *Legum Doctores quofcunque*,
Og, the great Commiffarie, alias Doctor *Roan* onely excepted, to the high Court of Parliament, there to bee cherifhed
according to their merits and defervings. *Item*, I bequeath all my Regifters, Deputy Regifters, Proctors, Examinors, and
publike notaries, to the court of Common-Pleas, at Weftminfter, to be admitted Attournies, (if no prohibition be granted to the contrary.) *Item*, I will and bequeath all my fifty pound Clearks, to their Friends in the Country, or to the Jufti-
ces of the Peace and *Quorum*. *Item*, I will and bequeath all my Journey-men Clearks, Hackney, and fub-hackney Clerks,
to *Chancery-lane*, and *Brittanick S. Hugh Preftar*, to the Star-Chamber. *Item*, I will and bequeath all my Purfuants, Appara-
tors, Promooters, &c. to under-Sheriffs, but in cafe they have no need of them, then I bequeath them to their ghoftly Father, unto whom they have moft relation. *Item*, I will and bequeath all my writings and records, as followeth : my bonds
to large meafuring Taylors, my Bils, Tranfmiffions and the like, to retailing Tobacconifts, my incontinent Articles to
Bloomesbury, Long-Acre, and other like places of good fellowfhip, my libels of diffamation, to the penitentiall
fcolds, there to be ordered according to their difcretions, all my Commiffions of Appeale to the parties appellant, for
they have the moft right unto them, in regard they have paid for them : *Item*, I will and bequeath all my large Bookes of
Acts, to them of the Fortune Play-Houfe, for I hold it a deed of charity, in regard they want good action ; my decrees to
the courts of *Chancery*, in cafe they want any ; My fentences to thofe Orators that imitate *Tullies quanquam te Marce fili*,
&c. for they are fomething long ; And laftly, I will and bequeath my Cannons, charged with &c. to the Tower, to de-
fend him that made them, and all the reft of my writings, efcripts, manufcripts, and fuperfluous papers whatfoever to
Cookes, Bakers, Grocers, and Chandlers. *Item*, I make the Scotch-men my Executors, (who I doubt not) but with all
diligence will fee the execution of this my laft will and Teftament, and defire they will fee thefe my Legacies, paid and per-
formed immediately after my deceafe : In Witneffe whereof, I the faid Doctors Commons have hereunto fet my hand and
Seale this 26 of June, in the yeare of our Lord, 1 6 4 1.

Signed, fealed, publifhed, and declared
in the Prefence of

W. C.
R. P.
B. K.

'The late will and testament of the Doctors Commons.' A 1641 tract using the style of a
will to satirize the alleged corruption and inefficiency at Doctors Commons, the home
of the Prerogative Court of Canterbury. *British Library: Thomason Tracts, 669. f. 4 (30)*

Wills and Other Probate Records

A practical guide to researching your ancestors' last documents

Karen Grannum and Nigel Taylor

the national archives

First published in 2004 by

The National Archives
Kew, Richmond
Surrey, TW9 4DU, UK

www.nationalarchives.gov.uk

The National Archives (TNA) was formed when the Public Record Office (PRO) and Historical Manuscripts (HMC) Commission combined in April 2003

ISBN 1 903365 49 X

Front cover illustrations: Will of Charles Nightingale proved January 1758 (PROB 10/2222); will of Cornelius Vanderstop of Saint George Hanover Square proved December 1789 (PROB 10/3134); photograph of Lady Davy reading, 1892 (COPY 1/409).

Back cover illustration: Several lines from the will of John Hedges written in verse, 1737 (PROB 10/1850, f. 72).

All document references are TNA: PRO unless stated otherwise.

Typeset by Textype, Cambridge, Cambridgeshire
Printed in the UK by Antony Rowe, Chippenham, Wiltshire

Contents

Preface

Wills have long been recognized as a valuable source of information for family historians. They can help fill gaps in your knowledge and open up fresh lines of research. They can also provide further information into family relationships and possessions.

Our own interest in wills and probate records developed from the start of our National Archives careers, when we worked in the old Public Record Office in Chancery Lane, in the heart of legal London. In a room called the Rolls Room, and later the Rolls Chapel, we helped readers find wills, inventories, and documents relating to disputes.

Wills and other associated probate records are also a key source for local, social, financial and economic historians and for biographers and historians generally. Associated records such as inventories and accounts often provide an intriguing glimpse of how our ancestors lived and may give the value of their personal property in minute detail.

Although wills can be dry and formulaic, they are also one of the few 'official' records that convey personal feelings and thoughts. From what other source could you learn that David Davis despised his wife to such an extent that in 1788 he left her 'the sum of five shillings', which he thought 'sufficient to enable her to get drunk for the last time at my expense'? Some wills are even written in the hand of the deceased themselves – for example, that of Jane Austen.

Our experience helping people with their enquiries highlighted the need for a practical guide that reveals how to find probate records, including less well-known records such as administration bonds and probate accounts. This guide explains the content of these records and places them in context with the relevant legislation. It also covers the primary sources for wills and related records from the earliest to the most modern – from wills found among ancient documents to those of the recently deceased.

In addition to the holdings of the National Archives and the Borthwick Institute of Historical Research, at the University of York, we have covered those of the various county archives throughout the country. The book's coverage also extends to the records held at institutions such as the Bank of England and the British Library, and looks beyond England to holdings in other parts of the British

Isles and in the Republic of Ireland. Nowadays no publication in the genealogical field can afford to ignore the growing number of wills or catalogues available online. This publication is no exception, with special mention being made of DocumentsOnline, the National Archives' collection of more than a million Prerogative Court of Canterbury wills.

Included too are chapters on death duty records – a key source for measuring wealth – and on litigation over wills, which can reveal unexpected aspects of an ancestor's life and character. As well as covering disputes brought before the church courts, this guide also refers to those dealt with by the secular courts, such as the Court of Chancery and Court of King's Bench, and explains some of the complexities of what was heard where, in language that can be understood by readers not familiar with ecclesiastical and legal history.

Karen Grannum and Nigel Taylor

Acknowledgements

We are indebted to the following colleagues at the National Archives for their assistance with this publication: Rosemary Amos, Stella Colwell, Sean Cunningham, Carol Dickson for her assistance in extracting statistical data from DocumentsOnline, Guy Grannum, Sheila Knight, Peter Leek, Malcolm Mercer for his help on Latin translations, Sarah Stark and Suzanne Woodley. We would particularly like to thank Amanda Bevan, who gave valuable help and assistance.

Outside TNA, we would like to thank Jackie Hill and Gary Wright of Iron Mountain for finding and providing an image of the will of Lily Langtry, and Kevin Donnelly of the Court Service for kindly photographing the National Probate Calendar entry for Lily Langtry at the Probate Searchroom in London. We would also like to thank Gary Beirne of the Court Service for his advice on modern records and plans for digitization.

Using The National Archives

The National Archives (TNA) was created on 2 April 2003, when the Public Record Office (PRO) and the Historical Manuscripts Commission (HMC) joined together to form a new organization. The National Archives is the national repository for central government records in the United Kingdom.

The main site at Kew holds British central government records ranging from the Domesday Book (1086) to the present day. There are millions of records, occupying more than 175 kilometres of shelving, and another 2 to 3 kilometres of documents are added at the beginning of each calendar year. Records of military and naval service, legal proceedings, charters, wills, photographs and one of the world's great accumulations of maps and plans are just a sample of the types of document that make the National Archives an invaluable resource for family and local historians.

The Family Records Centre (FRC) in central London is administered jointly by the National Archives and the General Register Office. It provides access to some of the most important sources for family history research in England and Wales, including birth, marriage and death certificates from 1837 onwards and the population census returns from 1841 to 1901.

Contact details

The National Archives
Kew
Richmond
Surrey
TW9 4DU

Telephone: 020 8876 3444
Website: **www.nationalarchives.gov.uk**

The Family Records Centre
1 Myddelton Street
London
EC1R 1UW

Telephone: 020 8392 5300
Website: **www.familyrecords.gov.uk/frc**

Enquiries and advance ordering of documents at Kew (with exact references only):

Telephone: 020 8392 5200
Fax: 020 8392 5286
Email: **enquiry@nationalarchives.gov.uk**

Opening times

Monday	9 a.m. to 5 p.m.
Tuesday	10 a.m. to 7 p.m.
Wednesday	9 a.m. to 5 p.m.
Thursday	9 a.m. to 7 p.m.
Friday	9 a.m. to 5 p.m.
Saturday	9.30 a.m. to 5 p.m.

The reading rooms are closed on Sundays and public holidays, and for annual stocktaking – usually the first week of December.

Note that the last time for ordering original documents for same-day production is 4 p.m. on Monday, Wednesday and Friday; 4.30 p.m. on Tuesday and Thursday; and 3.00 p.m. on Saturday.

The National Archives at Kew

The National Archives main site is about 10 minutes' walk from Kew Gardens station, which is on the London Underground District Line and the North London Line Silverlink Metro service. A number of bus routes pass nearby. The site is signposted from the South Circular Road (A205); a free car park is available.

Facilities include a restaurant, a bookshop, a cyber café, a reference library and a small museum.

The National Archives may seem a confusing place on your first visit, but staff are knowledgeable, friendly and happy to help. It is always best to bring with you as much relevant information as you can. If you have access to the Internet, it is worth doing some preliminary research on our website before you come: there are research guides on many of the most popular areas of research, and a searchable online catalogue of the records, as well as much general information about our services.

You do not need to make an appointment to visit, but a reader's ticket is required to gain access to the research areas and to order documents. To obtain a reader's ticket, you need to bring some means of personal identification, such as a banker's card, passport or full UK driving licence, if you are a British citizen; and a passport or national identity card, if you are not.

To protect the documents, most of which are unique, eating, drinking and smoking are not permitted in the reading rooms. No personal bags may be taken into the reading rooms: free self-service lockers are available. You may take a laptop computer into the reading rooms as well as graphite (black lead) pencils, a notebook and up to 20 loose sheets of paper; the use of rubbers, pens (including felt-tips) and coloured pencils is not permitted. Mobile phones may not be used. All original records and reference books should be handled with great care.

Identifying and ordering documents

To view a document at the National Archives, either in its original form or on microfilm or microfiche, you need first to identify its document reference. TNA (PRO) document references usually consist of three parts: department code, series number and piece number. When they are transferred to the National Archives, the records of a government department are normally assigned a department code reflecting their provenance: for example, records created by the Prerogative Court of Canterbury commence with the department code PROB. Each category of records transferred by a department is then assigned a series number: for example, PROB 2 is the series of Prerogative Court of Canterbury records that contains inventories compiled between 1417 and 1668. Each separate document (known as a 'piece') within a series is given its own individual piece number: for example, the reference for the piece that contains the inventory (dated 1559) of John Abyn, a merchant from Salisbury, is PROB 2/356. This is the full reference you need to order the document.

Document references can be found by using the printed *PRO Guide* and series lists in the reading rooms or by searching TNA's online catalogue, which is accessible via the National Archives website or through computer terminals in the reading rooms at Kew and in the Census and Wills Reading Room at the Family Records Centre. The online catalogue can be searched using keywords such as a person's name or a place name. More specific searches can be carried out by specifying dates and/or series references. Do bear in mind, however, that the catalogue was not designed to give the detailed information about individuals that the documents themselves may contain. So, for example, the catalogue entry for PROB 2/356 does not itemize the personal estate of John Abyn: you will have to look at the actual document to discover this. If an online catalogue search is successful, document references relevant to your research will be listed on screen.

Once you have the necessary reference, original documents may be ordered via a computerized ordering system and are usually delivered within 30 minutes. Documents on microfilm can be accessed on a self-service basis in the Microfilm Reading Room.

All probate catalogues are in the Research Enquiries Room and are duplicated in the Map and Large Document Reading Room. The supplementary finding aids are divided between the Research Enquiries Room and the Microfilm Reading Room. DocumentsOnline can be searched from any terminal in the public areas.

Records held elsewhere

Many records of value for family and local history are held in other record offices and libraries. The National Register of Archives – maintained by TNA and available on the National Archives website – contains information about the whereabouts of records in local record offices and local studies libraries and in other repositories in England and Wales. Probate records held by the British Library and the Bank of England are described in sections 10.8 and 10.9.

For the whereabouts of records relating to Scotland, Northern Ireland, the Republic of Ireland, the Channel Islands and the Isle of Man, see Chapter 11.

1
Introduction

This chapter answers basic questions such as 'What is a will?' and defines other important terms associated with wills. It provides an introduction to the various kinds of information that can be obtained from wills (with an emphasis on family history), briefly explains the reasons why some people or bequests were legally excluded, and includes a section on the process of probate.

Chapters 1–10 are primarily concerned with England and Wales. Scotland, Northern Ireland, the Republic of Ireland, the Channel Islands and the Isle of Man are dealt with in Chapter 11.

1.1 Wills as sources

Wills are documents in which people try to exert control over their property – and their heirs – after their death. Over the centuries, what would happen to property in the absence of a will has been governed by a variety of laws and customs, generally allowing so much to support the deceased's widow and other dependants, so much to go direct to the next heir, and so on. A will gives greater scope, allowing the testator to support a wider range of people and to leave property exactly as he or she wishes – for example, to a best friend, a trusted servant, the poor of the local parish, or even to a home for wayward boys and girls.

Centuries or decades after the creation of a will, we are able to use it as a prime source for finding out more about the testator's life, family and times. As with all documents that serve as sources for family history, this is not the purpose the writer had in mind. We therefore need to learn what can be taken at face value and what is merely traditional wording; what is meaningful and what is not necessarily significant; whether all close relatives or property that might be of interest are likely to have been mentioned; and if not, where else to look. It can be very easy to jump to conclusions – and not necessarily the right ones.

Every so often, over the centuries, the state displayed an interest in wills, whether to inhibit avoidance of taxes or dues payable to the Crown or to try to eliminate fraud. But making a will has never been obligatory. In some instances where no will was made, the transfer of property took place according to local knowledge or custom, perhaps through manorial courts or informally. In other cases, the next of kin or creditors were able to go to court to obtain authority to administer and dispose of the deceased's property – again, according to set rules.

1.1.1 Who made wills?

What kind of people left wills?
People from all strata of society, from the highest (the titled gentry) to the lowest, even paupers. Wills were more common among wealthy people because they were more likely to have complicated estates and financial matters that needed putting in order prior to death. Also, they were more likely to be able to afford the often complained about fees of the ecclesiastical courts. Having less to dispose of, the poor had less need to make a will.

But it should not be assumed that because a family was poor there would not be a will. In the days of the ecclesiastical courts, which court would consider an application for probate depended on the value of the estate. The poorer members of society were therefore more likely to have had their wills proved by an archdeacon's or bishop's court, rather than by the archbishop's court (see 2.1.4).

If you think your ancestor may not have left a will as his or her occupation was too lowly, you may be encouraged by the range of testators whose wills were proved by the lower courts. In the eighteenth century, the archdeaconry court in Berkshire proved wills of brewers, bricklayers, broadweavers, collar makers, cordwainers, drapers, gardeners, grocers, harness makers, labourers, servants, tanners and waggoners.

Other occupations mentioned in old wills include baker and gingerbread baker, barrister, innkeeper, surgeon, merchant and tailor. Often men are simply described as gentleman, and women as widow or spinster.

How many people left wills?
It is not easy to say what proportion of the population left wills. The most straightforward method of determining this would be to compare the number of wills with the number of adults buried, given in records such as parish registers. Unfortunately this is not as straightforward as it sounds. Many burial records give only the name and date of death of the deceased, so it is impossible to tell whether the death was of a child or an adult. Also, certain members of society, such as married women, were barred from making wills (see 1.5.1).

Since 1858 – when the church courts ceased to have jurisdiction over probate (see 1.1.2) – the number of people making wills has steadily increased (see 5.1.2). In particular, the number of women leaving wills grew following the Married Women's Property Act of 1882 (see 6.1.7.3).

Why did people leave wills?
People would decide to draft a will in order to settle their affairs, to ensure that their family or dependants were provided for, to make charitable bequests, and to remember friends.

Generally, people did not make wills early in life. There was much superstition among the medieval and early modern populace, and it may have been thought that to make a will too early in life might tempt fate and accelerate death.

Some people sorted out their estate and any marriage settlements years before they died, thus making the necessity for a will redundant. However, a will may have been considered a prudent precaution if there was the possibility of the wife remarrying (especially if she was young) – in which case her possessions would have become the property of her new husband (see 1.5.1). Also, a will may well have been judged necessary if it seemed likely there would be a dispute.

1.1.2 What courts did they use?

Before a will could be put into effect, it had to be 'proved' (accepted as valid) and registered by one of a number of courts.

- Until 1858, these were church courts – more than 200 of them, in all. Most people lived within reach of a church court of some kind. Unfortunately for family historians and other researchers, all these courts kept separate registers of wills and there was no central index.
- From 12 January 1858, the state took over, with the establishment of a new Court of Probate based in London. The new court had an extensive local network, consisting of 40 district registries where wills could be proved. In addition, wills of lower value could be proved at more than 250 offices of the Inland Revenue, scattered across England and Wales. Details of all wills were sent up to the central court for inclusion in a union index.

1.1.3 Wills for family history

The information contained in wills is rich with genealogical value. Indeed, it has been estimated that every will gives the names of 10 people associated with the deceased – though wills vary from the very short, naming maybe just one beneficiary, to extensive documents, running to as much as a hundred pages, with many individuals mentioned.

Wills can give an insight into the lifestyle and status of a family. For example, a series of bequests of scholarly books would indicate an interest in learning. They may display deeply felt emotions: love, hate, exasperation, or protectiveness. References to non-family members – trusted servants, business associates, local worthies – can help to reveal aspects of family life and may provide clues to a wider story.

Also, if one member of a family has left a written will, it is likely that other members of the family, from earlier and later generations, may have left wills, too.

1.1.4 Wills for local, social and economic history

Perhaps because of the difficulties in locating wills according to trade or place, until recently they were not generally regarded as a prime source for local, social or economic history. But now many more wills are searchable online (see 3.3) by place or occupation, and so the types of research for which they can be used have been greatly extended. Wills can, for example, be a helpful source in plotting the growth of a village or a trade, or the influence of landed families in an area or the spread of business contacts.

Identifying farmers, yeomen, butchers, wheelwrights, clergymen or lawyers and examining their wills in conjunction with linked evidence, such as inventories and accounts, can allow the identification of social trends, or patterns of activity such as booms and slumps, across places and time. A number of important studies (some on a national basis and others on a regional basis) of the various social classes have drawn extensively on such records. (For some of the academic publications that have used these sources, see Further Reading, p.213.)

Charitable bequests – including those that actually create a charity – can offer an insight into the religious and philanthropic nature of society. In addition a particularly generous bequest may prompt further research, to try to ascertain the motive for the testator's generosity.

1.2 Some key terms

Are a will and a testament the same thing?
Basically, a will is a declaration of the testator's wishes and instructions regarding his or her property that are to be put into effect after death. Strictly, the terms

'will' and 'testament' – which are often used together in the preamble to a will – relate to different categories of property:

- Originally, under common law, the *will* was solely concerned with land held on a freehold basis (see 1.5.3), also referred to as *real estate*. This was *devised*, not bequeathed. However, by the sixteenth century the expressions 'will' and 'testament' had become interchangeable.
- Originally, the term *testament* dealt with the testator's *personal estate* (or *personalty*) – including cash, credits, leases, goods and chattels (moveable possessions) – which are *bequeathed* as *bequests*.

For a long time there were severe restrictions on the willing of land, as land transfer was governed by strict rules – initially to protect the Crown's rights to feudal and other dues. To get round this and other problems, a wide variety of trusts and 'uses' (special kinds of trust – see 1.5.3) were developed by lawyers over the centuries. If you come across these and are not sure what is being intended, consult a legal dictionary. You may find *An Introduction to English Legal History* by J. H. Baker (Butterworth, 3rd edn 1990) helpful, too.

What is a nuncupative will?
- A *nuncupative will* is an oral or 'spoken' will, subsequently written down from evidence given by witnesses.

What is an estate?
- Not as grand as it sounds! The possessions of the deceased – whether a humble cottage or a stately home, a single cooking pot or a porcelain dinner service and an array of valuable paintings – are collectively known as his or her estate.

What is a codicil?
- A codicil is a properly witnessed supplement to a will, containing anything that the testator wishes to add. Notes and insertions cannot be added to a will without making it invalid.
- A codicil can be used to explain the contents of the will or make additional bequests, or to revoke, revise or cancel any of the provisions of the will.
- Codicils are treated as part of the will.

What is a testator? And an intestate?
- A *testator* is a person who leaves a will. A female testator is sometimes referred to as a *testatrix*.
- An *intestate* is someone who dies without making a will, or who leaves a will that is not proved to be valid. The legal term for such a situation is *intestacy*.

What is a beneficiary?
- A *beneficiary* is someone who is to benefit from the will – someone who has been left a *bequest* or a *legacy* by the testator.

What is an executor?
- An *executor* is someone nominated by the testator to put the provisions of the will into effect, by *executing* (carrying out) the wishes of the testator. The testator may nominate one or more executors. A female executor is sometimes referred to as an *executrix*.
- In order to put the provisions of the will into effect, an executor has to obtain a grant of *probate*.

What is probate?
- Probate is the official recognition by a relevant court of law that a will has been *proved* – accepted as legally valid, in that it has been properly witnessed, has not been tampered with, and conforms to all other requirements of the law.
- Probate does not concern itself with the detailed contents of the will.
- The granting of probate allows the executor or executors to *administer* the will – the legal term for putting the provisions of a will into effect.

So what is 'a probate'?
- Generally the court would give an executor a copy of the will with the text of the grant of probate added to it to work from as he or she administered the testator's estate. Such a copy of the will is sometimes referred to as a *probate*.

What are administrations? And administrators?
- An *administration* (sometimes abbreviated to *admon*) is a grant, made by a relevant court, authorizing an appropriate person to administer the estate when no valid will has been left by the deceased.
- *Letters of administration* may be granted to the widow or next of kin or to a creditor. They allow the *administrator* nominated by the court to collect rents and debts and to distribute the estate.
- The estate has to be distributed according to fixed rules (see 4.1.2 and 4.1.3) under the supervision of the court.
- This process would not take effect in all cases of intestacy – only if an appropriate person applied for letters of administration.
- Sometimes administrations may be granted after the granting of probate – for example, if an executor dies and someone else needs to be appointed to distribute the estate.

1.3 Administrations as sources

Although grants of administration do not contain as much information as wills, they can be very valuable for family historians, as they often mention underage children and other next of kin. For local or economic historians, they can be helpful in that administrators were quite often creditors, trying to get back money owed them from various enterprises.

1.4 Early wills

Documents described as wills or testaments survive from the Anglo–Saxon ninth century, although the immediate origins were from the Germanic peoples on the Continent, who brought over a will-making tradition when they invaded and settled in Britain that can be traced back to the Roman Empire. The early history of wills is not clear and has generated much discussion among academics. For more about early wills, see Michael M. Sheehan's *The Will in Medieval England* (Pontifical Institute of Mediaeval Studies, Toronto, Studies and Texts No. 6, 1963) and Dorothy Whitelock's *Anglo–Saxon Wills* (Cambridge University Press, 1930).

It is not known to what extent wills were made orally, even after the Norman Conquest. These oral wills may have been just a few sentences spoken in the presence of witnesses, and not always committed to writing. It is likely that this kind of will (or rather testament – see 1.2) persisted among the poor and those unable to make wills (such as married women – see 1.5.1) for centuries, with relatives and husbands disposing of small possessions and keepsakes quite informally.

The church developed a virtual monopoly on the probate of wills. Over the centuries, it used a mixture of ecclesiastical law (comprising civil law and canon law), common law and statute law. Priests made it clear that the dying man was duty bound to make atonement for the wrongs he had committed – particularly the non-payment of tithes (church taxes) – and to use part of his wealth for the relief of the poor. In fact, testaments developed first and were only later joined by wills. Charitable bequests were a notable feature of pre-Reformation testaments, often tied in with requests for prayers for the testator's soul. Unfortunately, this meant that the charitable bequests were appropriated by the Crown when prayers for the dead were forbidden by Henry VIII and Edward VI. Later charitable bequests were framed so as not to fall foul of laws against 'superstitious uses'. See 2.5 for origins of the medieval will.

1.5 Restrictions on will making

1.5.1 Invalid testators

Not everybody could make a valid will. Some people were barred from doing so or considered incapable:

Married women
- Until the Married Women's Property Act of 1882, married women were deemed to have no legal existence separate from their husband during his lifetime. Consequently, a married woman was only able to make a will with her husband's specific permission. A woman who acquired property after a judicial separation or protection order was allowed to make a will for that property only.

Children and adolescents
- girls under 12 until 1837
- boys under 14 until 1837
- anyone under 21 from 1837
  – except any soldier on active military service or any mariner or seaman at sea

Those incapacitated by disabilities or insanity
- deaf from birth (and therefore dumb)
- lunatic or idiot

Criminals
- including traitors, libellers, usurers, felons and suicides
  (these restrictions were abolished by the 1870 Forfeiture Act)

For further details, see 6.1.7.

1.5.2 Changing rules on will validity

Witnesses
- From 1677, the signatures of three witnesses were required.
- From 1837, only two witnesses were needed.
- If an otherwise valid will had not been witnessed, the court would accept affidavits (sworn statements) that the will was in the testator's handwriting or that it was intended as a valid last will.

Oral wills
- From 1677, nuncupative wills (see 6.1.3) involving estates worth more than £30 had to have been made at the time of the last sickness of the deceased and in the

deceased's own dwelling house or where he or she had resided 10 days before. In addition, they had to be proved by three witnesses.
- From 1837, oral wills were no longer valid, except for those made by soldiers on active service or by sailors (both naval and merchant seamen) at sea.

Date of effect
- Before 1837, a gift of the testator's estate was taken as the real estate as it existed when the will was made, and the personal estate as at the time of death.
- From 1837, a gift of the testator's real or personal estate was taken as that existing at the time of death.

1.5.3 Wills of land

Before 1540, freehold land could not be left by will. Instead, it descended by the laws of inheritance, usually to the eldest son. A man wishing to vary the strict rules of land inheritance (to provide for a gaggle of younger sons, for example) had to set up a kind of trust called a *use* that transferred ownership of the land to trustees who would hold the land for the purposes specified in his will. Henry VIII tried to block this, but eventually in 1540 he had to give way and allow at least some land to be devisable by will, under the Statute of Wills of that year.

Leases of land did not count as real estate but as personalty (see 1.2) and so could be bequeathed by will. Land held by copyhold tenure (manorial land held by copy of court roll) was not transferable by will until 1926. See 3.5.2.

1.6 The process of gaining probate

By an act of 1529 ('concerning fines and sums of money to be taken by ministers of bishops and other ordinaries of Holy Church for the probate of Testaments') it was specified that probate was to be granted with 'convenient speed without any frustratory delay'. Although the exact procedure and practices varied between the various courts, the act did serve as a general template. It set out the court fees that had to be paid and stipulated that the certification of the oath, sometimes called a *jurat*, had to be written on the back of the will, declaring when, where and before whom it was sworn.

This had to be done before the executor presented him/herself to be sworn by the surrogate (deputy judge) on behalf of the archbishop, bishop or archdeacon (depending on the type of church court) as to the due execution of the will. The executor's oath states that he/she would faithfully execute the same, paying debts and legacies, and bring in a 'true and perfect inventory'. After the swearing of the oath, a transcript or copy of the will was copied on parchment and delivered to the register scribe or other officer of the bishop, etc. (For more about the role of the executor, see 6.1.9.)

By the second half of the nineteenth century, simple instructions on how to gain probate were given in publications such as *Whitaker's Almanack*. The 1896 edition advised that when applying for probate executors should bring a registrar's certificate of death or an official certificate of burial, together with the will and full details of the property and debts of the deceased. It added that if there was no will, or no executor appointed, then two sureties would have to attend and enter into a bond for the faithful administration of the estate (see 4.5).

2

Church Courts and Records before 1858

Before 1858 the task of proving wills and granting administrations was the responsibility of the church. This chapter looks at why this came about and how the will evolved into a complicated legal document. Chapter 3 will explain how to find wills and administrations before 1858. For wills and administrations in Scotland, Northern Ireland, the Republic of Ireland, the Channel Islands and the Isle of Man, see Chapter 11.

2.1 Ecclesiastical courts

2.1.1 Authority of the church

Ecclesiastical courts were established as a separate entity from the secular courts from at least the reign of William the Conqueror. The church courts operated under canon law (see 2.1.2), and as well as dealing with testamentary affairs they were responsible for:

- the discipline of the clergy
- the fabric of church buildings
- suppressing recusancy (refusal to attend the parish church)
- non-payment of tithes
- matrimonial disputes
- defamation
- heresy

The main punishments administered by the church were excommunication and public penance. Secular courts would hear more serious offences, such as rape, as they had the power to execute or imprison.

Before 1858, there were more than 200 church courts scattered across the country and there was no single, united pattern of church administration.

Like the secular courts, the church courts operated in a hierarchy. England and Wales were divided into two provinces: York and Canterbury. Each province consisted of a number of dioceses and was presided over by an archbishop. Each of the dioceses consisted of several archdeaconries and was presided over by two or more bishops. Each archdeaconry was presided over by an archdeacon and consisted of a number of rural deaneries.

2.1.2 Canon law

The rules for the proving of wills and the granting of administrations were a combination of statute and ecclesiastical canon law, which existed side by side. Canon law consisted of proclamations issued by convocations (assemblies of the clergy gathered by their representatives to discuss ecclesiastical affairs). Ecclesiastical canons are certain rules and regulations, mostly concerning conduct or belief, defined by the church.

Despite England's break with Rome in 1534 following the divorce of Henry VIII and Catherine of Aragon, convocations for the provinces of Canterbury and York remained in operation. However, after the Act for the Submission of the Clergy (1533), they lost most of their power and independence. Convocations could only meet by royal command, and only with royal permission could new canons be made. In addition, the king could review all new and existing canons and prevent their execution or enforcement.

2.1.3 Origins of the medieval will

It may seem odd to modern observers that the church was once responsible for the proving of wills and the granting of administrations. Originally, the management of the will would have interested both the ecclesiastical authorities (the last confession and any charitable bequests) and the lay authorities (distribution of property at death).

The church was in an excellent position to take responsibility for the process of proving wills. On a person's deathbed, a priest would have been called to administer the last sacrament and hear the final confession. At this point, the individual would have made his final wishes regarding his estate known. The majority of these early medieval wills were nuncupative (spoken). See 6.1.3.

It is not known whether there was a conscious decision to grant the clergy responsibility for the probate of wills, or whether this simply evolved. Certainly secular courts would have been unable to grant probate without the help of the church. When a written will was made, it was likely that an educated priest would have been the one to draft it; and it was the clergy who would have received the will or heard the testator's final wishes during his or her last hours (see 6.1). Following the testator's death, it was the clergy who, if necessary, clarified points within the will. And when someone died without leaving a will, it was the clergy who advised on the wishes of the deceased regarding his or her estate.

The role of the secular courts in the probate process should not, however, be overlooked. Although the ecclesiastical courts were responsible for the proving of wills and the granting of administrations, they had jurisdiction over personal goods only – such as furniture, livestock, leaseholds, crops, jewellery and fabrics. Secular courts claimed jurisdiction over real estate (see 1.5.3).

2.1.4 *The rule of* bona notabilia *(noteworthy goods)*

Before 1604 archbishops claimed exclusive rights to administer estates where a person had goods (*bona*) in more than one diocese. Attempts by bishops and archdeacons to curb the power of the archbishops, and so increase their own revenues, resulted in the influential canons of 1604. These specified that:

- All witnesses, administrators and executors were to take an oath declaring whether or not there were any goods or debts in any other diocese within the province and their value. If there were goods in more than one diocese, then the case had to be referred to the archbishop's court within 40 days. No oath was required from executors or administrators by the archbishop's court unless there were objections.
- Only the estates of people dying with *bona notabilia* ('noteworthy goods') totalling £5 or more (the practice in London was £10) in more than one diocese were to be dealt with by the archbishop's court. Any person without goods in more than one diocese to the value of £5 or more was considered not to have *bona notabilia*, and so his or her estate would be dealt with by a lower ecclesiastical court (such as a bishop's or an archdeacon's court).

It is important to keep in mind the rule of *bona notabilia*, as it forms a crucial part of the probate and administration process. It was this rule that determined which court a will would be proved in, and consequently where the documents are now located.

2.2 How to find a will or administration

2.2.1 Which ecclesiastical court?

As explained above, before 1858 the amount of goods and property left by the deceased and where those goods were (in terms of ecclesiastical jurisdictions) determined in which court a will was to be proved.

To further complicate matters, testamentary court records are arranged by the date on which the probate or administration was granted, rather than by the date of death or the date on which the will was written – and, although wills were often written when the testator was on his or her deathbed, there is sometimes a large discrepancy between these dates. Straightforward wills might take a couple of months to prove, whereas complicated or disputed estates could take many years.

It is therefore important to try to establish:

- the name of the person
- the approximate place where the testator or intestate was living
- the approximate date on which the testator or intestate died

Chapter 3 explains the practicalities of how to find a will, but as a broad rule of thumb:

- If the testator or intestate lived in the north of England (the dioceses of Carlisle, Chester, Durham and York, covering the counties of Cheshire, Cumberland, Durham, Lancashire, Northumberland, Nottinghamshire, Westmorland and Yorkshire) and was reasonably wealthy (having goods totalling £5 or more in more than one diocese), the will or administration would be granted by the **Prerogative Court of York** (see 2.3).

- If the testator or intestate lived in the south of England or in Wales (Berkshire, Buckinghamshire, Cambridgeshire, Cornwall, Derbyshire, Devon, Dorset, Essex, Gloucestershire, Hampshire, Herefordshire, Hertfordshire, Huntingdonshire, Kent, Leicestershire, Lincolnshire, London, Middlesex, Norfolk, Northamptonshire, Oxfordshire, Rutland, Shropshire, Somerset, Staffordshire, Surrey, Sussex, Suffolk, Wales, Warwickshire, Wiltshire and Worcestershire) and was reasonably wealthy (having goods totalling £5 or more in more than one diocese), the will or administration would be granted by the **Prerogative Court of Canterbury** (see 2.4).

- If the testator or intestate had goods in more than one archdeaconry but all in the same diocese, the will or administration would be granted by the **bishop's court** (known as a **consistory court** or **commissary court**). If the goods were in just one archdeaconry, the will or administration would be granted by the **archdeacon's court.**

- The records of archdeacons' and bishops' courts will generally be found in the local county or diocesan record office for the county of the deceased's residence, but changing boundaries and jurisdictions complicate this and it is worth consulting a guide to probate jurisdictions. For further information, see *Probate Jurisdictions: Where To Look For Wills* by Jeremy Gibson and Else Churchill (FFHS, 5th edn 2002).

- In the event of someone dying with *bona notabilia* (see 2.1.4) in both the northern and the southern province, separate grants of probate or administration would be issued to cover the effects in each. This was because the jurisdiction of each archbishop was confined to his own province (see *A Brief Treatise of Bona Notabilia Within the Province of York* by George Lawton, 1825).

Over time the archbishops started to encroach upon the territory of the bishops, and in turn the bishops encroached upon the territory of the archdeacons. The archbishops' courts gradually began to prove wills and grant administrations irrespective of the rule of *bona notabilia*, until eventually the boundaries were eroded. In addition, the £5 threshold set in 1604 did not fluctuate over time. Consequently, in the eighteenth and nineteenth centuries many people who previously would have been excluded from the archbishops' courts had their testamentary business conducted there, and many of the smaller courts were superseded before the act of 1857 abolished them.

Relevant court?

Location of property	Relevant court	Location of records
In more than one diocese (with *bona notabilia* – goods amounting to £5 or more)	Archbishop's Prerogative Court	*York:* Borthwick Institute *Canterbury:* The National Archives (can also be viewed at the Family Records Centre and on DocumentsOnline)
In more than one archdeaconry, but all in the same diocese	Bishop's court (known as a consistory or commissary court)	Local record office
Within one archdeaconry	Archdeacon's court – or possibly a 'peculiar court' with local jurisdiction (see 3.5.1)	Local record office

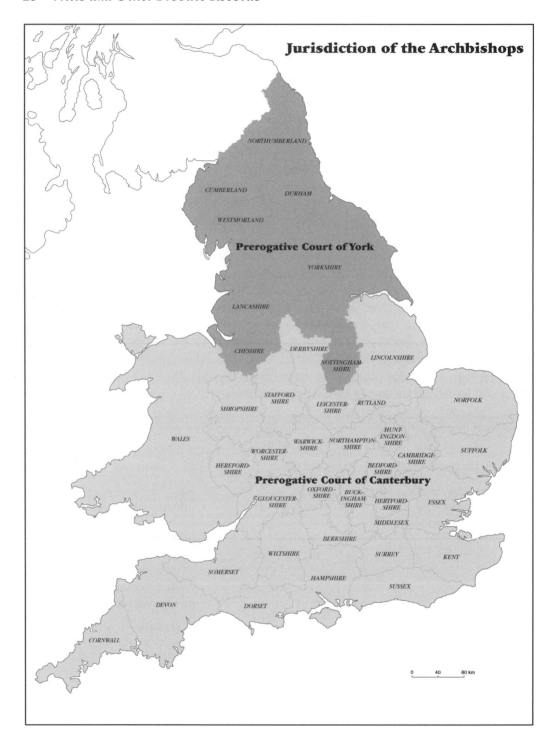

Jurisdiction of the Archbishops

NORTHUMBERLAND

CUMBERLAND   DURHAM

WESTMORLAND

Prerogative Court of York

YORKSHIRE

LANCASHIRE

CHESHIRE   DERBYSHIRE   LINCOLNSHIRE

NOTTINGHAM-
SHIRE

STAFFORD-   NORFOLK
SHIRE   LEICESTER-   RUTLAND
SHROPSHIRE   SHIRE

HUNT-
INGDON-
WARWICK- NORTHAMPTON- SHIRE
WALES   SHIRE   SHIRE
WORCESTER-   CAMBRIDGE-   SUFFOLK
SHIRE   SHIRE
HEREFORD-   BEDFORD-
SHIRE   SHIRE
Prerogative Court of Canterbury
OXFORD - BUCK-
GLOUCESTER- SHIRE   INGHAM- HERTFORD-   ESSEX
SHIRE   SHIRE   SHIRE
MIDDLESEX

BERKSHIRE
SURREY
WILTSHIRE   KENT

SOMERSET   HAMPSHIRE
SUSSEX

DEVON   DORSET

CORNWALL

0   40   80 km

2.2.2 Interregnum

At the beginning of the English Civil War (May 1643 to November 1644) wills were not proved in London but in Oxford, where the judge of the Prerogative Court of Canterbury was based, along with Charles I. In November 1644 the Parliamentarians declared all grants of probate made in Oxford invalid, but allowed people to have the wills proved (or administrations granted) for a second time by a parliamentary court based in London.

In 1646 the records of these two courts (Oxford and London) were amalgamated, following the fall of Oxford to the Parliamentarians. The Oxford court did not keep registered copies of wills (see 2.2.3) – so unless the will proved in Oxford was proved and registered again in London, you will need to look for the original will (at the National Archives, in PROB 10/639–642).

When Parliament abolished the episcopacy in 1646, most ecclesiastical testamentary business went into abeyance. Then, following an act of 8 April 1653, all testamentary matters were transferred to a single court for England and Wales called the Court for the Probate of Wills and the Granting of Administrations, based in London. Records created by this court were written in English, instead of Latin (at that time the normal language of court records). The court ceased to function in 1659, and after the monarchy was restored in 1660 the records were incorporated into those of the Prerogative Court of Canterbury.

This effectively means that for a brief time (1653–60) all probate records for England and Wales are held centrally by the National Archives and from 1651–60 are in English. However, some executors and administrators in the north of England avoided the new court because of the expense and inconvenience of travelling to London. In such cases the wills – now held at the Borthwick Institute in York (see 2.3) – either seem to have been implemented without formal probate or were proved retrospectively following the restoration of the ecclesiastical courts in 1660.

The document E 315/483 at the National Archives contains copies of a number of wills and letters of administration extracted from the registers of the Prerogative Court of Canterbury during the Interregnum. These mainly relate to people in the service of the Commonwealth, either in the army or otherwise, the copies having been obtained by the government for the purposes of settling arrears of pay.

2.2.3 Types of records

Although there were lots of different types of records generated during the course of testamentary business, the main records are:

Original wills

In order to obtain probate, the executor submitted the original will to the court. Generally it was retained by the court once the process was complete, though some courts made a copy of the will and returned the original to the executor (this was certainly the case with some wills in the Prerogative Court of Canterbury before 1600). Original wills are usually signed by the testator, but are generally not written in the testator's own hand. They are usually written on paper, or sometimes on parchment. As they are loose documents, their survival rate is not as great as that of registered copies. They tend not to survive in large numbers before 1600, although this varies from court to court.

Registered copies

Once the probate process was complete, the executor could pay to have a copy of the will entered into the probate register. The registers are large bound ledgers, with wills copied into them page after page. It is these that many archives have microfilmed, and not the original wills. Check with the archive whether the records you are consulting are the original wills or the clerk's copies in the register. The survival rate of the registered copies is quite good, often extending back further than the original wills. Ordinarily there is little difference between looking at the clerk's copy and the original. However, it is worth bearing in mind that:

- The clerk's copy never includes the signature or seal of the testator. The testator's signature or seal will only be found on the original will – though it should be pointed out that a seal at the end of a will is not always the testator's but sometimes that of the scribe or his office.
- Some executors did not pay to have the will copied. In which case, there will be either no entry in the registered copy will indexes or an entry but no corresponding will. In such circumstances the only full record will be the original will, if it survives. If the original will has not survived, then the only available source will be the probate act book.
- The original will and the registered copy would always have been written by different people, so the handwriting will be different. If the handwriting on either document is difficult to read, consult the other. Occasionally the clerk making the copy missed lines or names from the original document. If the registered copy seems not to make sense, or something appears to be missing from it, compare the registered copy with the original will.

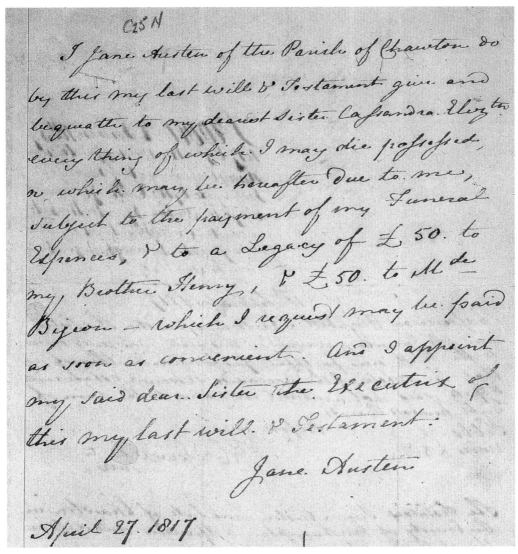

Figure 1 Comparison of two documents: **(a)** Jane Austen's original will in PROB 1/78 and **(b)** The registered copy will in PROB 11/1596.

The original will, which was written on 27 April 1817, reads as follows:

I Jane Austen of the Parish of Chawton do by this my last Will and Testament give and bequeath to my dearest Sister Cassandra Elizth every thing of which I may die possessed, or which may be hereafter due to me, subject to the payment of my Funeral Expenses, & to a Legacy of £50 to my brother Henry, & £50 to M^{de} Bigeon which I request may be paid as soon as convenient. And I appoint my said dear Sister the Executrix of this my last Will and Testament.
Jane Austen
April 1817

The original will is holographic (in Jane Austen's own hand) written on a single sheet of paper, and includes her signature. Because it was unwitnessed, a sworn affidavit (not shown) accompanies this document. The affidavit, signed on 10 September 1817 by Mr John Grove Palmer and Miss Harriet Ebel Palmer (in-laws of Charles-John Austen, Jane's brother), swears to the authenticity of the signature and the will. The will was proved on 11 September 1817.

Cassandra Elizabeth Austen, Jane's sister, was the executrix and heiress. She was also responsible for the preservation and subsequent distribution to her brothers, nephews and nieces of Jane Austen's letters, manuscripts and memorabilia.

(b) The registered copy (PROB 11/1596) was entered into a large ledger, a third of the way down the page. It provides details of the grant of probate and of the affidavit signed by the Palmers. Because it is a copy, made by a clerk, it does not include a signature.

Probate act books

These books contain the ecclesiastical courts' own records of the initial grant of probate and of later *letters of administration with will annexed* (see 4.7.1) and *administration with will annexed of goods not administered* (see 4.7.2).

The grant of probate was issued to the executor requiring him or her to:

- Produce an inventory of the personal estate within six months of the grant.
- Produce an account within 12 months of the grant, giving details of monies expended.
- Administer and distribute the personal estate of the deceased testator in accordance with the terms of the will.

When the grant of probate was issued, it was recorded on the original will (see 6.2.6), which was usually retained by the court. A record of the grant of probate was then copied into the probate act book. The probate act book may contain a valuation in the margin of the entry, alongside the date when the inventory was to be exhibited. This valuation can be useful if the inventory does not survive, although it will only relate to the personal estate of the deceased.

If the original will has not survived and the executor failed to pay the required fee to have the will copied into the probate register, then the probate act may be the only surviving item of testamentary documentation.

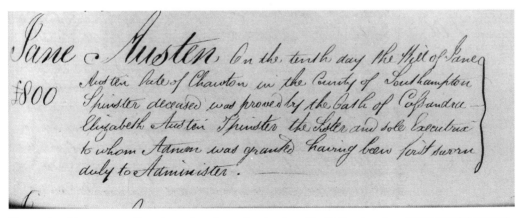

Figure 2   The grant of probate for Jane Austen's will, 11 September 1817 (PROB 8/210).

Administration act books

When a person died intestate, the next of kin (most often the widow) or another appropriate person (see 4.1.2) could ask the relevant ecclesiastical court to grant letters of administration. When making such a grant, the court would require the administrator to:

- Produce an inventory of the personal estate within six months of the grant.
- Produce an account within 12 months of the grant, giving details of monies expended.
- Distribute the residue according to the law of intestacy at the time.

The court kept copies of grants of administration in its administration act books, and it is these that are available in record offices. The original letters of administration rarely survive in archives unless the principal administrator revoked his or her right to administer the estate, or they were used as evidence in a law suit. In terms of information letters of administration are fairly disappointing, as they normally simply state that a named individual has been granted permission to distribute the estate. This may be accompanied by an administration bond providing slightly more information about the oath the administrator had to take before he or she could administer the estate. However, this extra information is likely to relate to the administrator (not always the next of kin), rather than the testator. Additional information regarding the estate may be obtained from the inventory and the account.

For more about administrations, see Chapter 4.

Inventories and accounts

As part of the probate process, the executor or administrator was charged with providing an inventory of the deceased's goods and an account of how his or her debts were discharged, so that the balance could be distributed among the beneficiaries. These can be extremely interesting documents, as they give a glimpse of our ancestors' lives. Moreover, they are useful for social historians because of the information they yield about how people lived and their personal possessions, and for financial historians as they provide an idea as to the value each item would have fetched at auction. A more accurate picture of a testator's wealth can be gained from an inventory or account than from a will, which is by its nature only a statement of intent.

For more about inventories and accounts, see Chapter 7.

2.3 Prerogative Court of York (PCY)

The testamentary records of the Archbishop of York are held at the Borthwick Institute of Historical Research, see Useful Addresses, p.211. PCY records survive from the fourteenth century to 1858, when the court was abolished. The Borthwick Institute also holds the records of minor church courts within the province of York.

Bishops dealt with the majority of probate business, and their court in northern England was known as the Exchequer Court of York. However, the Prerogative Court of York claimed jurisdiction over estates in the northern province where the rule of *bona notabilia* applied (see 2.1.4).

Jurisdiction

The jurisdiction of the Archbishop of York comprised the dioceses of Carlisle, Chester, Durham and York, covering the counties of Cheshire, Cumberland, Durham, Lancashire, Northumberland, Nottinghamshire, Westmorland and Yorkshire. The Dean and Chapter Court exercised jurisdiction on behalf of the archbishop during his absence (their records are also held by the Borthwick Institute).

Both the large number of peculiar courts (see 3.5.1) and changing boundaries complicate the jurisdiction of the Archbishop of York. More detailed information about the structure of the ecclesiastical courts in the north of England can be found on the Borthwick Institute's website (**www.york.ac.uk/inst/bihr**) and in *Probate Jurisdictions: Where To Look For Wills* by Jeremy Gibson and Else Churchill (FFHS, 5th edn 2002).

Copies of probate records can be ordered from the Postal Reprographic Service, Borthwick Institute (see Useful Addresses, p. 211).

2.3.1 Records

Original wills 1427–1858
Although the original wills series begins in 1427, there are only one or two surviving items before 1591. From 1591 there are some original wills surviving for most years, and the series is generally complete from 1660 onwards. These records also include administration bonds, inventories, tuition bonds, renunciations, and other testamentary paperwork. Few inventories survive before 1688. The records are in chronological bundles arranged according to month of probate by either the Prerogative Court or the Exchequer Court of York.

Administrations
See probate act books.

Probate registers 1389–1858
These contain registered copies of wills. Inventories and grants of administration were never registered after the medieval period. There are gaps in the probate registers series during the fifteenth and seventeenth centuries.

Probate act books 1502–1858
From 1502, grants of probate and administration were entered in the act books of the various rural deanery courts. The earliest surviving act book of the Prerogative Court is dated 1587; before that date, prerogative business will be found in the act books of York City Deanery, held at the Borthwick Institute. There are gaps in the probate act books series during the sixteenth and seventeenth centuries.

2.3.2 Printed and typescript indexes

1389–1688
Indexed by the Yorkshire Archaeological Society Record Series, in vols 4, 6, 11, 14, 19, 22, 24, 26, 28, 32, 35, 49, 60, 68, 73, 78, 89 and 93. See Appendix 2 for a list of PCY printed indexes. These will be found at both the Borthwick Institute and the National Archives.

1688–1731
Typescript indexes.

1731–1858
There are 29 name indexes arranged chronologically by date of probate, which will be found at the Borthwick Institute.

2.3.3 Wills and administrations not held by the Borthwick Institute

Location of records	Church court
York Minster Library	Peculiar of St Leonard's Hospital, York Prebend of Riccall
Hull City Record Office	Corporation of Kingston upon Hull
Leeds Archive Department	Peculiar of Marsham Consistory Court of the Commissary of Richmond (eastern deaneries) Manor of Arkengarthdale Deanery and Royal Peculiar of the Collegiate Church of Middleham Honour of Knaresborough Peculiar of Altofts in Normanton Manor of Hunsingore
University of Durham	Consistory Court of Durham with the Peculiar of Crayhe
Lancashire Record Office	Consistory Court of the Commissary of the Archdeaconry of Richmond (western deaneries) Consistory Court of Chester in the Archdeaconry of Chester
Nottingham Record Office	Exchequer Court of York in the Archdeaconry of Nottingham
Bradford Central Library	Manor of Batley

2.4 **Prerogative Court of Canterbury (PCC)**

The Prerogative Court of the Archbishop of Canterbury began to claim its right to grant wills and administrations as early as the reign of Henry III, although it was not until the fifteenth century that it emerged as an administrative organization in its own right. The court was based at Doctors' Commons in London and until 1858, when the court was abolished, it exercised jurisdiction where the deceased had *bona notabilia* (see 2.1.4) within the southern province amounting to £5 or more.

The testamentary records of the Prerogative Court of Canterbury are held by the National Archives, whereas records of minor ecclesiastical courts within the jurisdiction of the archbishop are held by either the local county record office or the diocesan record office (see 3.2).

During the first half of the fifteenth century, the Archbishop of Canterbury could also prove wills on his own account. These wills date from 1312 to 1637, although there are few after 1500. They are now held in Lambeth Palace Library, but have been published in the following:

- *Index of Wills Recorded in the Archiepiscopal Registers at Lambeth Palace*, edited by J. C. Smith (reprinted from *The Genealogist*, vols 34–5, 1919)
- *Calendar of Lambeth Palace Administrations Recorded in the Archbishops' Registers* (reprinted from *The Genealogist*, vols 7–8 (1883–4)
- *Micropublication of the Archbishops' Registers 1272–1640* (available from World Microfilms Publications)

For further information, see the Lambeth Palace Library website (**www. lambethpalacelibrary.org**).

Jurisdiction

The jurisdiction of the Prerogative Court of Canterbury covered Berkshire, Buckinghamshire, Cambridgeshire, Cornwall, Derbyshire, Devon, Dorset, Essex, Gloucestershire, Hampshire, Herefordshire, Hertfordshire, Huntingdonshire, Kent, Leicestershire, Lincolnshire, London, Middlesex, Norfolk, Northamptonshire, Oxfordshire, Rutland, Shropshire, Somerset, Staffordshire, Surrey, Sussex, Suffolk, Wales, Warwickshire, Wiltshire and Worcestershire. The PCC was the largest and busiest of all the testamentary courts, and because of its seniority and the weight of its judgments testators wanted their wills proved by the court.

In addition to its main jurisdiction, the PCC also claimed jurisdiction over soldiers and sailors who died abroad. From 1817, the value of the estate had to exceed £20 before the PCC could act. Soldiers and sailors will be found either at the end of the indexes to registered copy wills (in the series PROB 12) or as a separate section following each letter of the alphabet. The abbreviation *pts* ('parts', or *in partibus transmarinis*) accompanying an entry means died abroad.

Initially wills proved by the PCC would have attracted the wealthier sections of society, as the £5 limit would have acted as a barrier. The Prerogative Court of Canterbury also attracted business that strictly should perhaps have gone to lower ecclesiastical courts but because of the PCC's prestige were directed to it. Eventually due to inflation the £5 threshold became less of a restriction, as the stipulated sum was not increased. From 1810 until the abolition of the court in 1858, the Bank of England would only accept probate from the PCC (see Chapter 10).

2.4.1 Records

See Appendix 1 for a complete list of PCC record series, with references.

Original wills 1484–1858 (PROB 10)
These survive sporadically before about 1600. Up to 1600 many of the so-called 'original wills' are in fact copies, since the original was returned to the executor.

Original wills of famous people 1552–1854 (PROB 1)
The wills in this series were removed from PROB 10 due to the celebrity of the testators. They include the wills of Jane Austen, William Shakespeare and Samuel Pepys. They can be accessed via DocumentsOnline as either the original will or the registered copy.

Registered copy wills 1383–1858 (PROB 11)
These are clerks' copies of original wills (see 2.1.3) and only exist if the executor paid for the will to be registered. Before 1803 they include the 'sentence' (the final judgment in a cause) if the victorious party paid for it to be registered. The PCC registered copy wills have now been digitized in their entirety and are available on the National Archives website (see 3.3.1).

Administrations 1559–1858 (PROB 6)
From 1719, administrations were arranged by a 'seat' system. Before 1719, they are arranged by handwritten folio numbers. For further information on PCC administrations and the seat system, see 4.3.1.

Indexes to wills and administrations 1383–1858 (PROB 12)
The indexes (known as 'calendars') to PCC wills and administrations list the names of testators and intestates for whose estates grants were made during each year. They are arranged by year of probate and then by the initial letter of the

surname. Each calendar was given a name. For wills registered before 1651, this was the name of the first person whose will was entered in the register. After 1650, the name was chosen from the names of testators and is usually that of an eminent person. Will registers for the years 1841 to 1858 are not identified by names but referred to by calendar years. Many of the published name indexes available at the National Archives, Family Record Centre and elsewhere provide a reference based on the old register name. For example, the name John Small in the published index for 1649 gives the reference 64 Fairfax. This comprises the quire number and the name of the register which can be converted to a modern TNA reference using the PROB 11 catalogue. A quire is a traditional numbering system. It comprises eight folios (or 16 pages). The number is written at the top right-hand corner of the first page of the quire in roman numerals (early registers) or Arabic numbers. The index entry is to quire, and so the will should be in the following 16 pages. See also 2.4.2.

Probate act books 1526–1858 (PROB 8)
These record the day-to-day business of the probate court and provide confirmation that probate was granted. If the original will has not survived and was not copied into the probate register, then this is likely to be one of the few documentary sources available.

Other sources
Initial applications for a grant of probate are in PROB 14 (1657–1858). These records provide the executor's signature and an approximate date of the deceased's death.

If the executor was sworn by commission – and many executors were as they could not afford the expense of travelling to London – the name and address of the local clergyman who administered the oath will be found in the commissions to swear executors in PROB 52 (1796–1858) and PROB 56 (before 1796), although this series is currently unavailable. These series can be used as a guide to the executor's place of residence. PROB 52 is arranged by 'seat' (see 4.3.1).

If the court took over the distribution of the estate, details of this can be found in the Muniment Books in PROB 16 (1610–1858).

2.4.2 Published Prerogative Court of Canterbury wills

In addition to DocumentsOnline (see 3.3.1), the following four volumes list all of the wills in a particular PCC register for a single year, either as abstracts or in index form:

Year	TNA references	Author	Title
1620	PROB 11/135–136	J. H. Lea	*Abstract of wills in the Prerogative Court of Canterbury: Register Soame 1620* (Boston, Mass., 1904). Available at the FRC only.
1630	PROB 11/157–158	J. H. Morrison	*Prerogative Court of Canterbury: Register Scroope* (London, 1934). Available at the FRC only.
1658	PROB 11/ 272–285	W. Brigg	*Genealogical abstracts of wills proved in the Prerogative Court of Canterbury: Register Wootton 1658* (Leeds, 1894–1914). Available at the FRC only.
1750	PROB 11/776–784	G. Sherwood	*A list of persons named in the PCC wills proved in the Year 1750: Register Greenly* (London, privately published, 1918). Available at the Society of Genealogists only.

In addition to these volumes, the Richard III Society is currently indexing and transcribing all the wills from the PCC register Legge (1383–1499). See the society's website (**www.richardiii.net**) for further information.

2.4.3 Published Prerogative Court of Canterbury Indexes

For a list of published PCC indexes to wills and administrations, see Appendix 2.

2.5 Non-Anglican wills

2.5.1 Jewish wills

Wills of first-generation Jews can be particularly rewarding, as they often leave legacies to relatives living in their country of origin. A very useful source is *Anglo–Jewish Notabilities, Their Arms and Testamentary Dispositions*, compiled by A. P. Arnold (Jewish Historical Society of England, 1949). It includes a section giving details of wills and letters of administration of prominent members of Anglo–Jewry. Since a high percentage of Jewish wills were registered with the

Prerogative Court of Canterbury (reflecting the concentration of Jews in London), these wills have become more accessible through DocumentsOnline (see 3.3.1).

A search of the DocumentsOnline database under the name Cohen produces nearly 60 names for individual wills. Most are from London or Middlesex, although there are entries for Amsterdam and Lisbon and even for Charleston, in South Carolina. The most frequently mentioned profession is merchant.

2.5.2 Quaker wills

The wills of Quakers, like those of Jews, were proved or registered in the normal way – but before the Affirmation Act 1696 Quaker executors would have been prevented by their beliefs from swearing an affidavit, because this entailed swearing an oath of allegiance to the monarch. However, some Quakers were not happy with the affirmation specified in the 1696 act and had to wait until the Affirmation Act 1722 for satisfactory wording. Sometimes affirmation is mentioned in the probate clause of the will, but there are also instances of clerks using the word *jurat* to indicate that an oath was sworn by Quaker executors, who would probably not have sworn an oath.

2.5.3 Roman Catholic wills

For wills of Roman Catholics, see 6.1.7.2.

3

Finding a Will before 1858

There is no single place to look for wills and administrations before 1858. Many different church courts were able to prove wills and grant administrations. Consequently, it is not always straightforward to find the documents you are looking for. To find a will before 1858, you need to have some idea of the family name and the area where they lived – but families do not always stay put, and records of individuals may appear in unexpected areas because of church court rules.

This chapter is primarily concerned with England and Wales. Scotland, Northern Ireland, the Republic of Ireland, the Channel Islands and the Isle of Man are dealt with in Chapter 11.

3.1 Search strategies

First of all, try a search of the Prerogative Court of Canterbury (PCC) registered wills on DocumentsOnline (**www.documentsonline.nationalarchives.gov.uk**), which includes more than 1,016,000 wills from 1383 to 1858 (see 3.3.1). The powerful search engine makes searching easy – and as the PCC was the largest of all church courts (see 2.4), it is worth eliminating.

If your DocumentsOnline search proves unsuccessful, the next step is to identify the present location of wills proved by the local church courts for the county of residence. For the location of wills and administrations by county, see the table below.

Finally, check the will indexes of the likely local church courts. Some of these are available online (see 3.3). Also, many of them are published and can be found at the National Archives, the Family Records Centre or the Society of Genealogists, as well as the relevant local record office. For Useful Addresses, see p.211. If the will was proved between 1796–1858, it may be worth using the death duty registers as a shortcut. See 8.2 for more information.

3.2 Finding wills and administrations before 1858

Wills and administrations are arranged by the church court that proved the document. But some ecclesiastical jurisdictions covered more than one county. For example, someone who died in Berkshire could have had his or her will proved by the Archdeaconry Court of Berkshire, the Consistory Court of Salisbury or the Prerogative Court of Canterbury, depending upon the value and the location of his or her goods; and the records of these three courts are to be found in different locations.

The table below offers a basic guide to finding wills and administrations before 1858. Detailed guidance will be found in *Probate Jurisdictions: Where To Look For Wills* by Jeremy Gibson and Else Churchill (FFHS, 5th edn 2002).

Where to look?

England

Deceased's place of residence	Where to look?
Bedfordshire	PCC records at TNA and FRC and on DocumentsOnline (**www.documentsonline.nationalarchives.gov.uk**) *Local court records at:* Bedfordshire and Luton Archives and Record Service
Berkshire	PCC records at TNA and FRC and on DocumentsOnline (**www.documentsonline.nationalarchives.gov.uk**) *Local court records at:* Berkshire Record Office Oxfordshire Record Office Wiltshire and Swindon Record Office *Online source:* **www.wiltshire.gov.uk** (see 3.3.3) Due soon
Buckinghamshire	PCC records at TNA and FRC and on DocumentsOnline (**www.documentsonline.nationalarchives.gov.uk**) *Local court records at:* Buckinghamshire Record Office Oxfordshire Record Office Hertfordshire Archives
Cambridgeshire	PCC records at TNA and FRC and on DocumentsOnline (**www.documentsonline.nationalarchives.gov.uk**)

	Local court records at: Cambridgeshire Record Office Cambridge University Library Suffolk Record Office
Cheshire	PCY records at Borthwick Institute *Local court records at:* Cheshire and Chester Archives and Local Studies Service *Online source:* **www.cheshire.gov.uk** (see 3.3.5)
Cornwall	PCC records at TNA and FRC and on DocumentsOnline (**www.documentsonline.nationalarchives.gov.uk**) *Local court records at:* Cornwall Record Office
Cumberland	see Cumbria
Cumbria	PCY records at Borthwick Institute *Local court records at:* Cumbria Record Office Lancashire Record Office
Devon	PCC records at TNA and FRC and on DocumentsOnline (**www.documentsonline.nationalarchives.gov.uk**) *Local court records at:* Devon Record Office Cornwall Record Office Dorset Record Office Wiltshire and Swindon Record Office *Online source:* **www.wiltshire.gov.uk** (see 3.3.3) Due soon
Dorset	PCC records at TNA and FRC and on DocumentsOnline (**www.documentsonline.nationalarchives.gov.uk**) *Local court records at:* Dorset Record Office

Durham	PCY records at Borthwick Institute *Local court records at:* Durham University Library Archives and Special Collections
Essex	PCC records at TNA and FRC and on DocumentsOnline (**www.documentsonline. nationalarchives.gov.uk**) *Local court records at:* Essex Record Office London Metropolitan Archives Guildhall Library
Gloucestershire	PCC records at TNA and FRC and on DocumentsOnline (**www.documentsonline. nationalarchives.gov.uk**) *Local court records at:* Gloucestershire Record Office Bristol Record Office *Online sources:* **www.bristol-city.gov.uk** (see 3.3.7) **www.gloucestershire.gov.uk** (see 3.3.8)
Hampshire	PCC records at TNA and FRC and on DocumentsOnline (**www.documentsonline. nationalarchives.gov.uk**) *Local court records at:* Hampshire Record Office
Herefordshire	PCC records at TNA and FRC and on DocumentsOnline (**www.documentsonline. nationalarchives.gov.uk**) *Local court records at:* Herefordshire Record Office National Library of Wales *Online source:* **www.llgc.org.uk** (see 3.4) Due soon
Hertfordshire	PCC records at TNA and FRC and on DocumentsOnline (**www.documentsonline. nationalarchives.gov.uk**) *Local court records at:* Hertfordshire Archives and Local Studies Huntingdon Record Office

	Essex Record Office London Metropolitan Archives Guildhall Library
Huntingdonshire	PCC records at TNA and FRC and on DocumentsOnline (**www.documentsonline. nationalarchives.gov.uk**) *Local court records at:* Huntingdon Record Office
Kent	PCC records at TNA and FRC and on DocumentsOnline (**www.documentsonline. nationalarchives.gov.uk**) *Local court records at:* Centre for Kentish Studies London Metropolitan Archives
Lancashire	PCY records at Borthwick Institute *Local court records at:* Lancashire Record Office
Leicestershire	PCC records at TNA and FRC and on DocumentsOnline (**www.documentsonline. nationalarchives.gov.uk**) *Local court records at:* Leicestershire Record Office
Lincolnshire	PCC records at TNA and FRC and on DocumentsOnline (**www.documentsonline. nationalarchives.gov.uk**) PCY records at Borthwick Institute *Local court records at:* Lincolnshire Archives
London	PCC records at TNA and FRC and on DocumentsOnline (**www.documentsonline. nationalarchives.gov.uk**) *Local court records at:* London Metropolitan Archives Guildhall Library Corporation of London Record Office Lambeth Palace Library City of Westminster Archives Centre
Middlesex	see London

Norfolk	PCC records at TNA and FRC and on DocumentsOnline (**www.documentsonline. nationalarchives.gov.uk**) *Local court records at:* Norfolk Record Office
Northamptonshire	PCC records at TNA and FRC and on DocumentsOnline (**www.documentsonline. nationalarchives.gov.uk**) *Local court records at:* Northamptonshire Record Office Leicestershire Record Office
Northumberland	see Durham
Nottinghamshire	PCY records at Borthwick Institute *Local court records at:* Nottinghamshire Archives Some may also be found among PCC records at TNA and FRC
Oxfordshire	PCC records at TNR and FRC and on DocumentsOnline (**www.documentsonline. nationalarchives.gov.uk**) *Local court records at:* Oxfordshire Record Office, Bodleian Library
Rutland	see Northamptonshire
Shropshire	PCC records at TNA and FRC and on DocumentsOnline (**www.documentsonline. nationalarchives.gov.uk**) *Local court records at:* Lichfield Record Office Herefordshire Record Office National Library of Wales
Somerset	PCC records at TNA and FRC and on DocumentsOnline (**www.documentsonline. nationalarchives.gov.uk**) *Local court records at:* Somerset Archives and Record Service Bristol Record Office *Online source:* **www.somerset.gov.uk/archives/** (see 3.3.6)/ **www.bristol-city.gov.uk** (see 3.3.7)

Staffordshire	PCC records at TNA and FRC and on DocumentsOnline (**www.documentsonline. nationalarchives.gov.uk**)
	Local court records at: Lichfield Record Office
Suffolk	PCC records at TNA and FRC and on DocumentsOnline (**www.documentsonline. nationalarchives.gov.uk**)
	Local court records at: Suffolk Record Office, Ipswich Suffolk Record Office, Bury St Edmunds Norfolk Record Office
Surrey	PCC records at TNA and FRC and on DocumentsOnline (**www.documentsonline. nationalarchives.gov.uk**)
	Local court records at: London Metropolitan Archives Lambeth Palace Library Hampshire Record Office
Sussex	PCC records at TNA and FRC and on DocumentsOnline (**www.documentsonline. nationalarchives.gov.uk**)
	Local court records at: West Sussex Record Office East Sussex Record Office
Warwickshire	PCC records at TNA and FRC and on DocumentsOnline (**www.documentsonline. nationalarchives.gov.uk**)
	Local court records at: Lichfield Record Office Worcestershire Record Office Shakespeare Birthplace Trust Warwickshire Record Office
Westmorland	see Cumbria
Wiltshire	PCC records at TNA and FRC and on DocumentsOnline (**www.documentsonline. nationalarchives.gov.uk**)
	Local court records at: Wiltshire and Swindon Record Office Hampshire Record Office Gloucestershire Record Office

	Online source: **www.wiltshire.gov.uk** (see 3.3.3) Due soon
Worcestershire	PCC records at TNA and FRC and on DocumentsOnline (**www.documentsonline. nationalarchives.gov.uk**) *Local court records at:* Worcestershire Record Office Hertfordshire Record Office ??
Yorkshire	PCY records at Borthwick Institute *Local court records at:* Cheshire and Chester Archives and Local Studies Service Cumbria Record Office Durham University Library Archives and Special Collections Nottinghamshire Archives National Library of Wales Lancashire Record Office Leeds District Archives West Riding Registry of Deeds *Online source:* **www.cheshire.gov.uk** (see 3.3.5)

Wales

Deceased's place of residence	Where to look?
North Wales: Anglesey, Caernarvonshire, Denbighshire, Flintshire, Merionethshire, Montgomeryshire	PCC records at TNA and FRC and on DocumentsOnline (**www.documentsonline. nationalarchives.gov.uk**) *Local court records at:* National Library of Wales *Online source:* **www.llgc.org.uk** (see 3.4) Due soon
South Wales: Brecknockshire, Cardiganshire, Carmarthenshire, Glamorganshire, Monmouthshire, Pembrokeshire, Monmouthshire	PCC records at TNA and FRC and on DocumentsOnline (**www.documentsonline. nationalarchives.gov.uk**) *Local court records at:* National Library of Wales Herefordshire Record Office *Online source:* **www.llgc.org.uk** (see 3.4) Due soon

3.3 Online sources

Because of their popularity among family and social historians and their relevance for one-name searches, wills make good indexing projects and are becoming more common on the Internet.

The following sites have indexes to wills, or are in the process of placing their indexes online. Some of them have digitized images of the wills themselves that can be downloaded for a small fee.

The Internet is a good tool for one-name searches. To find out whether someone else has done relevant research already, try typing the surname you are looking for into a search engine along with the word 'wills'.

3.3.1 DocumentsOnline (www.documentsonline.nationalarchives.gov.uk)

All PCC registered wills from 1383 to 1858 (over 1,016,000 wills) are now available on DocumentsOnline, which is part of the National Archives website. The index is free to search and, as the Prerogative Court of Canterbury was the busiest of all the church courts, it is worth searching this database first. Currently the wills cost £3.50 each to download from the Internet and, as a pilot scheme, can be viewed free of charge at the Family Records Centre and the National Archives.

A powerful search engine enables you to search for surnames, specific date ranges, occupations and other information, using the keyword search facility. The easiest way to search is to type the name of the person you are looking for into the Quick Search box and click on the 'Go' button. You will find lots of search tips and detailed information on searching in the help files.

Up to 200 characters can be entered in the Quick Search box, which can accommodate between 20 and 30 search terms, depending on the length of the words you enter. You can significantly narrow down your search by entering even four keywords – for example, 'james taylor innkeeper middlesex'. Simply separate the words with spaces; there is no need to use capital letters.

The Quick Search results are ordered by relevance and ranked by matches to the name field first. In some cases you will see that there is an alternate name given – for example, 'Will of James or James Brown Lynch of Carrick on Suir, Tipperary'. In this case, the individual will rank slightly higher because the name is repeated in the description. If you are looking for a place that might also be somebody's name, you may find it easier to use the Advanced Search.

You can reorder your search results by date or description by clicking on the appropriate headings at the top of the search results table.

It is worth remembering that the wills available online are reproductions of the registered copies and not the original wills. As the executor had to pay to have the will copied into the register, there may be some gaps in the series. DocumentsOnline does not include administrations.

Extracting statistical information

Online access to more than a million wills has made it possible to undertake some valuable statistical analysis. Where a county is identified within the will (for example, James Taylor of Bow Lane, Middlesex), it was included in the database. Consequently, DocumentsOnline has been able to reveal that from 1383 to 1858 the most common counties of residence for testators were:

1.	Middlesex	202,419
2.	London	87,702
3.	Surrey	70,571
4.	Kent	53,247
5.	Somerset	31,205
6.	Gloucestershire	30,932
7.	Essex	27,672
8.	Devon	27,039
9.	Hampshire	23,923
10.	Wiltshire	19,800

Female wills

Although it is not possible to search DocumentsOnline by gender, most women were identified by their occupation or status. Adding together the most common female identifiers – for example, (by status) single lady, lady, dowager, widow, spouse, gentlewoman, mistress, spinster, wife, and (by occupation) dressmaker, nurse, housekeeper, school mistress, laundress – it is possible to estimate that at least 21% of all PCC testators were female.

3.3.2 English Origins (www.englishorigins.com)

English Origins provides online access to the records of the Society of Genealogists. In terms of probate records, the site holds:

● Prerogative Court of Canterbury will index 1750–1800
● Bank of England will extracts 1717–1845 (see 10.9)
● Archdeaconry Court of London will index 1700–1807

There is a charge to access the database, and a further charge should you wish to see the images. The site also includes indexes to marriages, depositions and apprenticeship records.

3.3.3 Wiltshire wills project (www.wiltshire.gov.uk)

The Wiltshire wills project (1560–1858) aims to digitize wills from the whole of Wiltshire and Berkshire, parts of Devon, and Uffculme in Dorset. The project is supported by the Heritage Lottery Fund. The wills have been catalogued and put onto a computer database, and are being flattened and repaired where necessary. The index will be available on site by autumn 2004, and placed on their website some months after then. Currently one fifth of 105,000 wills have been digitized, but it has been estimated that it will take 12 years to complete the digitization project. Check their website for progress.

3.3.4 Welsh wills (www.llgc.org.uk)

The National Library of Wales (see 3.4) is in the process of digitizing the wills of 200,000 testators between the mid 1550s and 1858. The aim is for the wills to be searchable and viewable online. Approximately 300,000 records (wills, administrations, inventories, etc., comprising over a million images) will be digitized. Check their website for progress.

3.3.5 Cheshire wills (www.cheshire.gov.uk)

This database covers the years 1492 to 1940 and contains over 130,000 entries. It covers most probate documents held at the Cheshire and Chester Archives, including wills, administrations, administration bonds, inventories, codicils and other documents. It is not possible to view the documents themselves, but they can be copied and posted to you for a small fee.

3.3.6 Somerset wills (www.somerset.gov.uk/archives)

The majority of probate records before 1858 for Somerset (and Devon and Cornwall) were destroyed during enemy action in the Second World War. Despite this, many original and registered copy wills do survive. For further information, consult *Somerset Wills Index: Printed and Manuscript Copies* by Sir Mervyn Medlycott (1993).

Somerset Estate Duty wills (1812–57)

From 1796, 'death duties' – Legacy Duty, Succession Duty or Estate Duty, depending on the date (see 8.1) – were payable on estates in England and Wales over a certain value. 'Estate Duty wills' (copies of wills relating to estates subject to death duties) were made from 1812 to 1857 (see 8.4.2). Somerset Archive and Record Service have created an online index to Estate Duty wills (but not administrations or copies made by peculiar courts) for Somerset for the period 1812–57. The database covers indexes to abstracts of wills that were recorded locally before being passed to the Estate Duty Office for the payment of death duties.

3.3.7 Bristol wills (www.bristol-city.gov.uk)

This is an index of all wills proved in Bristol between 1793 and 1858. It includes wills previously unindexed and supersedes all other indexes of Bristol wills for this period. It is an electronic version in PDF format of a printed index; to access it, you need to have Acrobat Reader (downloadable from **www.adobe.com**) installed on your computer.

The wills themselves are available at Bristol Record Office. To obtain a copy of a will, either write to Bristol Record Office, 'B' Bond Warehouse, Smeaton Road, Bristol BS1 6XN or send an email to **bro@bristol-city.gov.uk**, or visit the record office in person.

3.3.8 Gloucestershire wills (www.gloucestershire.gov.uk)

This database currently comprises an index of all wills proved in Gloucester between 1541 and 1858.

If you find a will for a person you are interested in, you can apply for a copy by writing to Gloucestershire Record Office, Clarence Row, Alvin Street, Gloucester GL1 3DW or sending an email to **records@gloucestershire.gov.uk**. Although the record office does not yet offer an online service, you can download an order form, complete it and, after signing the copyright declaration, submit it by post.

3.3.9 Access to Archives (A2A) (www.a2a.org.uk)

This is a collaborative project between the National Archives and the British Library, designed to bring indexes from archives throughout England into a single database. It allows you to search for information about records dating from the tenth century to the present day held by local record offices and libraries, universities, museums, and national and specialist institutions across the country.

The catalogues range from very detailed individual files to summary information. It is possible to find, for example, catalogues of the family archives of named families and catalogues of archives relating to the study of genealogy as a subject. Via the A2A site you can search for records from particular ecclesiastical courts.

The database is updated regularly, so is worth revisiting from time to time for newly included catalogues.

3.4 Welsh wills

Many Welsh testators had their wills proved at the Prerogative Court of Canterbury.

Records of those that were proved in minor Welsh church courts are held at the National Library of Wales, Aberystwyth (see Useful Addresses, p. 211). These include the probate records of the church courts at:

Bangor   (from 1635)
Brecon   (from 1543)
Chester   (from 1547 – Welsh wills only)
Hawarden   (from 1554)
Llandaff   (from 1568)
St Asaph   (from 1565)
St David's   (from 1556)

3.5 Other testamentary jurisdictions

3.5.1 Peculiar jurisdictions

Some clergy had the right to hold their own courts – for example, holders of monastic and abbey lands following Henry VIII's dissolution of the monasteries. Lords of the manor, universities and cathedrals also sometimes inherited such rights. These 'peculiar courts', as they were called, were exempt from the authority of their local archdeacon and sometimes even from the authority of the bishop. Examples of peculiar jurisdictions in the county of Dorset include Wimborne Minster, Sturminster Marshall, Great Canford and Poole, and Corfe Castle. Records of peculiar courts are deposited at the local or diocesan record office for the county.

3.5.2 *Manorial courts*

Under the feudal system, in theory all land was held by the Crown and therefore the disposal of land, either through sale or inheritance, was a matter for the royal or manorial courts. Manorial courts recorded the passing on of title of copyhold land (literally 'held by copy of court roll') and the acquisition of copyhold land. Copyhold land could not be transferred to another person (whether by sale, mortgage or inheritance) without the permission of the manor court.

In some parishes the manorial courts were virtually defunct by the eighteenth century, in others they continued until 1926 when copyhold tenure was abolished by the Law of Property Act 1922.

You can find the location of manorial court rolls and other documents by consulting the Manorial Documents Register located at the National Archives. For Wales, Isle of Wight, Hampshire and the three Ridings of Yorkshire, you can search coverage and availability on the National Archives Website. Court rolls for some manors are located at TNA. A will could be proved by a church court and enrolled on a manorial court roll. However, from 1815 there was no legal necessity to surrender (transfer) the copyhold and subsequently there may be no enrolment. For more information consult M. Ellis, *Using Manorial Records* (PRO revised edn, 1997).

3.6 Can't find the will or administration?

If the most likely sources have been exhausted, there are other avenues to try.

Research tips

If you are fairly confident a will would have been left, but cannot find it among the records of the registered copy wills:

- Try searching the registers for at least three years from the date of death of the testator or intestate. Although a straightforward will would have been proved within a few months of the date of death, a complicated or disputed estate could take several years.
- Look for the original will, rather than a registered copy. Probate courts required the executor to pay for the original will to be copied and not all executors would have done this, although it appears that the majority did.
- Try variant spellings of surnames.
- Some courts indexed titled people by title, rather than by name, and some of the indexes to wills are idiosyncratic. So try more unusual combinations. For example, you may find that the Bishop of Rochester is indexed under 'B' for 'Bishop'.

Try the death duty indexes

If the testator or intestate died between 1796 and 1858, try the indexes to the death duty registers in IR 27 (see 8.2) available on microfilm at the Family Records Centre and the National Archives. The indexes – which are arranged by the first three letters of the surname of the testator or intestate and the year of probate – cover the whole of England and Wales, irrespective of which court proved the will. The documents provide the name of the testator/intestate and the name and address of the executor(s) or administrator(s). The limitations of these records is that they include only estates subject to death duties, and before 1858 that would have been a relatively small proportion of all estates.

No will?

It is always possible that no will was left at all, even though the individual was quite wealthy. This may be for one of the following reasons:

- Property may have been disposed of before death, making a will redundant.
- The person whose will you are seeking did not own the capital he was living off, but merely a life interest.
- He or she may have died suddenly at a relatively young age.
- Sometimes, superstitious testators felt that to write a will might encourage death.

4
Administrations before 1858

This chapter looks at what happened before 1858 when someone died without leaving a valid will. It discusses what types of records exist and what information can be obtained from them. It also explains what happened to estates where revenues reverted to the Crown. For administrations in Scotland, Northern Ireland, the Republic of Ireland, the Channel Islands and the Isle of Man, see Chapter 11.

4.1 Intestacy

As mentioned earlier, in legal terminology a person who dies without leaving a will or whose will proves to be invalid is known as an *intestate*. When someone leaves a valid will, they are able to specify exactly what they want to happen to their personal estate, following payments to creditors. Both statute and common law govern the distribution of the personal estate of an intestate, which means that next of kin have little control over its distribution.

In instances of intestacy, not all estates before 1858 were subject to administration, as the process was time-consuming and costly. Next of kin were most likely to apply for a grant of administration if the estate was complicated or subject to dispute, or if it was necessary to establish a clear legal title to property.

If no one applied for letters of administration, then there will be no formal record of the distribution of the personal estate.

4.1.1 Process of granting an administration

Before 1858, an individual with a claim on an estate would apply to the appropriate ecclesiastical court for authority to act as administrator. The administrator was required to take an oath promising to distribute the estate in accordance with the law. He – or most likely she, as the majority of administrators were widows – would then be issued with a document sealed with the seal of the court. This document, known as letters of administration, authorized the administrator to:

- Exhibit an inventory of the deceased's estate.
- Collect any sums owed to the deceased.
- Pay the deceased's debts and any legitimate expenses (such as medical bills, funeral costs, and the maintenance of the deceased's dependants) and submit an account of expenditure to the court.
- Distribute the estate in accordance with the law of intestacy at the time.

The law required the administrator to compile an inventory of the personal estate within six months from the date of the grant of administration and an account within 12 months from the grant of administration. For more about inventories and accounts, see Chapter 7.

It should be remembered that, as with wills, originally the ecclesiastical courts only had jurisdiction over the deceased's personal estate or moveable goods. Until the 1837 Wills Act they did not have complete authority over real estate (see 6.2.7).

4.1.2 Who could administer the estate?

When appointing administrators, the courts had to follow the order of precedence laid down by statute in 1529:

- husband or wife
- children
- father or mother
- brother or sister
- next of kin (e.g. uncle or aunt)
- creditor
- others, at the discretion of the court

4.1.3 Distribution of the estate

In order to tighten procedures for administrators and force them to distribute the estate fairly, from 1670 the administrator was required to distribute the personalty (personal estate) as follows:

- One third to the deceased's widow and the remainder to the deceased's child or children. If there were several children, the remainder would be shared among them equally.

- If there were no children, half to the widow and the remainder equally to the remaining next of kin.
- If there was no widow, then the remainder went to the children.
- If there were no children, the administration could be granted to someone with an interest in the estate (e.g. a creditor).
- If there were no next of kin and no one wished to claim administration, the estate would revert to the Crown (see 4.8).

Real estate descended to *the heir(s) at law* – normally to the eldest son or, if there were daughters only, then to all of them equally. Local custom in a manor could alter this; for example, where the custom of *Borough English* persisted (by which the youngest son inherited) or in those parts of Kent where *gavelkind* prevailed (by which all sons inherited equally).

Distribution of the estate could not take place until one year after the grant of administration had been made, so that all debts could be fully discharged.

4.2 The records

The letters of administration – or often brief summaries of them – were copied into an *administration act book* by the appropriate ecclesiastical court. These served as the court's registered copies and are what will be found at record offices. Unfortunately the letters are very formulaic and usually supply little in the way of information about the family or the distribution of the estate. However, additional details may sometimes be obtained from the inventory, account and administration bond, if they survive, or from death duty records.

Administration act books normally give the following information:

- date of the grant of administration
- name of the intestate
- parish of residence of the intestate
- name of the administrator and his or her relationship to the intestate
- dates by which the inventory and account had to be returned to the court

For more complicated estates or later administrations, they may also include:

- place of death of the intestate
- marital status and/or occupation of the intestate
- conditions limiting the grant (if applicable)
- name of the special commissioner before whom the administrator was sworn
- marginal notes referring to previous or subsequent grants

The original letters of administration handed to the administrators rarely survive. However, they might have been returned to the court when an administrator renounced his or her right to administer or as an exhibit in the event of litigation. There are examples of original letters of administration at the National Archives in the records of the courts of Exchequer and Chancery, which can be searched using the National Archives' online catalogue.

Example of an administration, in Latin, 1720

Before 1733, except during the Interregnum (see 2.2.2), all administrations were written in Latin. Below is an example of a Latin administration (PROB 6/96, f. 97) translated into English.* As the records are formulaic legal documents, this can be used as a basis for translating other Latin administrations.

Johannes Bayly	*Tricesimo die Emanavit Commissio Elizabethae Bayly viduae Relictae Johannis Bayly nuper parochiae Sanctae Mariae Rotherhithe in Comitatu Surriae sed in Nave Regia Le Dreadnought defuncti habentis &c [dum vixit et mortis suae tempore bona jura sive credita in diversis diocesibus sive peculiaribus jurisdictionibus sufficientia ad fundandum jurisdictionem Curiae Praerogativae Cantuariensis] ad Administrandum bona jura et credita dicti defuncti De bene &c [et fideliter administrando eadem ad sancta Dei evangelia] juratae*	*ultimus [dies] Novembris* *ultimus [dies] Maij 1721*
John Bayly	On the thirtieth day a commission was issued to Elizabeth Bayly, widow relict of John Bayly formerly of the parish of St Mary Rotherhithe in the county of Surrey but in HMS *Dreadnought* deceased, having [while he lived and at the time of his death goods, rights or credits in different dioceses or peculiar jurisdictions sufficient to the foundation of the jurisdiction of the Prerogative Court of Canterbury], to administer the goods, rights and credits of the said deceased, having been sworn [on the holy gospels] to well [and faithfully administer the same].	last [day] of November last [day] of May 1721

* Letters omitted from the original text on account of abbreviations have been supplied underlined. Words omitted from the original – including those implied by *&c* (etc.) – have been supplied in square brackets.

The first date in the right-hand margin is the date by which the administrator was required to exhibit an inventory of the intestate's personal estate. The second date is the date by which the administrator was required to present an account of his or her administration of the estate.

4.3 Finding an administration

Administrations can be more difficult to find than wills, as administrations are less likely to have either an online index or an alphabetical surname index. As administrations provide less social and genealogical information, indexing projects are less common. For many courts, a handwritten index arranged by the first letter of the intestate's surname may be the only means of locating the document. In trying to identify the current location of an administration, use the table in Chapter 3. Remember that DocumentsOnline (see 3.3.1) does not include administrations.

4.3.1 Prerogative Court of Canterbury (1559–1858)

There is no single comprehensive index to PCC administrations. Instead, there is a combination of different personal-name indexes. To find an administration, you will therefore need to examine one of the many indexes, in different formats for different periods, listed below (some of which cover both administrations and wills):

Indexes to administrations

1559–1660	Published indexes, in several date sequences.
1661–2	Calendars in PROB 12, arranged annually.
1663–4	Typescript indexes.
1665–1700	Calendars in PROB 12.
1701–49	Index compiled by Friends of The National Archives.
1750–1852	Calendars in PROB 12. Index covering 1750–1800 available at the Society of Genealogists and the FRC.
1853–8	Two alphabetical calendars in PROB 12.

The indexes to administration acts supply:

- calendar year of grant
- month of grant
- place of residence of the deceased

Early published indexes give a folio number (each folio has a recto and a verso, so the folio number relates to both sides of the page), which corresponds to a small handwritten number in the act book. Before 1719, if there is no folio number you will need to make a note of the month of the grant given in the index and search through the particular month in the act book. After 1719, administrations are arranged by seat (see below).

PCC seat system (1719–1858)

From 1719 to 1858, the PCC divided the business of granting probate and administration between five 'seats', each with its own distinct geographical area of responsibility. During this period, the seat system was also applied to the organization of limited administrations in PROB 7, probate acts in PROB 8, limited probates in PROB 9, administration bonds in PROB 46, and commissions to swear executors in PROB 52.

Similarly, from 1719 to 1743 the administration act books in PROB 6 are divided into seats corresponding to the five seats of the court.

The seat sections usually appear in the following order: Registrar's seat, Surrey seat, Welsh seat, Middlesex seat, and London seat. Each seat is arranged in calendar order, and the entry should appear in alphabetical order by the initial letter of the intestate's surname. The administrative areas of the five seats were as follows:

Registrar's seat	Testators or intestates dying overseas or at sea, except in cases where the grant was made to the widow and she lived in an area within the jurisdiction of one of the other seats, in which case probate or administration was granted at that seat. Such entries will be indicted by *'pts'* (*in partibus transmarinis* – meaning died abroad) or *ser* or *serv* (*in servitio regis* – in the service of the Crown). Testators or intestates living outside the province of Canterbury. Estates that were, might be, or had been subject to litigation within the PCC. (If, however, a subsequent grant of probate or administration was made, it was issued at the seat that would have been responsible had there been no litigation.)
Surrey seat	Cornwall, Devon, Dorset, Hampshire, Somerset, Surrey, Sussex, Wiltshire.
Welsh seat	Berkshire, Derbyshire, Gloucestershire, Herefordshire, Leicestershire, Northamptonshire, Oxfordshire, Rutland, Shropshire, Staffordshire, Warwickshire, Worcestershire, Wales.
Middlesex seat	Bedfordshire, Buckinghamshire, Cambridgeshire, Essex, Hertfordshire, Huntingdonshire, Kent, Lincolnshire, Middlesex (except parishes listed below), Norfolk, Suffolk.

London seat	The city of London, including the following parishes and administrative areas (some of them in Middlesex or partly in Middlesex and partly in London):
	Charterhouse; Furnivall's Inn; Glasshouse Yard; Gray's Inn; Holy Trinity Minories; Liberty of the Rolls; Liberty of the Tower of London; Lincoln's Inn; Old Artillery Ground; Precinct of Norton Folgate; Precinct of St Katherine by the Tower; Precinct of the Savoy; St Andrew Holborn; St Anne Soho; St Botolph Aldersgate; St Botolph without Aldgate; St George Bloomsbury; St George the Martyr Holborn (Queen Square); St Giles Cripplegate; St Giles in the Fields; St James Clerkenwell; St James Westminster; St John Clerkenwell; St John the Evangelist Westminster; St John Wapping; St Leonard Shoreditch; St Luke Old Street; St Margaret Westminster; St Mary le Strand; St Mary Matfelon Whitechapel; St Sepulchre.

It is also necessary when using the seat system to bear in mind the following anomalies:

- If the place of residence is given as Middlesex and it is not possible to tell whether the deceased lived in an area subject to the Middlesex seat or the London seat, you may need to search both.
- The city of Bristol was partly in Somerset (Surrey seat) and partly in Gloucestershire (Welsh seat). It may therefore be necessary to search both.
- In some act books the term *walk* is used, rather than *seat*.

Other sources

As information contained within administrations can be scant, other potential sources may be worth considering.

The initial application for a grant of administration (these are in PROB 14, 1657–1858) bears the administrator's signature and gives an approximate date of the intestate's death.

If the court took over the distribution of the estate, details of this can be found in the Muniment Books in PROB 16 (1610–1858).

For information about administration bonds, see 4.5.

Estates of intestates may have been subject to death duties from 1796–1858. See 8.3 for more information.

Administrators were required to produce an inventory and account of the distribution of the estate. See Chapter 7 for more information.

4.3.2 Prerogative Court of York (1502–1858)

Administrations are included in the PCY probate act books. As mentioned in 2.3.1, from 1502 grants of probate and administration were entered into the act books of the various rural deanery courts. The earliest surviving act book of the Prerogative Court is dated 1587; before that date, prerogative business will be found in the act books of York City Deanery, held at the Borthwick Institute. There are gaps in the probate act books series during the sixteenth and seventeenth centuries.

Printed sources

Published indexes to wills proved in the Exchequer and Prerogative courts will be found in Appendix 2.

4.4 Additional information that administrations may contain

Records that reflect variations to the normal process of the granting of administrations include:

- Grants of administration of goods not administered (*administratio de bonis non administratis*, often abbreviated to *admon dbn*). These occurred following the death or refusal or inability to act of the initial administrator, and will be found in the administration act books in the normal way.

- Grants where the administration was granted to a creditor.

- Grants relating to minors (*administratio durante minore aetate*). Where an estate was administered in the name of a minor (under 21), the name of the minor is given.

- Grants that were disputed. If an entry is prefixed by the abbreviations *dec* (by decree), *int dec* (interlocutory decree) or *sent* (sentence), then the estate was the subject of litigation. See Chapter 9 for further information.

4.5 Administration bonds

From 1529, administrators – including those responsible for administrations with will annexed (see 4.7) – were required to enter into a bond for a sum of money, with two or more guarantors, whereby they undertook to faithfully perform the tasks assigned to them by the probate court. This was to ensure that the estate was administered properly. The appropriate ecclesiastical court would keep a copy of the bond, and another copy would be given to the administrator.

Administration bonds usually include the following:

- the place of residence of the administrator
- the places of residence of his or her guarantors
- the signature (or mark) of the administrator
- the signatures (or marks) of the guarantors

The value of the bond is often double the valuation of the personal estate and may be annotated (formally noted) in the administration act books. Sometimes the value of the bond was less than double, though it was usually greater than the value of the personal estate. A second bond was sometimes entered into if the original valuation was inaccurate.

Although administration bonds can be used to give a rough estimate of the value of an individual's estate, a more accurate indicator would be either the death duty (see 8.3.2) or the inventory and account (see 7.2). Bonds can supply additional information about an estate, but their genealogical value is normally limited to providing details about the administrator rather than the intestate.

Bonds for the Prerogative Court of Canterbury before 1601 are to be found in PROB 51. Some bonds in this series predate the earliest surviving PCC administration act book (PROB 6), which dates from December 1559. This series has only been partially sorted and catalogued. The majority of bonds are therefore not available. PCC bonds from 1601 to 1713 are in PROB 54, though a catalogue for these records is not yet available. The bonds from 1714 to 1858 will be found in PROB 46, arranged by the month of the grant and by seat (see 4.3.1). PROB 46 is stored off site, so please allow three working days for the document to arrive.

Generally, bonds for the Prerogative Court of York (and other ecclesiastical courts) are found together with the administration itself.

4.6 Special or limited administrations

Sometimes the court limited the grant of administration to a particular part of the deceased's estate or to a specified period of time. Instances include administrations granted during the absence (usually abroad) of the obvious administrator and those limited to the payment of seamen's wages.

From 1810 to 1858, limited administrations granted by the Prerogative Court of Canterbury are to be found in PROB 7. Before that date, they will be found in PROB 6, preceding the relevant monthly section. Cross-references in PROB 6 to entries in PROB 7 are identifiable by the term *'entered at length'* in the administration act book.

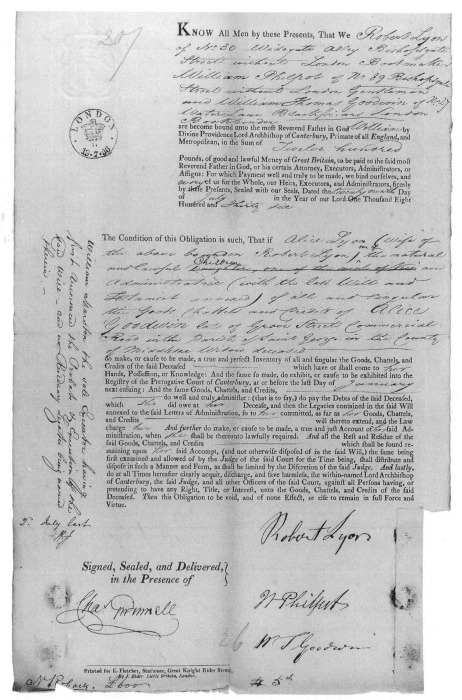

Figure 3 Administration bond with will annexed, relating to the estate of Alice Goodwin, 1836 (PROB 46/852). William Marston, the sole executor of her will, had renounced his right to administer the estate. Instead the administration was granted to Alice Lyon, Alice Goodwin's daughter and residuary legatee. The sureties are Robert Lyon (husband of Alice Lyon), William Philpot and William Goodwin, who were bound to the court for the sum of £1,200 (double the value of the estate, which is given as £600 at the foot of the page).

Limited administrations granted by the Prerogative Court of York and minor church courts will be found with the main administration.

For special or limited grants of probate, see 9.18.1.

4.7 Administrations granted as part of the probate process

In certain cases, an administrator would be appointed (instead of an executor) to administer a testator's estate. The two main examples of these are *letters of administration with will annexed* and *administration with will annexed of goods not administered*. Although the same procedure would be followed as for the administration of an intestate's estate, the record of the grant is copied into the probate act book and not the administration act book. Such PCC grants are annotated (formally noted) in the name indexes to wills. Prior to 1781, letters of administration with will annexed and letters of administration of goods not administered issued by the PCC were recorded in the ordinary Probate Act Books (PROB 8) 1526–1858. From 1781, such grants are in PROB 9 (1781, 1800, 1802–1858). Administrators of such estates were required to enter into bonds for the proper administration of the estate (see 4.5).

4.7.1 Administration with will annexed

These grants relate to valid wills where probate could not be granted because the executor refused to act or was unable to do so. The Latin name for them is *administratio cum testamento annexo*, often abbreviated to *AW*.

Situations of this kind would occur when:

- The nominated executor failed to respond to the summons asking him to prove the will.
- The nominated executor renounced the right to administer.
- The nominated executor died before the testator.
- The testator failed to nominate an executor in the will.

In such cases the administrator would usually be the next of kin (under the same laws as intestacy), but the distribution of the estate would follow the terms of the will and not the various intestacy laws.

Example of an administration with will annexed, in Latin, 1720

Before 1733, except during the Interregnum (see 2.2.2), all grants of administration with will annexed were written in Latin. Below is an example of a Latin administration (PROB 8/113, f. 97), translated into English.* As the records are formulaic legal documents, this can be used as a basis for translating other such documents.

Rogerus Pocock	*Decimo Septimo die Emanavit Commissio Gulielmo Sussex Legatario Principali nominato in Testamento Rogeri Pocock nuper de Felfam in Comitatu Sussexiae Clerici defuncti habentis &c [dum vixit et mortis suae tempore bona jura sive credita in diversis diocesibus sive peculiaribus jurisdictionibus sufficientia ad fundandum jurisdictionem Curiae Praerogativae Cantuariensis] ad administrandum bona jura et credita dicti defuncti juxta tenorum et effectum Testamenti ipsius defuncti (Eo quod Rebecca Collier executrix et Legataria residuria in dicto Testamento nominata oneri Execucionis ejusdem expresse renuntiaverit) De bene &c [et fideliter administrando eadem ad sancta Dei evangelia] jurato*	*ultimus* [dies] *Novembris* *ultimus* [dies] *Maij 1721*
Roger Pocock	On the seventeenth day a commission was issued to William Sussex, principal legatee named in the will of Roger Pocock formerly of Felpham in the county of Sussex, clerk, deceased, having [while he lived and at the time of his death goods, rights or credits in different dioceses or peculiar jurisdictions sufficient to the foundation of the jurisdiction of the Prerogative Court of Canterbury], to administer the goods rights and credits of the said deceased according to the wording and effect of the said will of the deceased (since Rebecca Collier executrix and residuary legatee named in the said will shall have expressly renounced the burden of the execution of the same), having been sworn [on the holy gospels] to well [and faithfully administer the same].	last [day] of November last [day] of May 1721

* Letters omitted from the original text on account of abbreviations have been supplied underlined. Words omitted from the original – including those implied by *&c* (etc.) – have been supplied in square brackets.

The first date in the right-hand margin is the date by which the administrator was required to exhibit an inventory of the intestate's personal estate. The second date is the date by which the administrator was required to present an account of his or her administration of the estate.

4.7.2 Administration with will annexed of goods not administered

A second or further grant of administration – called *administratio de bonis non administratis* (often abbreviated to *admon dbn*) – was issued when the administration of the estate was incomplete.

Grants of this kind were made when:

- The executor died or renounced his or her executorship before the administration of the estate was complete.
- The previous executor had died.
- The grant had been revoked by the court.
- The grant was issued during the minority of the next of kin, which had since expired.

● The residuary legatee or next of kin was inaccessible because abroad and the executor was dead.

If a former grant had been made, this would be recorded – usually annotated with the year and month of the previous grant, which will help to identify other references to the same estate. Some estates were subject to a large number of grants, sometimes years after the first grant.

4.8 Estates without next of kin (*bona vacantia*)

If someone dies intestate and is not survived by a lawful heir, or dies leaving a will but fails to dispose of the residue of his or her estate, the estate (or residue) reverts to the Crown. Such estates are known as *bona vacantia.*

The National Archives holds selected case papers relating to estates of this kind administered by the Treasury Solicitor (the government lawyer) and HM Procurator General. Among them you will find papers relating to property in England and Wales belonging to dissolved companies and to trusts that failed or were wound up.

The main series is TS 17 (*Bona Vacantia*, Administration of Estate Papers, 1698–1981), which contains selected case papers (TS 17/1–301 and TS 17/1245–1390) and letters of administration (TS 17/302–1244) extracted by HM Procurator General in favour of the Treasury Solicitor. The files are arranged by the name of the person or organization whose estate is under administration, but later files within the series relate to the wider policy questions concerning *bona vacantia.*

Other records of the Treasury Solicitor and HM Procurator General concerning *bona vacantia* business include:

TS 8:   Letter Books, 1804–15
TS 9:   Letter Books, 1815–44
TS 30:   Royal Warrants and Treasury Authorities, 1804–1936
TS 33:   Pedigrees, 1794–1944

TS 8 and TS 9 also include details of wills. See 10.7.9.

For details of *bona vacantia* estates in Scotland and Ireland, see 11.6.

5
Wills and Administrations from 1858 Onwards

The period from 1858, when the present-day Probate Registry was formed, can be considered the modern era for the history of wills and administrations. This chapter describes the court structure, and gives practical advice on how to find wills and administrations and obtain copies of them. Only England and Wales are covered here. For wills and administrations in Scotland, Northern Ireland, the Republic of Ireland, the Channel Islands and the Isle of Man, see Chapter 11.

5.1 The Probate Act 1857

This act took away the probate jurisdiction of the ecclesiastical courts and set up a secular national Court of Probate for England and Wales. However, there was no change to the law of probate, and the new court followed the rules, orders and practice of the Prerogative Court of Canterbury. For the wider implications of the act, see 9.16.

Although often described as a centralized court, the new Court of Probate was also a very local institution, with a network of 40 district registries to cover wills of lower value. Indeed, by 1879, three fifths of all grants of probate and administration were issued by the district registries.

One of the advantages of the post-1858 Court of Probate, compared with the church courts, was that it was much easier for executors to appear in person. Previously, specialized ecclesiastical lawyers called proctors appeared on behalf of executors, especially for probate of wills at the Prerogative Court of Canterbury and some of the London courts.

The general impression of a single universal court was created by the production of a union index of all wills and administrations (see 5.2.1 and 5.2.2). This was compiled annually by the Principal Probate Registry from information sent in by the local registries. The new court made its first grants of probate and administration on 12 January 1858.

In 1873, under the Supreme Court of Judicature Act, the Court of Probate became part of the Probate, Divorce and Admiralty Division of the High Court of Justice. The implications of this act, too, are referred to in 9.16.

5.1.1 *The Court of Probate: Principal Registry and District Registries*

As already mentioned, in addition to the Principal Registry, which served London and the surrounding counties, the Court of Probate had 40 district registries. See below for a list of district registries by county.

Within a county, poorer people did not even have to travel to the district registry. An executor of a will of low value could apply for probate at the local Inland Revenue Office, if that was more convenient. Taking one year at random, 1899, we find that 'low value' was then defined as where the gross real and personal estate did not exceed £500. So in Middlesex, for example, many people had the option of going to Inland Revenue offices at Acton, Enfield, Kilburn, Staines, Sudbury, Tottenham and Uxbridge; and in Devon low-value wills could be proved at Barnstaple, Bideford, Honiton, Ilfracombe, North Tawton, Okehampton, Parracombe, Plymouth, South Molton, Tiverton and Totnes, as well as Exeter. Although local church courts had gone, there was still local provision for getting wills proved as cheaply as possible. This was of great importance for the success of the court, and also for the extension of death duties (see Chapter 8). There was even a provision allowing applications for administrations to be made to the registrar of a county court, if the value of the estate was small (for example, £100 in 1896) and the applicant lived more than 3 miles from a district registry.

Today, there are 30 district and sub-district registries. Contact details for these registries are given on the Court Service website, **www.courtservice.gov.uk**.

District registries by county

England

Deceased's place of residence*	District registry
Bedfordshire	Northampton
Berkshire	Oxford
Bristol and Bath	Bristol
Buckinghamshire	Oxford
Cambridgeshire (including the university)	Peterborough
Cheshire	Chester
Cornwall	Bodmin
Cumberland	Carlisle
Derbyshire	Derby
Devon	Exeter
Dorset	Blandford
Durham	Durham
Essex, northern division	Ipswich
Gloucestershire (except the Bristol area – see Bristol)	Gloucester
Hampshire	Winchester
Herefordshire	Hereford
Huntingdonshire	Peterborough
Isle of Wight	Winchester
Kent, eastern division (including Cinque Ports and their dependencies in Kent)	Canterbury
Lancashire (except Manchester and the hundreds of Salford and West Derby)	Lancaster
Lancashire (Manchester and the hundred of Salford)	Manchester
Lancashire (the hundred of West Derby)	Liverpool
Leicestershire	Leicester
Lincolnshire	Lincoln
Norfolk	Norwich
Northamptonshire, northern division	Peterborough

Deceased's place of residence*	District registry
Northamptonshire, southern division	Northampton
Northumberland and Berwick-upon-Tweed	Newcastle upon Tyne
Nottinghamshire	Nottingham
Oxfordshire (including the university)	Oxford
Rutland	Leicester
Shropshire	Shrewsbury
Somerset, eastern division (except the Bristol and Bath areas)	Wells
Somerset, western division	Taunton
Staffordshire	Lichfield
Suffolk, eastern division	Ipswich
Suffolk, western division	Bury St Edmunds
Sussex, eastern division (including Cinque Ports and their dependencies in Sussex)	Lewes
Sussex, western division	Chichester
Warwickshire	Birmingham
Westmorland	Carlisle
Wiltshire	Salisbury
Worcestershire	Worcester
Yorkshire, East Riding (including the city of York and Ainsty, and the town and county of Kingston upon Hull)	York
Yorkshire, North Riding	York
Yorkshire, West Riding	Wakefield

* For counties not mentioned (such as Hertfordshire, western Kent or southern Essex), the registry to use was the Principal Registry in London.

Wales

Deceased's place of residence	District registry
Anglesey	Bangor
Brecknockshire	Hereford
Caernarvonshire	Bangor
Cardiganshire	Carmarthen
Carmarthenshire	Carmarthen
Denbighshire	St Asaph
Glamorganshire (except for the Bath areas)	Llandaff
Glamorganshire (deaneries of East and West Gower)	Carmarthen
Merionethshire	St Asaph
Monmouthshire	Llandaff
Montgomeryshire	Shrewsbury
Pembrokeshire	Carmarthen
Radnorshire	Hereford

5.1.2 Do all wills go to probate?

Probate does not have to be sought if the sum involved is small (currently the threshold for England and Wales is £5,000 for money held in accounts). However, many wills involving smaller amounts go to probate, as this is often the easiest way to fulfil the instructions contained in the will.

Using the National Probate Calendar (see 5.2), in his annual report for 1861 the Registrar General produced an analysis of the number of wills that went to probate during 1858 and the number of administrations granted. The number of persons who died during the year was 210,972. Out of these, some 21,653 left wills (since the new Court of Probate was not operative for the first 10 days of 1858, this figure had been adjusted to compensate for the missing days). Therefore only one person in 10 left a will. The average value of property disposed of was £2,998 by will and £759 by administration.

During 1858, out of the 102,049 men aged 21 or over who died in England and Wales, 15,558 (15.2%) left personal property by will and 5,896 (5.8%) by administration. So 21% of adult males left personal property and 79% made no bequests.

Out of the 108,923 women who died aged 21 or over, 6,095 (5.6%) left personal property by will and 3,274 (3%) by administration. So for women, the average amount left by will was £1,793 and the average amount left by administration was £587. However, it should be borne in mind that this was before the Married Women's Property Act of 1882, and so a large percentage of adult women were still excluded from making wills.

5.2 Finding wills proved in England and Wales from 1858

From the outset, the Principal Registry of the Court of Probate published an annual index, known as the National Probate Calendar (also referred to as the Probate Calendar, the National Probate Register or the National Index), listing all wills proved and administrations granted during the year by the whole court. As a result, finding wills proved since 12 January 1858 is much easier than finding wills proved before then.

5.2.1 The National Probate Calendar

There are National Probate Calendars for each year from 1858 to the current year. From 1871, wills and administrations are indexed in a single sequence: before then they were given in separate indexes. All are arranged in strictly alphabetical order.

From 1858 to 1968, the following information appears:

- full name and address of the deceased (and sometimes occupation)
- full name and address of executors or administrators (and addresses up to 1892)
- their relationship, if any, to the deceased (not given from 1892)
- date and place of death
- date and place of grant of probate or administration
- value of estate
- for women, marital status of the deceased, often with name of husband if still alive at time of probate or administration (husband's name not given from 1958)

From 1968 onwards, the only information given is:

- name and address of the deceased
- date and place of death
- date and place of grant of probate or administration
- value of estate

Figure 4(a)   Photograph of the actress Lily Langtry, née Emilie Charlotte Le Breton. Born in Jersey (hence her nickname 'the Jersey Lily'), she married Edward Langtry first, who died in 1897, and subsequently Hugo Gerald de Bathe. (COPY 1/ 402)

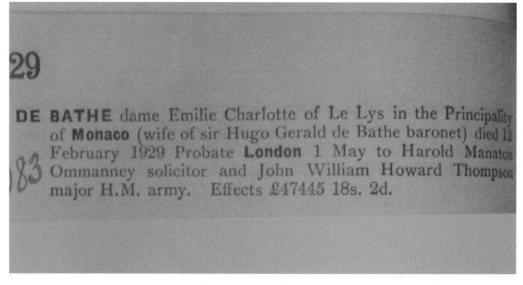

Figure 4(b)   Entry in the 1929 National Probate Calendar for Dame Emilie Charlotte de Bathe (Lily Langtry). *Reproduced by courtesy of the Court Service*

DAME
EMILIE
CHARLOTTE
DE BATHE

13.

THIS IS THE WILL made the twenty second day of October one thousand nine hundred and twenty eight of me LADY EMILIE CHARLOTTE DE BATHE of Le Lys Monaco in the Principality of Monaco Whereby

1. I revoke all former Wills and Codicils and declare this to be my last Will

2. I appoint my friends Harold Manaton Ommanney of 3 and 4 Great Winchester Street in the City of London Solicitor and Major John William Howard Thompson of 25 a North Audley Street in the County of London to be EXECUTORS AND TRUSTEES of this my Will and I give to the said Harold Manaton Ommanney and John William Howard Thompson a legacy of five hundred pounds each as such Executors free of duty

3. I give the following pecuniary and specific legacies and annuities all free of duty (a) To the Museum situate at St Helier in the Island of Jersey the following furniture at present in my Villa Le Lys Monaco in the Principality of Monaco viz Suite of Dining Room painted furniture including buffet two tables glass cupboard and six chairs the drawing room set of eight Louis XVl fauteuils and settee the tapestry panel in the drawing room Louis XVl Cabinet the bust of Diana and pedestal the drawing room "mantle clock my bed and hangings the Brittany wardrobe my gilt and turquoise toilet service my silver gilt mirror my Buhl linen cupboard all my coloured glass my Viennese dinner service and the portrait of myself painted by Sir Edward Poynter and in the event of the Museum not accepting the above articles then I bequeath them unto Mathilde Marie Peat (b) To my cousin Maud le Breton Butler a legacy of five hundred pounds (c) To Clara Purr a legacy of one hundred pounds (d) To my Godson Michael Melford a legacy of one hundred pounds (e) To Louis d'Albani late Major in the First 123rd Rifles a legacy of two thousand pounds (f) To Dr Gavin of 5 Berkeley Square in the County of London a legacy of one thousand pounds (g) To Peter Faskally of 2 Warterton Street in the County of London a legacy of one hundred pounds (h) To Mrs Hardacre of 33a Grenfell Road Gorringe Park Mitcham a legacy of two hundred pounds (i) To George Ian Malcolm a legacy of one thousand pounds and silver Epergne inscribed to Sir Thomas le Breton (j) To Victor Neilk Malcolm a legacy of five thousand pounds and Jockey Club Cup (k) To Angus Christian Edward Malcolm a legacy of five thousand pounds and Georgian tray inscribed to my father (l) To Helen Mary Malcolm a legacy of five thousand pounds and my diamond pearl and emerald clock (m) To E_ F_ Treen of Drummonds Bank 49 Charing Cross London a legacy of five hundred pounds (n) To the Honourable Evelyn Lady Miller my oval opal ring (o) To my daughter Lady Malcolm all silver (with the exception of any articles of silver otherwise bequeathed by this my Will) and my mother of pearl dessert service (p) To my friend Mathilde Marie Peat as a token of affection and gratitude a legacy of ten thousand pounds all my wearing apparel furs jewellery electro plate Sheffield plate silver tea pot milk jug sugar basin and hot water jug generally used by me my motor car my Villa known as Le Lys Monaco aforesaid together with the entire contents with the exception of any articles otherwise specifically bequeathed by this my Will (q) To any domestic servants in my employ for a period of six months and if still in my service at the date of my death and not under notice to leave one years wages and in addition any unpaid wages that may have accrued due to the date of my death I declare that I have only given my Grandson George Ian Malcolm a small legacy not through any lack of affection for him but because being the heir he will be amply provided for on the death of his parents

Figure 4(c)   The first page of the will of Dame Emilie Charlotte de Bathe (Lily Langtry). *Reproduced by courtesy of the Court Service.*

5.2.2 Where to find the National Probate Calendar

The only **complete run** of the annual National Probate Calendars is held at:

The Probate Searchroom
Principal Registry of the Family Division
First Avenue House
42–49 High Holborn
London WC1V 6NP

Telephone: 020 7947 7000

They are in the following formats:

1858–1992:	in books
1993–5:	on microfiche
1996 onwards:	on computer (also available at Manchester District Probate Registry)

However, the National Archives, the Family Records Centre and a number of county archives/record offices and local studies centres hold microfiche copies of the National Probate Calendars for 1858–1943. The Society of Genealogists, in London, and some record offices have microfilm or microfiche copies for the slightly shorter period of 1858–1930. Additionally, hard copies that were held at district registries are now deposited at a number of local record offices.

The National Probate Calendars are also available at district probate registries (of which there are currently 11), although these registries are only required to hold the indexes to wills and administrations for the last 50 years and most do not hold any for earlier years. The addresses of the district registries and the network of sub-registries are listed on the Court Service website (**www.courtservice.gov.uk**).

Although the National Probate Calendars are not at present accessible via the Internet, there is currently a proposal to digitize the indexes to wills and administrations and to provide online ordering and payment for copies of wills and grants. Check the Court Service website (see above) for the latest developments.

5.3 Obtaining a copy of a will or administration after 1858

If you have found an entry in the National Probate Calendar for a will or administration that is of interest to you, in order to obtain a copy you need to note down the following:

- the name of the deceased
- the date
- the type of grant (i.e. will or administration)

For the years 1940–46, you may find Llandudno mentioned when you were expecting London to be given as the place of probate or administration. The reason for this is that the Principal Registry moved from London to Llandudno, in North Wales, as part of the evacuation of certain government records during the war years.

5.3.1 In person

You can go to the Probate Searchroom at the Principal Registry of the Family Division in London (see 5.2.2 for address) or any of the district registries to request a copy of a will, grant of probate or grant of administration.

If you are using the calendars for 1858–1930 at the Probate Searchroom in London, be sure to make a note of the handwritten folio number that appears in the margin of the index, as you will need it in order to request access to the will itself. These numbers do not appear on the microfiche or microfilm copies. Also, there are handwritten additions to show further grants of probate or where the original value of an estate was resworn, because it had been recalculated.

5.3.2 By post

The Probate Registry offers a postal search service. Applications for searches and copies of wills and administrations can be made to:

Postal Searches & Copies Dept
York Probate Sub-Registry
Castle Chambers
Clifford Street
York YO1 9RG

For more detailed information about the postal search service (including a downloadable application form), see **www.courtservice.gov.uk**.

5.3.3 Estates without next of kin (bona vacantia)

For details of estates without next of kin (see 4.8), contact the following.

For most of England and Wales:
The Treasury Solicitor (*Bona Vacantia*)
Queen Anne's Chambers
28 Broadway
London SW1H 9JS

If the deceased person lived in Cornwall:
The Solicitor to the Duchy of Cornwall
10 Buckingham Gate
London SW1E 6LA

If the deceased person lived in Lancashire:
The Solicitor to the Duchy of Lancaster
Lancaster Place
Strand
London WC2E 7ED

For details of *bona vacantia* before 1858 see 4.8. For details of *bona vacantia* outside England and Wales, see 11.6.

5.4 Location of records

When probate was taken out at a district registry, the registry would retain the original will and make a registered copy, which was bound into a volume. A further copy was then forwarded to the Principal Registry in London. The original wills and associated records – apart from those lodged during the last two years, which are still held by the district registries – are now held in a central repository in Birmingham. The centre receives requests for copies from the registries, scans a copy and sends it back electronically. It does not deal directly with members of the public.

Registered copies originally held by the relevant district registry that are more than 50 years old are now mainly held at local county archives. See the table on p. 69 for the holdings of registered copy wills at local record offices.

The central repository in Birmingham also holds associated records for the Principal Registry, including oath bonds and, in some cases, correspondence from solicitors and internal registry notes. These have been kept for the last 50 years (earlier records have been destroyed).

In addition, the repository in Birmingham holds surviving records for the last 50 years of wills and grants issued by courts in former British colonies and resealed (probate confirmed or grants of administration authorized) in the Court of Probate in London. These are for people who lived and worked abroad but held property in England or Wales. Again, earlier records have been destroyed.

Local record office holdings of registered copy wills

England

County	Registered copy wills	County	Registered copy wills
Bedfordshire	Up to 1930 at Northamptonshire Record Office	Lincolnshire	Up to 1941 at Lincolnshire Record Office
Cambridgeshire	Up to 1926 for Northamptonshire Record Office	Norfolk	Up to 1941 at Norwich Record Office
Cheshire	Up to 1940 at Cheshire and Chester Archives	Northamptonshire	Up to 1930 at Northamptonshire Record Office
Cornwall	Up to 1941 at Cornwall Record Office	Northumberland	Up to 1941 at Northumberland Record Office
Cumberland	Up to 1941 at Cumbria Record Office, Carlisle	Nottinghamshire	Up to 1939 at Nottinghamshire Record Office
Derbyshire	Up to 1928 at Derbyshire Record Office, Matlock	Rutland	Up to 1941 at Leicestershire Record Office
Dorset	Up to 1941 at Dorset Archive Service	Shropshire	Up to 1940 at Shropshire Records and Research Centre
Durham	Up to 1940 at Durham University Library Archives and Special Collections	Staffordshire	Up to 1928 at Lichfield Record Office
Essex	Up to 1941 at Suffolk Record Office, Ipswich	Suffolk	Up to 1928 for Bury St Edmunds at Suffolk Record Office, Bury St Edmunds Up to 1941 for Ipswich at Suffolk Record Office, Ipswich
Gloucestershire	Up to 1941 for Gloucester at Gloucestershire Record Office	Sussex	Up to 1928 (West Sussex) for Chichester at West Sussex Record Office

County	Registered copy wills	County	Registered copy wills
	Up to 1941 for Bristol at Bristol Record Office		
Hampshire and Isle of Wight	Up to 1941 at Hampshire Record Office	Warwickshire	Up to 1941 at Birmingham Reference Library, Local Studies Department
Herefordshire	Up to 1928 at the National Library of Wales	Westmorland	Up to 1941 at Cumbria Record Office, Carlisle
Huntingdonshire	Up to 1941 at Northamptonshire Record Office	Wiltshire	Up to 1928 at Wiltshire and Swindon Record Office
Lancashire	Up to 1941 at Lancashire Record Office	Worcestershire	Up to 1928 at Worcestershire Record Office
Leicestershire	Up to 1940 at Leicestershire Record Office	Yorkshire	Up to 1939 for Wakefield at West Yorkshire County Record Office

Wales

County	Registered copy wills	County	Registered copy wills
Anglesey	Up to 1941 at NLW	Glamorganshire	Up to 1940 at NLW
Brecknockshire	Up to 1928 at NLW	Merionethshire	Up to 1928 at NLW
Cardiganshire	Up to 1941 at NLW	Monmouthshire	Up to 1940 at NLW
Caernarvonshire	Up to 1941 at NLW	Montgomeryshire	Up to 1940 at Shropshire Records and Research Centre
Carmarthenshire	Up to 1941 at NLW	Pembrokeshire	Up to 1941 at NLW
Denbighshire	Up to 1928 at NLW	Radnorshire	Up to 1928 at NLW
Flintshire	Up to 1928 at NLW		

NLW = National Library of Wales

5.5 Resealing in London of Scottish and Irish wills

Wills of Scots and Irish persons with property in England and Wales had to be resealed (that is, the grant of probate had to be confirmed) in London and are therefore listed in the general indexes. From 1858 to 1876, these resealed wills are indexed after the letter Z in each year. However, only the grants of probate were lodged in London and these do not usually contain more information than included in the probate calendars. The wills themselves would have been lodged in the respective countries. For more information about Scottish and Irish wills, see Chapter 11.

5.6 Wills of the royal family

When an application for probate involving a member of the royal family is submitted, the will is sealed pursuant to an order by the President of the Family Division of the High Court. No one may inspect the original will and no copies may be made, though the grant of probate is usually made available (an exception was made in 1998, when both a will and a grant of probate were made available in respect of the estate of Diana, Princess of Wales).

A list of royal wills is kept by the Principal Registry of the Family Division, but this is not available to the public and approval from a senior district judge would be needed to release it. However, the now out of print *Wills, inventories and death duties: The records of the Prerogative Court of Canterbury and the Estate Duty Office, a provisional guide* by Jane Cox (Public Record Office, 1988) – copies of which are available in the library and Microfilm Reading Room at the National Archives – lists royal wills from the medieval period to the twentieth century. Also see 10.5 for a list of royal wills at the National Archives.

6

Understanding the Will

This chapter focuses on the information contained within the will or administration itself. It explains how wills were constructed and how to interpret the information. The final part of the chapter looks at the skills needed to read and interpret the documents.

6.1 Drafting a will

6.1.1 The process of drafting a will

Early wills were oral statements taken down in the presence of witnesses. Commonly, as death approached, a cleric would be sent for to help the dying person prepare for death, receive his or her last wishes in the form of a will, and administer the last sacrament.

Early wills often include a statement that the testator is of 'sound mind' but 'sick in body'. This reference to soundness of mind was to satisfy the legal requirement that testators had to be in control of their senses and free from coercion. As the majority of old wills carry some kind of declaration of poor health, it can be deduced that testators tended to leave the making of a will until they were close to death or dangerously ill. However, some people made wills much earlier in life – often following marriage or the birth of children, during an illness, or following an inheritance.

By law, at least two people were required to witness the signing of the will in order for the ecclesiastical courts to accept it as an authentic document. These witnesses were likely to be close or trusted friends. See 6.1.10 for details of who was not allowed to act as a witness. At the end of the will, the testator was required to name an executor – but the relationship (if any) between the executor and the testator did not have to be mentioned, which can be frustrating for family historians.

The law would accept deathbed wishes provided they were written down and witnessed. But before the ecclesiastical courts would grant probate for a spoken (nuncupative) will, it had to be established that the testator was in sound mind (see 6.1.3).

6.1.2 Scribes

During the medieval period, wills progressed from oral statements of intent to written documents. However, because the ability to read and write was relatively uncommon, very few people wrote their own wills. Traditionally such clerical work was the province of the parish priest, but over time it became common practice for scribes, lawyers, doctors and other professionals to undertake the task.

It was the responsibility of the scribe to translate the wishes and requirements of the testator into a legible, formal legal document. Sometimes numerous revisions had to be made before a satisfactory version was produced. Often, after completing the will, the scribe had to be called back in order to add codicils (see 6.1.5) – especially since child mortality rates were high, and frequently alterations or substitutions had to be made.

A good scribe was expensive, but it was essential to find someone reliable and competent. Mistakes in the drafting of a will could prove very costly in terms of litigation and disputes after the testator's death. Also, it was important that the person employed to write the will was trustworthy, especially if some of the bequests – or omissions – were likely to be controversial.

Books of pro forma wills would have been available for the scribes to consult, and could be used as a basis for drafting a straightforward will.

6.1.3 How wills were recorded

Wills were recorded in three ways.

In the testator's own hand
Also known as holograph. Originally, because literacy was rare, wills of this kind were unusual. In order for a will in the testator's own hand to be valid, it had to be signed by at least two credible witnesses. See page 74 for an example of a holographic will.

Third party
This was the normal method of drafting a will (see 6.1.2).

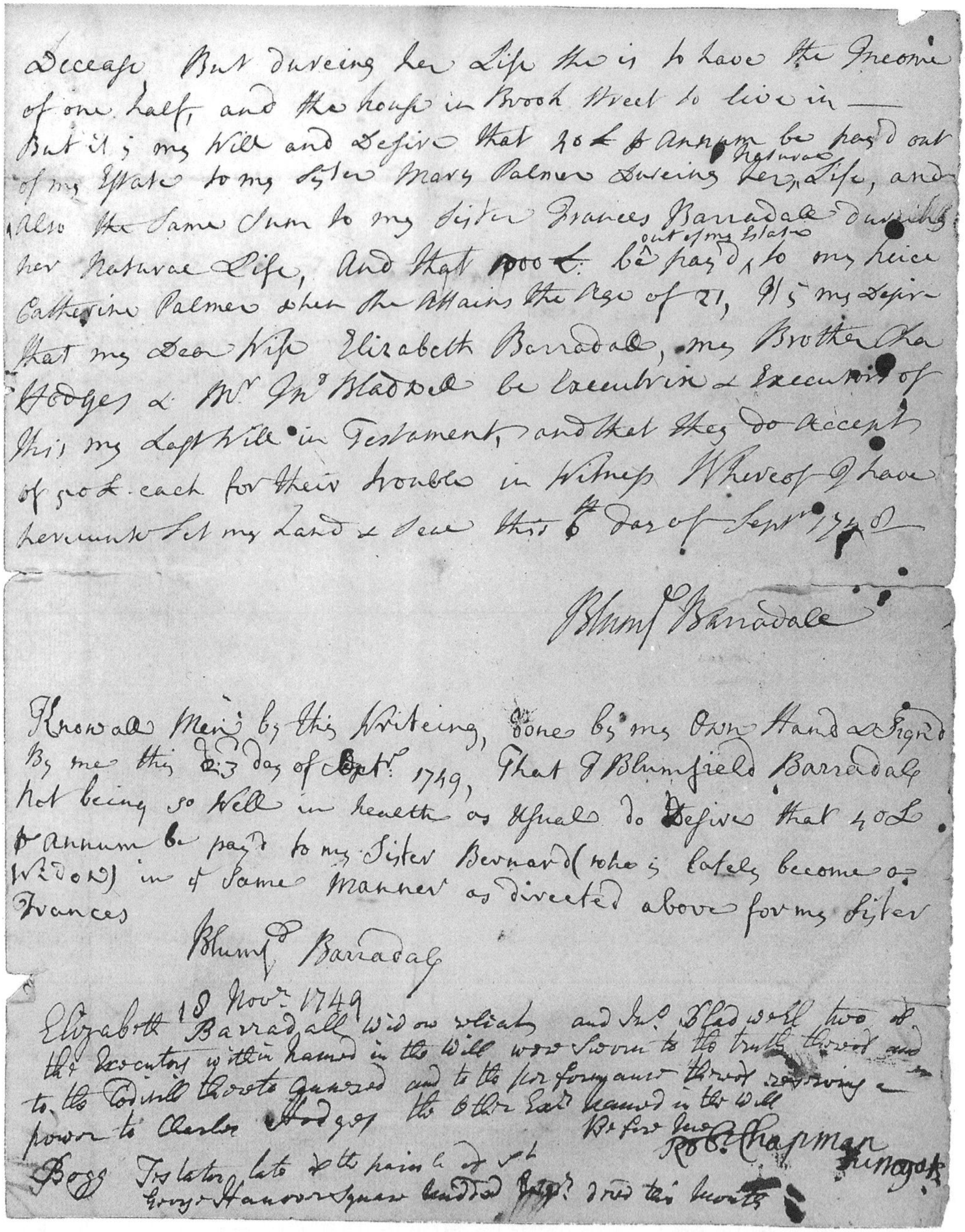

Figure 5   Holograph will of Blumfield Barradall, proved 19 November 1749 (PROB 10/2067). On 23 September 1749, a codicil had been added to the will bequeathing £40 per annum to his sister, as she had recently become a widow. Sadly he writes 'I Blumfield Barradall not being so well. . .' The will was proved less than two months later, after oaths from Elizabeth Barradall (widow) and John Bladwell (executor), who swore that the will and codicils were written by Blumfield Barradall.

Oral will

Also known as a nuncupative will or a spoken will. This usually occurred when the testator had left the drafting of a will to the last minute and was on his deathbed. It was necessary for at least two witnesses to be present when the words were spoken, and for them to be aware that the testator was making his will. The words were written down and signed as soon as possible, normally following the death of the testator.

In order to prevent fraud and give sufficient time for any other wills to be declared, probate would not be granted for this type of will until at least 14 days after the death of the testator. The ecclesiastical courts specified no precise form that nuncupative wills should take, but required that the meaning of the bequests be clear and free from ambiguity or obscurity. In 1676, the Act for Prevention of Fraud and Perjuries stipulated that if the estate totalled more than £30 a nuncupative will would no longer be acceptable unless at least three witnesses were present. Nuncupative wills are easily identifiable, as they usually begin with the word 'Memorandum'. In will indexes, they are sometimes identified as 'nunc'.

Following the Wills Act of 1837, nuncupative wills were declared invalid unless made by soldiers or sailors on active service.

The National Archives has a series of nuncupative wills (PROB 20), ranging from 1623 to 1838, where the Prerogative Court of Canterbury was asked to rule on authenticity.

Figure 6 Nuncupative will of Anne Marshall, 1620 (PROB 11/135). It commences with the words: 'Memorandum that Anne Marshall of Bisham in the Countye of Berkshire spinster being of good and perfect mynde and memorie made her last will and testament nuncupative in theis wordes followinge or the lyke in effect. . .'.

6.1.4 Appearance

Wills could be written on any material, although paper or parchment are normal. They could be written in any hand (for example, Secretary, Roman or Court hand) or language.

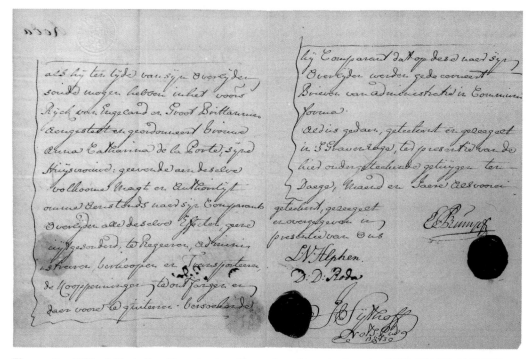

Figure 7   Will of Christian Constantyn Rumpf, written in Dutch, 1749 (PROB 10/2067). Attached to the original will is an English translation certified by the Prerogative Court of Canterbury. The registered copy (in PROB 11) is in English.

English, French and Latin are the most common languages. Examples of Portuguese, Italian and Dutch wills may also be found (a Dutch will dating from the eighteenth century is reproduced above). If written in a foreign language, the original will is usually accompanied by a certified English translation and the registered court copies are in English.

The essential requirement was that the will should be legible, and the sentiments within it clear and easily understood. In medieval times the language normally used for wills was Latin. By the middle of the sixteenth century this practice had died out – but, except during the Interregnum (see 2.2.2), the probate clause (see 6.2.6) continued to be written in Latin, which remained the official language of the courts until 1733.

The average will runs to less than six pages. However, there are wills that extend to several hundred pages, for example, and also those that are incredibly short. Sometimes the bequests may provide clues to the testator's character, but more commonly they simply detail the procedure to be followed after death.

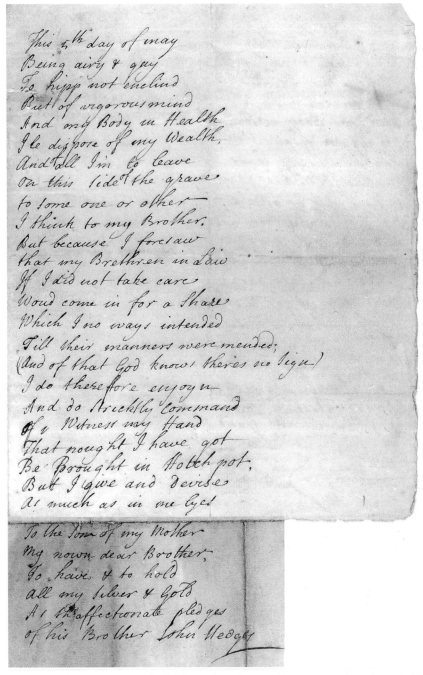

This 5th day of may
Being airy & gay
To hipp not enclind
But of vigorous mind
And my Body in Health
Ile dispose of my Wealth,
And all I'm to leave
On this side the grave
to some one or other —
I think to my Brother.
But because I foresaw
that my Brethren in Law
If I did not take care
Woud come in for a Share
Which I no ways intended
Till their manners were mended;
(And of that God knows theres no Sign)
I do therefore enjoyn —
And do strickly command
O, Witness my Hand
That nought I have got
Be Brought in Hotch pot,
But I give and devise
As much as in me Lyes

To the Son of my Mother
My nown dear Brother,
To have & to hold
all my silver & gold
As th'affectionate pledges
of his Brother John Hedges

Figure 8 Wills are usually laid out in a formulaic way, so that there is little to be learned about the personality and the individuality of the testator. Some testators, however, were undaunted by the legality and formality of the process – as witness the will of John Hedges of St George Hanover Square, London, who in 1737 wrote his will in verse (PROB 10/1850, f. 72). This will was duly proved, as it fulfilled all the legal requirements. However, John Hedges neglected to have his will witnessed. Consequently, attached to the original will are affidavits by two friends, who were called on to testify that the will was indeed written by him.

6.1.5 Codicils

Changes or revisions to a will could be made by adding a codicil. This was an attachment to the original will that avoided the need to submit a new document. There was no restriction on the number of codicils that could be made, and the addition of a codicil could be made either in writing or orally. The court granting probate was supposed to treat codicils as part of the original will.

6.1.6 Validity

For probate to be granted, it was essential that the will was valid. A will could be declared void, either fully or in part, if:

- it was made by a testator who was legally exempt from making a will (see 6.1.7)
- bequests were jointly owned
- the form of the disposal was unlawful
- the executor was incapable of acting as such
- the will was made in fear (the testator had been coerced into making a will)
- the will was fraudulent
- there was an error regarding either the person, name or quality of an executor or legatee, or the name, substance, quantity or quality of an item bequeathed
- there was uncertainty regarding either an executor or a legatee, or an item or items bequeathed, or the date of the will
- the quality and legibility of the will were imperfect

A will could be voided in its entirety if there was found to be a later will.

6.1.7 Exceptions to will making

6.1.7.1 Categories of people unable to leave a valid will

The following categories of people were either unable to leave a valid will or only able to do so if certain conditions were fulfilled:

Those proved not to be in full possession of their senses at the time the will was written, in which case the will would be declared void by the ecclesiastical courts. Within this category were:

- dumb or deaf (the court would grant probate only if it could be proved they had understanding and a desire to leave a will)
- drunks
- lunatics and idiots

The blind could make nuncupative wills provided they followed the normal legal requirements (see 6.1.3).

Those who had committed crimes:

- traitors (abolished under the Forfeiture Act of 1870 – until then those convicted of treason forfeited all goods and property to the Crown, so any will left by a traitor would be declared void)
- felons
- usurers
- libellers
- suicides (abolished under the Forfeiture Act of 1870)

Those who were not free:

- Slaves were considered to be the property of their master and so were their goods. They were therefore unable to make wills.

Those who were under age:

- Boys from the age of 14 and girls from the age of 12 could make wills. A girl's will would be declared void once she married, unless it was made with the consent of her husband (see 6.1.7.3). However, in 1540 the Statute of Wills forbade the devise of land by anyone under the age of 21, and in 1837 this was extended to all bequests. Under the Wills Act of 1837, the minimum age for leaving a will became 21.

Those barred for reasons of religion:

- excommunicates (abolished in 1813 – until then their wills were declared void)
- heretics
- apostates (those who did not believe in baptism)

6.1.7.2 Catholics

Following Henry VIII's divorce from Catherine of Aragon and the subsequent break with Rome in 1534, Catholics suffered increasingly hostile legislation. In the seventeenth century, a Catholic widow whose late husband was Protestant forfeited two thirds of her dowry as well as the right to be his executor.

In 1672, the Act for Preventing Dangers Which May Happen from Popish Recusants (commonly known as the Test Act) stipulated that in order for a Catholic widow to inherit her husband's estate she had to conform to the Protestant faith within four months of her husband's death. Further legislation in 1700 barred Catholics from buying or inheriting land.

Following an act of Parliament in 1716, deeds and wills of papists had to be enrolled in the law courts. Most of these are on the Close Rolls (series C 54) at the National Archives; others will be found on the Common Pleas Recovery Rolls (CP 43). See 10.6 for details on enrolled wills.

6.1.7.3 Married women

Before 1882, a married woman could only make a will with her husband's consent (which he could revoke at any time – even after her death, but before probate); and when he died, a further will had to be made. Widows and spinsters, however, could leave wills in their own right.

From 1882, the Married Women's Property Act allowed women to leave wills in their own right (see 1.5.1).

6.1.8 The armed forces

The Prerogative Court of Canterbury claimed jurisdiction for soldiers and sailors who died overseas, although from 1817 the estate had to be valued at over £20 before the PCC could act.

In 1837 the Wills Act allowed soldiers and sailors to make wills of personalty and from the age of 14 to make valid unwitnessed wills before going on expeditions. It also allowed them to make nuncupative wills (see 6.1.3) in the presence of two witnesses.

The National Archives series PROB 20 contains a number of precautionary wills made between 1623 and 1838 by sailors and others embarking on hazardous voyages. These are usually little more than letters of attorney authorizing a named person to dispose of the estate if the traveller failed to return.

6.1.9 The role of the executor

If the executor decided to act, there were certain tasks he or she had to fulfil.

These were to:

- compile an inventory of the deceased's personal estate
- pay the debts and legacies
- provide an account of the distribution of the estate

Following the death of the testator, the executor's first task was to find the last will and, before 1858, to identify the appropriate ecclesiastical court for probate (see 2.2.1). The executor and witnesses had to go to the court and swear that the exhibited will was the final one and that it had either been written or dictated by the testator (see 6.1). Executors unable to come to court in person could be sworn by commission (see 2.4.1). Assuming there were no problems or objections, the judge would then grant probate. Executors were charged with exhibiting the inventory in court within six months of the grant of probate and had to provide an account of expenditure within six months of exhibiting the inventory (for more about inventories and accounts, see Chapter 7).

An executor could be anyone except those barred from will making (see 6.1.7). He or she was seen as someone who would act as the testator would and who would carry out his or her wishes as stipulated. There was therefore effectively a moral agreement between the executor and the testator to see the distribution of the estate and the payment of the debts through to its conclusion, although this was not enforceable in law.

The testator was allowed to revoke his will at any time during his life, thus removing the executor from his or her obligation. Similarly, the executor was free to renounce his right to administer the estate.

An executor could be appointed either simply (without any requisites) or conditionally (e.g. for a certain period of time or to administer a certain part of the testator's estate). There was no limit to the number of executors that could be named in a will, and particular executors could be charged with dealing with particular aspects of the estate.

If an executor refused to act, it was improper for him or her to become involved with the testator's debts or to help with the distribution of the estate. However, the executor was permitted to help out with 'other acts of charitie', such as helping with cattle or looking after goods to prevent theft.

The naming of an executor is described by Henry Swinburne (c.1560–1623), Commissary of the Exchequer and judge of the Consistory Court at York, in his publication *A Brief Treatise of Testaments and Last Willes* (1611), as the 'foundation of the will'. Indeed, a testator who failed to name an executor ran the risk of being treated as having died intestate. The administration of the estate would then fall to the next of kin as prescribed in the various intestacy laws (see 4.1).

If the executor died before the administration of the estate was complete, an administrator for the goods left unadministered was appointed. This was known as an administration with will annexed (see 4.7.1).

6.1.10 Witnesses

The purpose of a witness was to authenticate the document and to prevent concealment of the will or fraudulent substitution by a third party.

Following the Act for the Prevention of Frauds and Perjuries in 1676, three to four credible witnesses were required. Before this, two witnesses were generally considered sufficient. However, if there was no question that the will was either written or dictated by the testator, witnesses were not always necessary, although affidavits would probably be taken from relatives or acquaintances familiar with the testator's handwriting.

Witnesses could be either male or female. According to Henry Swinburne (see 6.1.9), although some might think women would make poor witnesses due to their 'inconstancy and frailty', their testimony was so good that two women alone would be sufficient to witness a will.

The following were not allowed to act as witnesses:

- criminals (unless they had been living honestly for three years) and perjurers
- children, idiots and lunatics
- those who might be biased towards one party rather than another

Before 1858, it was considered acceptable for a witness to act even if he or she benefited from the will, although there had to be another witness to corroborate that bequest. After 1858, a will had to be witnessed by two people who were not going to benefit from the estate.

In order to validate a holographic will (see 6.1.3), at least two credible witnesses were needed.

6.2 Likely contents of a will

6.2.1 Form

The will would include some or all of the following:

- the name, place of residence and occupation of the testator
- a statement of health
- a statement of Christian faith (more likely in early wills)
- a statement of mental capability
- instructions for burial

- details of bequests (charitable bequests may come before family bequests) and any stipulations
- the testator's signature (witnessed)
- name(s) of witness(es)
- appointment of executor(s)
- date of will

Wills can vary from the simple and straightforward to the extremely complicated. If the testator makes contingency arrangements for his wife and children, that adds to the complexity and length of the will.

The will had to be signed, at the end, by the testator or by some person in the testator's presence or under his or her direction. The testator in the presence of witnesses would have acknowledged the signature, and they would have signed the will in his or her presence. Sometimes a will would have been signed at the bottom of every page, or at the foot of the final page with the loose pages sewn together at the top or along the side. Modern wills are often drawn up by a solicitor or on printed forms with the blanks filled in.

6.2.2 Religious preamble

6.2.2.1 The significance of religious preambles

There has been much debate and research regarding the religious preamble with which early wills begin. In medieval times religion formed a central part of people's lives, and it is not known to what extent these religious statements were a matter of personal belief or simply a formulaic insertion by the scribe. However, given that the scribe was supposed to read the will back to the testator before it was signed, it is likely that the religious statement would have broadly reflected the views of the testator, even if the words were not his or her own.

One aspect of a will that may provide evidence of a moral or religious outlook is the number and type of charitable bequests.

6.2.2.2 The religious denomination of the testator

Following the Reformation, preambles were often phrased to reflect a Protestant bias (Catholics were more likely to mention saints and the Virgin Mary). It is therefore sometimes possible to determine the denomination of a testator from the wording of the introduction – as can be seen by comparing the Catholic and Protestant preambles given below.

Catholic introduction, 1632

'. . . I give and recommend my soul into the hands of almighty God my maker hopeing by the death and passion of Jesus Christ my only Saviour and redeemer to have life everlasting and to live with his blessed Angels and Saints . . .'

Figure 9 Catholic introduction: the preamble to the will of John Wilkins, Temple, Bristol, 1632. (PROB 11/165)

Protestant introduction, 1651

'. . . I give my soule into the hands of almighty God my maker and creator hoping to be saved by the only merits of Jesus Christ . . .'

Figure 10 Protestant introduction: the preamble to the will of Richard Essex of London, 1651. (PROB 11/218)

6.2.3 Bequests

The terms bequest or legacy are used to describe something left by a testator. A beneficiary or legatee is someone who inherits. Items such as jewellery, plate, furniture and clothes, etc., are the most frequent types of bequest. Farm stock (sheep, cows, oxen, pigs, etc.) often feature as bequests in less wealthy early estates. Individual items may be mentioned, although this is more common in female wills. Many bequests were in the form of cash, and are therefore quite a good gauge of the value of the testator's personal estate.

A bequest may be bequeathed 'absolutely' (in its entirety, without conditions) or 'conditionally' (provided that certain conditions are adhered to or fulfilled). As mentioned earlier, a will is a statement of intent rather than an accurate indicator of the testator's wealth. So, when a testator lists a large series of bequests, it should not necessarily be assumed that at his death he had sufficient funds to pay them or that they were in fact paid. A more accurate indication of wealth can be obtained from the inventory and accounts (if they survive), or from the death duty registers for estates between 1796 and 1903 (see 8.3.2).

6.2.4 Provision for the widow

Older wills often mention widows' 'thirds'. This refers to a widow's entitlement, for life or until remarriage, to one third of her husband's property settled on her as dower at the time of their marriage. Sometimes the widow had already been provided for at the time when the will was written, and so it may not state the details. Often a husband's bequests to his widow were on condition that she did not remarry. This was because before the Married Women's Property Act of 1882 a woman's goods and property were forfeit to her husband on marriage (see 6.1.7.3).

You should not assume that the widow is necessarily the mother of all of the deceased's children (it was not uncommon for a man to remarry following the death of his wife).

6.2.5 Provision for the children

Usually the greater part of the estate went to the eldest son (or heir at law, see 4.1.3). However, this may not be stipulated in the will, such provision having already been recorded on deeds.

Married daughters may have already received their marriage portion and therefore be omitted from the will.

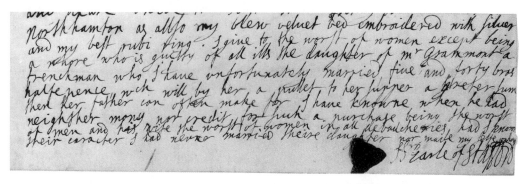

Figure 11   Bequests to widows were normally made by loving, sympathetic husbands, anxious to care for their spouse. However, occasionally husbands took the opportunity to vent their rage. A spiteful bequest of this kind was left by Henry, Earl of Stafford (1648–1719):

I give to the worst of women, except being a whore, who is guilty of all ills, the daughter of Mr Grammont a Frenchman, who I have unfortunately married, five and forty bras halfepence which will buy her a pullet for her supper, a greater sum then her father can often make, for I have knowne when he had neigther mony nor credit for such a purchase, being the worst of men and his wife the worst of women, in all their debaucheries had I known their character I had never married theire daughter nor made myself unhappy.
(PROB 10/1575)

Particular attention should be paid to phrases like 'when he reaches the age of...' – although they do not give the person's age, they are helpful as they confirm that he or she was under a certain age at the time when the will was written.

For more about guardianship of children, see Chapter 9.19.

6.2.6 Probate clause

Originally, the probate clause was attached to the will by seal following the grant of probate by the ecclesiastical court. Later, instead, the confirmation of probate would be annotated (formally noted), usually on the last page of the will. Probate clauses are formulaic and merely confirm that probate was granted on a particular day. As a result, they provide little in the way of personal information about the testator and his or her family. Before 1733 – except during the Interregnum (see 2.2.2) – probate clauses were written in Latin. For an example of a Latin probate clause and English translation, see p. 87.

Probate clause from the will of William Christie, proved on 22 February 1719/20

(PROB 11/572, f. 212v)

Probatum fuit hujusmodi Testamentum apud London coram Venerabili viro Roberto Wood Legum Doctore Surrogato Venerabilis et Egregij viri Johannis Bettesworth Legum etiam Doctoris Curiae Praerogativae Cantuariensis Magistri Custodis sive Commissarij legitime constituti Vicesimo Secundo die Mensis Februarij Anno Domini Millesimo Septingentesimo Decimo nono Juramento Thomae Willisee Executoris unici in dicto Testamento nominati Cui commissa fuit Administratio omnium et Singulorum bonorum jurium et creditorum dicti defuncti De bene et fideliter administrando eadem ad Sancta Dei Evangelia Jurato. Examinatur.

English translation

This will was proved at London before the worshipful Robert Wood LLD [Doctor of Laws], surrogate of the worshipful and wise John Bettesworth, also LLD, Master Keeper or Commissary of the Prerogative Court of Canterbury, lawfully constituted on the twenty-second day of the month of February 1719 by the oath of Thomas Willisee, named sole executor in the said will to whom administration of all and singular the goods rights and credits of the said deceased was granted being sworn on the holy gospels to administer the same well and faithfully. Examined.

6.2.7 Property bequests

Technically, a will was supposed to deal with real estate and a testament with personal estate, although this distinction was not strictly observed. Gradually these documents were merged into one – hence the term 'last will and testament' (see 1.2).

6.2.7.1 Real estate

Real estate was land-based property, as opposed to personal estate (goods and chattels). Real estate encompassed both the land and the buildings on it, together with the associated land rights. It might be held by freehold – which gave the holder the right to sell the property – or by copyhold, a type of tenancy whereby the land returned at intervals to the disposal of the lord of the manor.

Older wills are unlikely to mention real estate. However, the absence of any reference to it does not mean the land was not passed on. Real estate largely fell beyond the terms of the will. It had its own regulation through the manorial courts and common law courts. The heir at law (usually the eldest son) would inherit the land automatically. Only in 1540 (under the Statute of Wills) was the disposal of some types of real estate by will approved by statute. From 1837, all kinds of real estate could be disposed of by will.

6.2.7.2 Personal estate

Personal estate included leasehold houses and land, where the lease ran for a finite period. It also included personal possessions such as furniture and other household effects, and any farm animals or equipment. It might also encompass debts due to or by the testator. Executors (or, if there was no will, administrators) had to be appointed by the probate court before debts could be collected by lawsuit.

It is primarily this type of property that wills are dealing with – though there was a great incentive to minimize the amount of personal estate bequeathed by will, since duty on its value had to be paid to the church.

6.2.7.3 Trusts

A testator could set up a trust or trusts to settle property the way he or she wished. The trustees would be bound by the wishes of the original holder of the property, often (but not always) expressed in his or her will. Such trusts were often used to protect the interests of dependants; but they were flexible and could be used to protect property, too.

6.3 Interpreting wills

6.3.1 Misleading terminology and omissions

The terminology of wills can be misleading. *Father, brother* and *son, mother, sister* and *daughter* may be used to refer to in-laws as well as blood relatives. The term *cousin* was often used, indiscriminately, for all types of kin.

Omissions of family members may indicate that they were out of favour or dead. Or, as already mentioned, a previous settlement may have been made.

6.3.2 Indirect family information contained in wills

Wills can provide a certain amount of 'hidden' information.

- It may be possible to deduce whether a daughter was married (for example, if she is referred to by a different surname). This may narrow the range of a marriage register search to before the date the will was written.
- Make notes regarding legatees who are not directly connected to the family. If the wills of these individuals have survived, they may provide a cross-reference back to the original family.

- References may be made to individuals who were unmarried when the will was made but who later married. Information of this kind can narrow down searches in the marriage registers.
- Indirect reference may be made to people who died before the will was written (for example, 'To the children of my deceased sister. . .'). Such references provide an indication of the latest possible date of death.

6.4 Reading wills

6.4.1 Making it easier to decipher the document

There are a number of steps you can take to make it easier to read and understand a will, or other document.

- Try using a photocopier to enlarge the document. Sometimes enlarging even a small section can help. Be careful not to make the copy too large, as that may lead to distortion.
- Number the lines of the document, then take a fresh piece of lined paper (to serve as a worksheet for transcription) and number the lines to match those of the document. It is advisable to 'double-space' your worksheet, for clarity.
- If you have difficulty reading the will, start with words you can read and leave blanks in your worksheet to come back to later. This will allow you to 'get your eye in'. Once you have become used to the handwriting, you may find that you can decipher words that seemed incomprehensible at first.
- If there is a sentence where you cannot make out one of the words, try reading the sentence aloud. This may help put the word in context.
- If you find a document impossible to read, you may want to consider asking an expert researcher for help. Details of such researchers can be found on the National Archives website, at **www.nationalarchives.gov.uk/irlist**.

6.4.2 Abbreviations

Deciphering wills is made more difficult by the number of abbreviations and other devices employed by scribes in order to speed up the process of writing, thus saving time and money. Some of the standard abbreviations are described below (for publications that provide more detailed information, see Bibliography).

- A small letter positioned above the line (superscript) indicates an abbreviation. For example, y^r (your), w^t (with) and w^tout (without).
- Often, the letter 'x' (Greek *chi*) stands for Christ – particularly at the beginning of the will in phrases such as 'xian burial'.
- The scribe may miss out a letter and place the mark '~' over the top. The letters 'm' or 'n' are often omitted.

- If the letter 'p' has a curly tail or the downstroke is crossed, it is serving as an abbreviation for per, par, pro, pri or pre. Thus 'pish' with a curly or crossed 'p' stands for parish.
- 'u' and 'v' are often used interchangeably – as in 'vnto'
- 'i' and 'j' are often used interchangeably, especially in inventories and accounts (see 7.4) – for example, iiij is commonly used for 4
- Scribes often used 'is', 'ys' or just 's' in place of 'es' at the end of a word.

6.4.3 *Spelling and punctuation*

Punctuation is hardly used in the writing of wills. As a result the document may form one large flowing paragraph, not broken up at all until the probate clause at the end. To combat this, try to visualize the will in chunks. For example, most wills start with a preamble or introduction that includes the testator's name, the date of the will and an assertion that the testator is in sound mind, followed by burial instructions and charitable bequests. Next comes the main body of the will, usually with each bequest separated by the word 'item' (often used as a substitute for punctuation). Finally comes the formulaic probate clause (see 6.2.6).

Spelling was not standardized as it is now, and different rules applied. Often the letter 'y' was substituted for 'i' – for example, 'contaynyng', 'syke' (sick) and 'payed' – to make the handwriting easier to read.

6.4.4 *Minims*

When used together in words such as 'community', minims (downstrokes of the pen, as in the letters 'i', 'm', 'n' and 'u') could be difficult to read. To help overcome this problem, scribes often substituted the letter 'y' for 'i'.

6.4.5 *Obsolete letters*

There are two archaic letters that you are likely to encounter when reading old wills – namely the letter yogh (which looks like a cross between a '3' and a 'z') and thorn, which looks similar to a 'y'.

The yogh was used in Old and Middle English to represent a sound believed to have been close to the semi-vowel sound of the modern English 'y'. Confusingly, in Middle English it was also used to represent a guttural 'j', 'gh' or 'yh' sound similar to *ch* in the German word '*ich*'. It looks like a z with an extra loop descending below the line.

The thorn is similar in shape to the letter *y*. It is an abbreviation for *th* and was Germanic in origin. It may be found in such abbreviations as y^e (the) and y^t (that). It is often wrongly transcribed as 'ye', as in 'Ye Olde Shoppe'.

7

Inventories and Accounts

This chapter looks at inventories and accounts and their role in the probate process – especially before 1858, when probate was handled by the church courts. It also describes what kind of information inventories and accounts provide, and how they can supplement the information found in wills and administrations.

7.1 Inventories

7.1.1 What are inventories?

Inventories are detailed lists of articles such as goods and chattels found to be in the possession of a person at the time of their decease. Parcels of land (see 7.1.3) are also sometimes included. The production of an inventory as part of the process of probate and administration was required in ecclesiastical law from 1342 – following a canon by John Stratford, Archbishop of Canterbury – although there is documentary evidence of inventories being in existence before then. The bulk of surviving inventories, for estates of both testators and intestates, date from after 1529, when this requirement was laid down in statute.

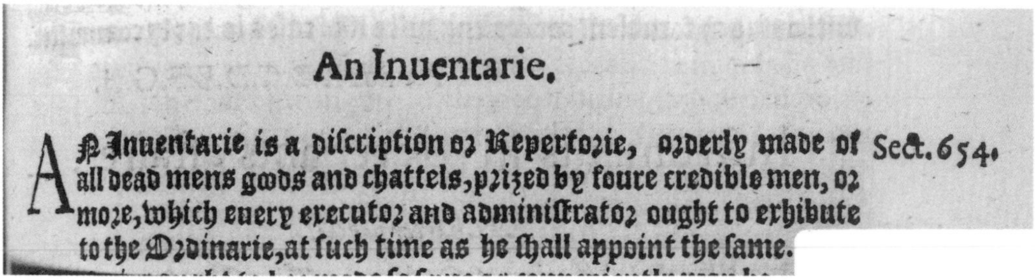

An Inuentarie.

An Inuentarie is a discription or Repertorie, orderly made of Sect. 654. all dead mens goods and chattels, prized by foure credible men, or more, which euery executor and administrator ought to exhibute to the Ordinarie, at such time as he shall appoint the same.

Figure 12 *Symboleography*, compiled by William West of London (1622), describes an inventory as 'a description or Repertorie, orderly made of all dead mens goods and chattels, prized by foure credible men or more, which every executor and administrator ought to exhibate to the Ordinarie, at such time as he shall appoint the same'.

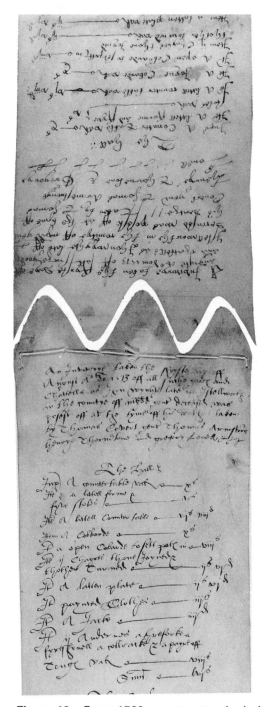

Figure 13   From 1529 executors and administrators had to produce an indented inventory of the deceased's estate, as a 'true and just account'. To create the indented document, two (or more) copies of the inventory were drawn up on a single sheet of parchment. The document was then cut in a jagged fashion, so the joining pieces would constitute proof of its validity. One of the copies was retained by the court, and one was given to the executor or administrator. The practice of producing indented inventories gradually died out. The example shown here, giving details of the personal estate of John Wyghte of Isleworth, Middlesex (1573), is rare in that both copies have survived. (PROB 2/395 and PROB 2/396)

The reason for the production of an inventory as part of the probate and administration process was to identify the value of the deceased's personal estate and make it public, and to facilitate payment of the deceased's outstanding debts. Once the court had accepted that a legitimate inventory had been produced and the deceased's debts paid off, the executor was required to distribute the balance of the estate to the next of kin. This measure was adopted to prevent dishonesty by the executor or administrator.

7.1.2 Procedure and appraisal

Executors and administrators were charged with exhibiting the inventory of the testator's or intestate's personal estate in court within six months of the grant of probate or administration.

The inventory was usually compiled within a few days of the death of the testator or intestate, generally by someone with an interest in the estate such as the next of kin or a legatee or creditor. It was supposed to list all personal estate or moveable assets – but not real estate, as this was outside the jurisdiction of the ecclesiastical courts. Personal estate included furnishings and other household items, clothing, leasehold property, livestock and crops.

The law stipulated that the appraisal of the deceased's goods was to take place openly and in the presence of witnesses. The goods included in the inventory were to be valued and priced by someone 'honest and skilful to their correct value', or to what they would fetch at auction at the time. Often the executor or administrator (usually the widow) would call in a neighbour to undertake the valuation; or if there were specialist items such as shop goods, an expert might be called in. These appraisers might be paid for their services, which could be claimed back from the estate.

The executor or administrator was required to swear a solemn oath when the inventory was submitted and declare that it was an accurate and true evaluation of the estate. Anyone wishing to state that items were missing from the inventory had to prove this was the case before an ecclesiastical judge, otherwise the inventory would be accepted as it stood.

7.1.3 Valuation

It is difficult to know whether the prices stated in an inventory accurately reflect the value of the items. It would have been possible for the appraiser to either overestimate or underestimate the value of the goods, either accidentally or intentionally. But as the inventory had to be submitted in court, appraisers would have been aware of the risk of deliberately giving a false valuation. Corrupt executors could and were brought to account by legatees or creditors and by the ecclesiastical courts.

Overvaluing of goods may occur because:

- There were goods in the deceased's house that belonged to someone else.
- The value of goods such as crops had fallen between the date of the valuation and the date they were sold.

7.1.4 *What goods were contained within the inventory?*

The inventory was, by law, supposed to cover everything due to the deceased at the time of his or her death, including:

- goods (moveable and immoveable), chattels, wares and merchandise
- leases
- crops (such as corn, hops and hemp)
- items attached to freehold property
- debts
- rent

Inventories were not supposed to include:

- grass
- trees
- glass in windows
- root vegetables (such as carrots, parsnips and turnips)

Leases and tenements were classed as immoveable goods.

Under civil law, a widow's *bona paraphernalia* – personal items such as her apparel (clothes), bed, jewels and ornaments – were to be excluded from the inventory. But the church courts generally interpreted *bona paraphernalia* as comprising her apparel only.

7.1.5 *Limitations of inventories*

Inventories are a list and statement of an individual's personal estate. They do not list debts, and therefore on their own cannot be used as an accurate indicator of the wealth of the deceased. A more accurate picture can be obtained when the inventory is used in conjunction with the account (see 7.2) and will.

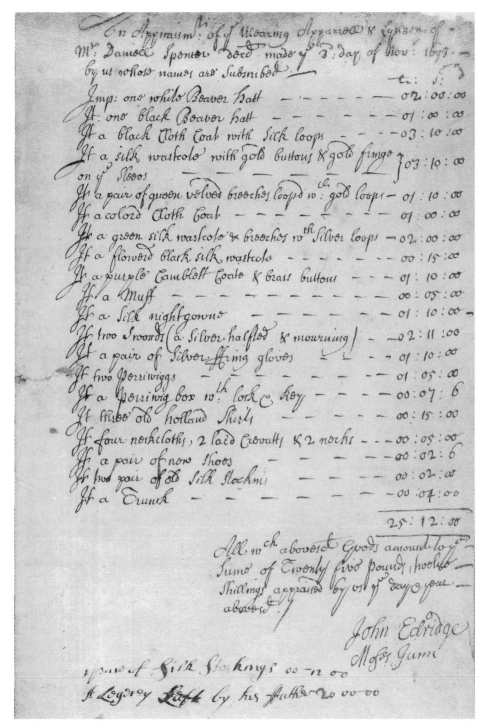

Figure 14 The inventory of Daniell Spencer (1693) itemizes wearing apparel. Other inventories provide detailed lists of shop items, books, farming equipment, etc. (PROB 5/4160)

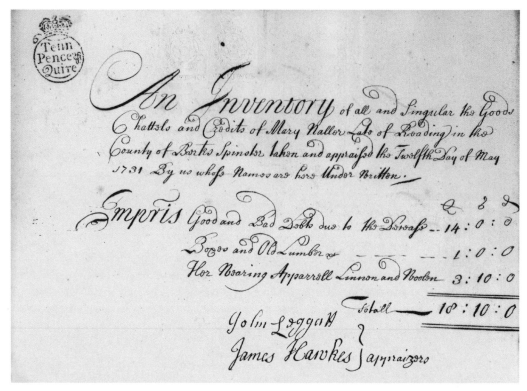

Figure 15   Some inventories contain very little detail (for example, poor estates may include nothing more than details of wages owed to the deceased). This inventory of the goods, chattels and credits of Mary Nallor, dated 1731, is such an example. (Archdeaconry of Berkshire, D/A1/102/186)

7.1.6 Format

As inventories are formal legal documents, the information contained in them is laid out in a formulaic way, although their exact nature varies from one church court to another. A detailed inventory may include:

- name, and occasionally place of residence and occupation, of the appraiser(s)
- a detailed room by room listing and valuation of the contents of the home
- stock from shops
- agricultural equipment, crops and livestock
- signature(s) of the appraiser(s)
- credits owed to the deceased

610   𝔚𝔦𝔩𝔩𝔰—*Account.*

Form of an Inventory.

A true and perfect inventory of all the goods, chattels, and personal estate of A. B., late of C., in the county of ——, and diocese of ——, yeoman, deceased, made by us whose names are hereunto subscribed, the —— day of ——, in the year of our Lord ——.

	£	s.	d.
His purse and apparel	15	0	0
Horses and furniture	20	0	0
Horned cattle	27	0	0
Sheep	20	0	0
Swine	0	13	0
Poultry	0	2	4
Plate and other household goods	18	0	0
One lease of, &c.	30	0	0
Rent in arrear	25	0	0
Corn growing at the time of his death	12	0	0
Hay and corn	10	0	0
Ploughs and other implements of husbandry	6	10	0
Debts	100	0	0
Total	284	6	4

Other debts, supposed to be desperate 25 2 6
Debts owing by the deceased 250l.

Appraised by us, the day and year above written,

A. B.
C. D.

Form of a Will of Lands and Goods (y)
[since Jan. 1, 1838.]

In the name of God, Amen. I, A. B., of ——, Esquire, do make and declare this my last will and testament in manner following.

First, I give and devise to my younger son, B. B., all that my whole freehold messuage and tenement, situate, lying, and being at ——, to

(y) [*Vide supra*, 226, 268.—Ed.]

Figure 16 Pro forma inventories were available in a variety of publications that offered assistance and guidance to executors and administrators. The example shown here is from *The Ecclesiastical Law* by Robert Burn (Vol. IV, 1842).

7.1.7 Survival

Unfortunately the survival of inventories is erratic, but the additional information they can provide makes them worth searching for. Prerogative Court of Canterbury inventories (see 7.3.1) survive from 1417 to 1858; however, from 1710 inventories were only required in cases of litigation. Few Prerogative Court of York inventories (see 7.3.2) survive before 1688.

7.1.8 Declaration (in lieu of inventory)

In some cases it was not possible to produce an inventory, so a document called a declaration was submitted instead. This often took the form of a sworn statement giving the reasons for the lack of inventory. These documents can be as detailed as an inventory or simply a statement by the executor(s) stating what, if any, of the deceased's property was in his or her (or their) control. A declaration was often used in lieu of an inventory when some time had elapsed since the death of a testator.

7.1.9 Inventories by commission

An executor was not always in a position to go to court to exhibit the inventory or account. The court had power to grant commissions or licences to local clergymen to administer appropriate oaths to executors or administrators. The clergyman would then return the appropriate document to court.

7.2 Accounts

7.2.1 What are accounts?

Within six months of the exhibition of the inventory (i.e. within 12 months of the grant of probate or administration), the executor or administrator was required to submit an account of his or her expenditure in the process of settling the deceased's estate.

The executor was required to:

- declare what goods and chattels belonged to the testator
- declare what debts and legacies she or he had paid for
- provide proof of every payment made

The ecclesiastical court would examine the account and check that it had been properly calculated, how much had been distributed, and what expenses had been claimed. If the account was accurate, the executor was released from any further obligation and could not be called to further account.

If the distribution of the estate took longer than a year, the court could send an official known as an apparitor to chase the executor or administrator. As the court would reclaim any costs thus incurred from the value of the estate, it was not in the interests of the executor or administrator to delay.

Submitting the account served three purposes, to:

- make the affairs of the testator public
- demonstrate that all debts had been paid
- confirm the residue available for distribution

The account reiterated the value of the personal estate as stated in the inventory. This was known as the charge (see 7.2.4). The account also gives the disbursements (what had been paid out) or discharge (see 7.2.5). The charge is usually formulaic and usually gives little more than a general overview of the value of the estate. The final valuation may differ from that cited in the inventory – for example, because:

- Sale prices had been either overestimated or underestimated.
- Items had been omitted from the inventory that were subsequently included.

Probate accounts are either filed as a separate document attached to the inventory, or copied at the end of the inventory.

7.2.2 *Format*

An account may include some or all of the following information:

- name of the executor or administrator
- relationship (if any) of the executor or administrator to the deceased
- place of residence of the executor or administrator
- name of the accountant (usually one, but sometimes more), and whether acting as an executor or administrator
- the 'charge' – the value of the deceased's goods based on the inventory (see 7.2.4)
- the 'discharge' – monies paid out by the executor or administrator, including legal fees and funeral costs (see 7.2.5)
- date when the account was presented in court (ecclesiastical courts seem to have followed legal terms and sat four times a year)

- total expenditure deducted from the charge to produce final amount to be distributed

Accounts can provide a fascinating insight into daily life and are therefore useful for both financial and social historians, especially when used in conjunction with the inventory and the will. Some accounts state expenditure as a lump sum, others give annual expenditure. The account can also flesh out a will, by providing details of family members not given in the will itself.

7.2.3 Survival

It is estimated that only 5% of probate accounts survive in relation to wills. They survive from around 1521 to 1685. From 1685 (An Act for the Reviveing and Continuance of Severall Acts of Parlyament), administrators of intestates' estates were no longer required to produce an account of the deceased's moveable goods unless either the next of kin or a minor or creditor specifically requested it. However, an inventory of the deceased's estate was still required. From this date, the numbers of surviving accounts for both estates of testates and intestates drop dramatically (in some jurisdictions more so than others), and their survival compared with inventories is poor. Accounts are more likely to survive if there was a court case.

7.2.4 Charge

The charge is the total value of the personal estate as cited in the inventory. Additions would have been made at this stage if extra goods had been sold or the inventory had been either undervalued or overvalued. An inventory may have been overvalued if the debts owed to the deceased could not be collected. 'Desperate debts' were normally included in the charge, even if they were thought not to be collectable (see 7.2.7). Debts are often totalled, without itemizing individual creditors.

7.2.5 Discharge

The discharge lists the expenditure incurred in settling the deceased's estate. This document can add an extra layer of information not obtainable from the will or inventory. It may detail such expenditure as:

- funeral costs
- medical expenses during the deceased's last illness
- administrative costs during probate (the drawing up of the inventory, the fee payable to the court for the granting of probate, payment for writing up the account, and court fees for the final presentation of the account)

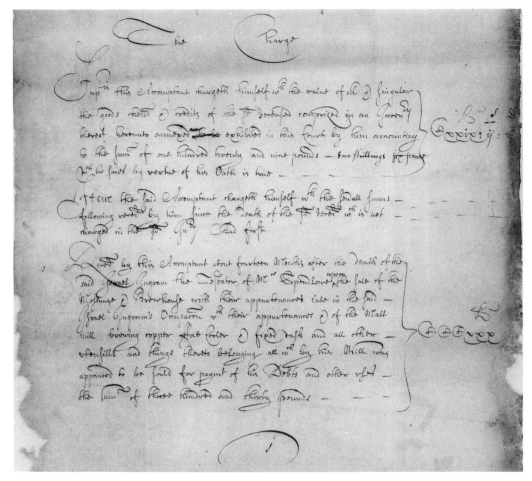

Figure 17 The charge of the estate of Israel Ingram, merchant of Great Yarmouth, Norfolk (1652). (PROB 2/432A)

- maintenance of the estate (for example, feeding and maintenance of livestock and payment of wages, rent and taxes)
- court costs
- debts owed by the estate
- maintenance of household expenditure for the deceased's family

7.2.6 Litigation

'Disputed accounts' were called for either during the course of a court case or at the end. In such cases several accounts might be produced, especially when a minor suing was an accountant (via a guardian) or an adult was suing an accountant. In either event, the account would concentrate on specific aspects of the executor's or administrator's expenditure.

Figure 18   The discharge of the estate of Israel Ingram, merchant of Great Yarmouth, Norfolk (1652). (PROB 2/432A)

Ecclesiastical courts had no power to enforce payment of money owed, and in such circumstances the case would have been heard by an equity court such as Chancery (see 9.13.1).

7.2.7 Debt

The executor or administrator was required to pay the debts of the deceased before any money could be distributed to the legatees. He or she was responsible for the maintenance of dependants (children, next of kin, apprentices) and the children's debts (lodgings, clothes, food, education, etc.). The estate could not be wound up until all the children had come of age.

Debts owed to the testator were included in the inventory, but debts incurred by the testator were not. Debts were often divided into two categories:

- Sperate debt (debts that were believed to be recoverable).
- Desperate debt (hopeless debts that could not be recovered).

7.3 Finding inventories and accounts (main sources)

7.3.1 *Prerogative Court of Canterbury (1417–1858)*

Year	TNA reference	Series	Indexes
1417–1668	PROB 2	Inventories, Series I	Name index searchable via TNA's online catalogue
1660–c.1720	PROB 4	Inventories submitted from 1660	Name index searchable via TNA's online catalogue
1641–1722	PROB 28	Cause papers	Name index to causes, testators and intestates searchable via TNA's online catalogue
1653–1721	PROB 36	Exhibits pre-1722	Card index to causes, testators and intestates. Partial name index searchable via TNA's online catalogue
1643–1836	PROB 5	Paper inventories	Name index searchable via TNA's online catalogue
1658–1723	PROB 32	Filed exhibits with inventories	Index with series list
1722–c.1900	PROB 33	Index to exhibits	Original indexes to exhibits in PROB 31 and PROB 37. Available in hard copy at TNA and arranged by year and name of testator. Not searchable on TNA's online catalogue. See 9.11.4
1701–82, 1718–82	PROB 3	Inventories, Series II	Name index searchable via TNA's online catalogue
1722–1858	PROB 31	Exhibits, main series	Card indexes (of names and places) to inventories See 9.11.4
1783–1858	PROB 37	Cause papers, later series	Partial name index to testators and intestates searchable via TNA's online catalogue

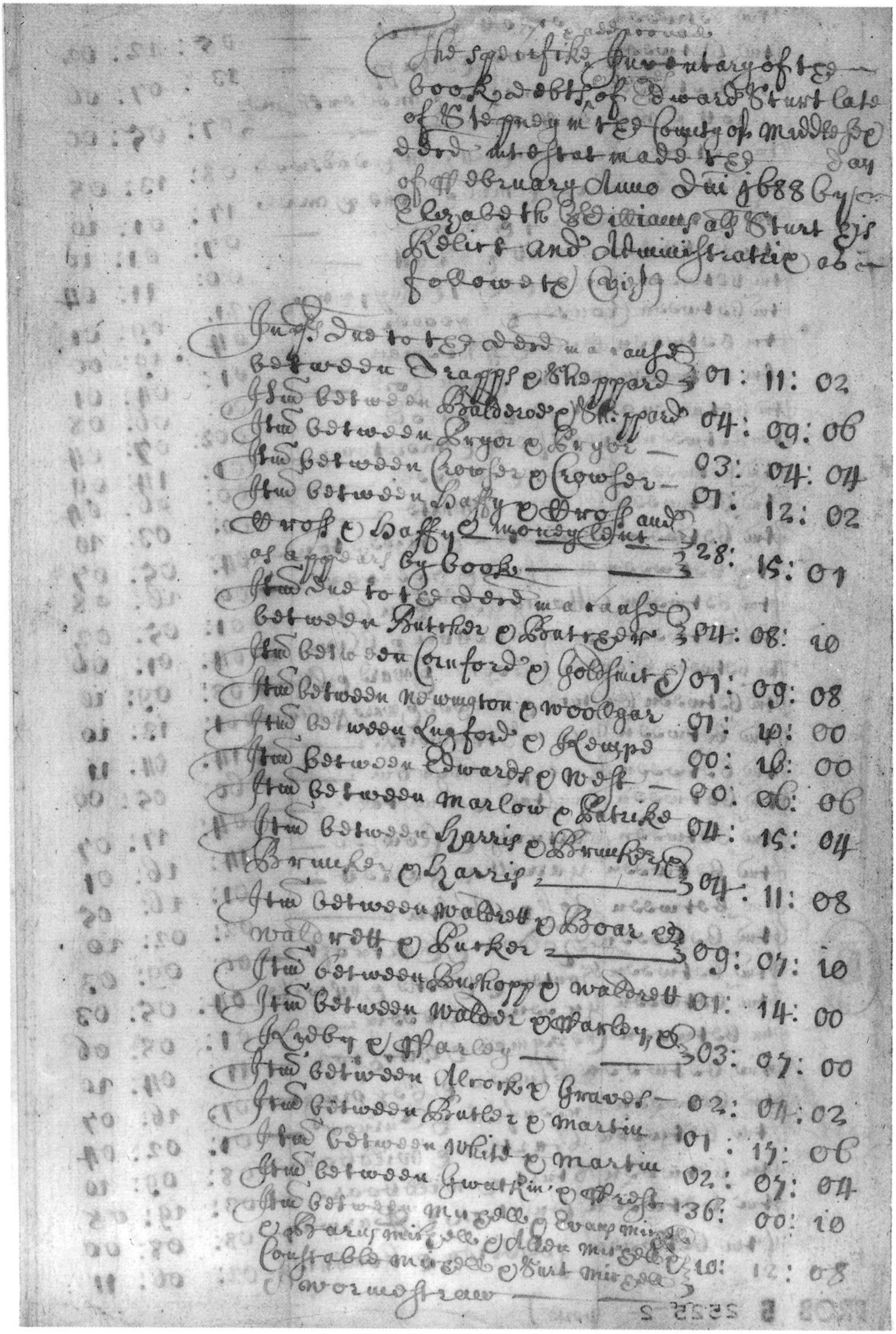

Figure 19 Inventory of Edward Sturt (1689). This is an example of a commission and inventory limited to a specific part of the deceased's estate – in this case, book debts. (PROB 5/2525)

7.3.2 Prerogative Court of York (1427–1858)

The arrangement of Prerogative Court of York inventories differs from that of the Prerogative Court of Canterbury. Whereas the various kinds of PCC probate records have been divided into separate series, PCY inventories – and the same applies to those in many local archives – are kept with the relevant will or administration, along with any other testamentary paperwork. Although a few date back as far as 1427, PCY inventories rarely survive before 1688.

7.4 Reading inventories

Medieval and early modern scribes used Roman numerals when calculating inventories. Some of the most common financial abbreviations are:

- *li (librae)*   =   pounds
- *s (solidi)*   =   shillings
- *d (denarii)*   =   pence

These abbreviations are used as a heading for columns of figures, for example:

li   s   d

xxx   viij   ij   (three pounds, eight shillings and two pence)

In early handwriting the letters 'i' and 'j' were used interchangeably, but perhaps most often in figure work. For example, j is 1, xj is 11, and cj is 101.

A raised (superscript) xx indicates a score. For example, iij^{xx} means 60.

Roman numerals

I or j	=	1
II or ij	=	2
III or iij	=	3
IV or IIII or iiij	=	4
V	=	5
VI or vj	=	6
VII or vij	=	7
VIII or viij	=	8
IX or viiij	=	9
X	=	10
XI or xj	=	11
XIX	=	19
XX	=	20
XXX	=	30
XXXX or XL	=	40
L	=	50
LX	=	60
LXXX or iiijxx	=	80
LXXXX or XC	=	90
XCIX or iiijxxxix	=	99
C	=	100
CI or cj	=	101
CC	=	200
CCC	=	300
CCCC or iiijc	=	400
D	=	500
DC	=	600
M or M^1	=	1,000
MM or M^{1}M^1	=	2,000

8
Death Duty Registers, 1796–1903

This chapter is primarily concerned with 'death duty' records in England and Wales. For Scotland, Northern Ireland, the Republic of Ireland, the Channel Islands and the Isle of Man, see Chapter 11.

8.1 Introduction to 'death duties'

The term 'death duties' encompasses a range of taxes levied on estates left by will or administration. Although generally referred to as death duty registers, the records relate to the payment of three different taxes: Legacy Duty, Succession Duty and Estate Duty.

The death duty registers – which contain brief details of the estate and to whom it was left – are to be found in the National Archives series IR 26. They extend from 1796 to 1903, with some gaps in the 1890s caused by a fire.

Before 1805 the registers cover about a quarter of all estates; but from 1857 there should be an entry for all estates except those worth less than £20. However, unless the assets were valued at £1,500 or more, the taxes were often not collected – and so not all the details were entered in the register.

During the period 1796–1903, death duties were not levied on the estates of people who lived abroad or who died in the service of their country. Also, until 1894 no death duties were payable on overseas property belonging to people resident in Britain. From 1894, Estate Duty (see 8.6) was levied on the personal estate (excluding leasehold property) held abroad of people resident in Britain at the time of their death.

After 1903, the death duty registers were discontinued and an individual file system was introduced. Under this new system, the individual files were retained for a minimum of 30 years following closure of a file and were then destroyed. The only surviving files are the ones for well-known people and others who were prominent in public life (see 8.8.1), in the series called Selected Death Duty Accounts (IR 59).

8.2 Death duty registers as a short cut to wills and administrations

Between 1797 and 1857 (as well as before) wills were proved and administrations granted in more than 200 church courts (see 2.1.1), with no union index. However, the National Archives series IR 27 consists of indexes to the death duty registers that show where the will was proved or the grant of administration issued – thus providing a very helpful short cut to finding the actual will or administration.

In addition, the National Archives have been digitizing all the 'country court' IR 26 death duty register entries (i.e. those deriving from courts other than the Prerogative Court of Canterbury) for the years 1796 to 1811 and they will soon be available on DocumentsOnline (**www.documentsonline. nationalarchives.gov.uk**).This will offer a free search facility for the name and place of residence of the deceased, occupation, date of probate or administration and the name of the church court. (For more about DocumentsOnline, see 3.3.1.) The National Archivist website, **www.nationalarchivist.com**, provides charged online access to the death duty indexes 1796–1903.

It should be stressed that not all wills and administrations figure in IR 27, as not all estates were subject to death duties. So the absence of an entry in IR 27 does not necessarily mean that no will or administration exists – simply that you will have to go the long way round to find it.

8.3 Death duty registers as sources

The information provided by death duty registers is not the same as the information given in probate records. Indeed, the details can be especially rewarding if you find the entry for an intestate, as most administrations give scant information. The administration entries normally list all the family members entitled to be included in the distribution of the estate.

The registers can be difficult to read and use, as they are roughly written and use many abbreviations (for guidance on interpreting the registers, see 8.7).

8.3.1 Information about people

The registers in IR 26 can give:

- name of the deceased, with address and last occupation
- date of the will (and, from 1889, date of death)
- place and date of probate
- name, address and occupation of executors or administrators

- details of estates, legacies, trustees, legatees and annuities, and the duty paid
- information about the people who received bequests (beneficiaries) or who were the next of kin (such as the exact relationship to the deceased)

Tax was not payable on bequests of personal estate to people within a closely defined family circle, and as a result the family relationship was often noted in the registers. In 1796 tax was not payable on bequests to offspring, spouse, parents and grandparents. In 1805 the exemption was restricted to spouse and parents; and from 1815 only bequests to the spouse were exempt from tax.

Because the registers could be annotated with additional information for many years after the first entry, they can include details such as:

- date of death of spouse
- dates of death or marriage of beneficiaries
- births of posthumous children and grandchildren
- changes of address
- references to law suits
- cross-references to other entries in IR 26

If any of the estate was left in trust before 1852, look at the reversionary registers as well, as trusts were set up to last for a long time (see table in 8.4.2).

Between 1853 and 1894 you may need to look at two series of registers to find all the entries relating to a person's estate – the Legacy Duty registers for personal estate and the Succession Duty registers for real estate.

From 1882, all wills proved and administrations granted are included in the indexes, regardless of any potential death duty: if there was no liability, the index reference will either be *NE* (no entry) or left blank. From 1889, the date of death of the deceased will be included.

8.3.2 *Evidence of value of the estate*

The death duty register entries include a valuation of the deceased's estate. However, this figure needs to be treated with caution, for the following reasons:

- Before 1853 it relates to the deceased's personal estate only and excludes freehold property – whereas from 1853 it should take into account both personal and real estate (see 8.5).
- It does not take into account the deduction of debts and expenses.
- Part of the personal estate may not have been taken into account, as the valuation figure only provides a record of the bequests as described in the will.

- The value placed on bequests may not be accurate.
- The valuations are expressed as an amount linked to the relevant tax band, and the tax bands were periodically changed by legislation. (From 1804 to 1815, a 'sum sworn under £10,000' means between £7,500 and £10,000.)

From 1853 to 1893 there may be both a Legacy Duty register entry (personal estate) and a Succession Duty entry (real estate), so the two valuations need to be added together.

8.4 Legacy Duty (from 1796)

8.4.1 Legacy Duty Acts

Although Legacy Duty was introduced by an act of Parliament in 1780, there are no registers for the pre-1796 period. Under the Legacy Duty Act of 1796, which applied to the whole of Britain, duties were payable on legacies and residues of personal estate but were restricted to certain types of bequest. The amount of duty payable was based on rates that varied according to degree of blood relationship (consanguinity) to the deceased. Spouses, children, parents and grandchildren were exempt.

During this period of British history the French Revolutionary Wars were causing considerable strain on state finances. However, this form of inheritance tax was very unpopular and it resulted in a number of disputes in the central courts at Westminster, particularly in the Court of Chancery and the Court of Exchequer (see Chapter 9 for information about these courts).

Subsequently, the taxation net was widened by a series of further acts. First the Legacy Duty Act of 1805 and then the Stamp Act of 1815 extended Legacy Duty to cash legacies and residues that were to be generated by the sale of real estate.

Legacy Duty continued until 1949, but from 1894 to 1903 you will need to look at the Estate Duty registers (see 8.6).

8.4.2 Legacy Duty records

Between 1796 and January 1858, the registers and indexes reflect the existence of many probate courts involved in the registration of estates for Legacy Duty. Each court had its own index of estates left by will between 1796 and 1811, and its own administration index for 1796 to 1857.

There is an alphabetical card index at the Family Records Centre for the consistory and lower courts of Bangor, Bath and Wells, Bristol and Dorset, Canterbury, Carlisle, Chester and Chichester. In addition, for 1796 to 1811 a typescript alphabetical index is available at the National Archives and the Family Records Centre for the consistory courts of Durham, Ely, Exeter and Oxford and lesser courts within those dioceses. However, these are in the process of being superseded by an online union index for 'country courts' – that is, courts other than the Prerogative Court of Canterbury – as part of DocumentsOnline (see 8.2).

From 1858, because there was only one probate court, the range of indexes drops.

The table below provides a quick guide to which part of the IR 27 and IR 26 series lists you will need to look at to identify the index or register you need. Please note microfilm copies are held at both TNA and Family Records Centre.

Date range	Category/content	Indexes IR 27	Registers IR 26	Form and access
1796–1811 1796–1811 1812–81	*Testators* PCC testators Country courts testators Testators	1–16 67–93 140–419	1–178 287–437 535–3292	Microfilm Microfilm Microfilm to 1860 and then original documents at the National Archives
1796–1857 1796–1857 1858–63 1864–81	*Intestates* PCC intestates Country courts intestates Intestates Intestates	17–66 67–139 420–429 No indexes	179–286 287–534 3293–3316 3317–3433	Microfilm Microfilm Microfilm to 1860 and then original documents at the National Archives Original documents at the National Archives
1882–94	*Both testators and intestates* All testators and intestates	430–531	3434–4855	Original documents at the National Archives
1812–52	*Long-running entries (e.g. for trusts)* Reversionary registers: outstanding claims as in 1899	No indexes	4856–4867	Original documents at the National Archives

The indexes can be a bit tricky. In particular, note that:

- The date given in the index entry is the date of probate or issue of grant of administration, not the date of death.
- Abbreviations such as *SP* (of the same place), *NE* (no entry), *& ors* (and others) and *& anor* (and another) are often used.
- The index entry will normally give you a folio reference to the corresponding register. Look at the IR 26 series list to convert the reference.
- An index entry without a folio reference means that no tax was payable, as does *NE* (no entry).
- A reference such as RR/41/J/12 is to the reversionary registers. It gives year (e.g. 41), initial letter of surname (e.g. J) and folio (e.g. 12), and needs to be converted using the IR 26/4856–4867 part of the series list.

Before 1812, the registers include abstracts of wills. After 1812, copy wills were made, but these have largely been destroyed. However, those from the major local probate courts in Cornwall, Devon and Somerset were sent to the respective record offices to fill some of the gaps in local probate records caused by enemy action during the Second World War (see 3.3.6). David Hawkings' *Index of Somerset Estate Duty Office Wills and Letters of Administration 1805–1811* (Weston-super-Mare, 1995) can be consulted at the Family Records Centre.

8.5 Succession Duty (from 1853)

The next significant date in the history of death duties is 1853, when under the Succession Duty Act the transmission of a family's main land holdings to the next heir – or to anyone else – became taxable for the first time.

Duty was now payable where a person became beneficially entitled to or interested in property upon the death of another (described as 'gratuitous acquisition of property'). The relevant registers are as follows:

Date range	Category/content	Indexes IR 27	Registers IR 26	Form and access
1853–94	Testators and intestates	See below	4868–6262	Original documents at the National Archives
1853–78	Succession Arrears (outstanding claims)	None	6263–6282	Original documents at the National Archives

In the Succession Duty registers, entries can relate to wills proved many years before the date of the register – for example, a register for 1865 could contain an entry relating to a will proved in 1830. The Succession Duty registers provide details of duty payable on intestate estates between 1858 and 1881; after 1881, details for intestates may be found in the will and administration registers for 1881–94 and the Estate Duty registers for 1894–1903.

Due to a fire (see 8.6), 11 of the Succession Duty registers for 1894 have not survived. Although Succession Duty continued to 1949, between 1894 and 1903 you will need to look at the 'Old Duty' registers (see 8.6).

There is an extra column in the IR 27 indexes 1889–99 giving the folio number in the corresponding Succession Duty registers. For other years the Legacy Duty register entries refer to Succession Duty register entries, often abbreviated to Succ. Reg. followed by a folio number.

8.6 Estate Duty (from 1894)

Introduced by the Finance Act of 1894, Estate Duty was payable on all property (both real and personal estate) passed on at death. This duty continued through to modern times, being finally replaced by Capital Transfer Tax in 1975.

After 1894, Legacy Duty and Succession Duty became known as 'Old Duty' and any property liable to these two duties was exempted from Estate Duty. The relevant registers are as follows:

Date range	Category/content	Indexes IR 27	Registers IR 26	Form and access
1894–1903	Testators and intestates	532–605	6283–8690	Original documents at the National Archives
1895–1903	Old Duty registers	None	8691–8743	Original documents at the National Archives

The index entry will give you a folio reference to the corresponding register. You then need to look at the IR 26 series list to convert the reference.

Approximately 500 Estate Duty registers (many of them relating to the period 1894–8) have not survived, mainly because of a fire in the Estate Duty Office building that housed the records.

8.7 The layout of the registers

8.7.1 Up to and including 1811

Before 1812, the registers are reasonably simple. An entry for the estate of a particular person occupies two facing pages and is divided into columns. Each column contains a specific piece of information, defined by a printed column heading, and has its own abbreviations.

8.7.2 From 1812

From 1812, an entry for the estate of a particular person still extends over two facing pages and is divided into columns. However, each entry now has two sets of headings.

- The first set of headings is printed at the very top of the page. Here you will find the name of the deceased, the date of the will and approximate value of the estate, details of the executors, the date of probate, and the name of the court where the will was proved. Equivalent information is given for an administration. The information given under this first set of headings is ruled off from the rest of the entry.

- The second set of headings – which are printed immediately below the first set of headings at the top of the page – gives the details of the will or administration.

After each entry there is a ruled line separating it from the next one.

8.7.3 What do the headings and abbreviations mean?

Below, to serve as a guide, we show what the various headings mean in a register dating from 1837 and what you can expect to find in each column. However, the registers changed over time, so you will find that the headings and the content of the columns vary a little, depending on the date of the register you are looking at.

An example of these differences is provided by comparing the headings described below with the death duty entry for Jane Austen (reproduced on p. 123), which dates from 1817. You will see that the column headings in this earlier register differ slightly, affording greater breakdown of types of legacies and providing individual columns for each year of annuity instalments. For more about Jane Austen's entry, see 8.8.3.

First set of column headings

Column	Heading	
1–2	Name and address, date of death	
3	Date of will/administration	
4	Executors/administrator	
5–6	Residence	• Residence of executors/administrator.
7–8	Description	• Occupation/rank of executors/administrator.
9–13	Where and when proved	• Name of court where grant of probate or administration was made and date on which the grant was made. **Sample of abbreviations used:** • *ArchCt/Totnes/archd'on* = Archdeaconry Court of Totnes • *BishCt/Lichfield /* = Bishop's (Consistory) Court of Lichfield • *ConCt/London* = Consistory Court of London • *ConstEpic/Wells* = Episcopal Consistory Court of Bath & Wells • *Deans/Lichfield* = Dean and Chapter of Lichfield • *Ecclesi/St Albans* = Archdeaconry of St Albans • *ExCt/York* = Exchequer Court of the Archbishop of York • *PC/Cant.y* = Prerogative Court of Canterbury • *PecuC/Biggleswade* = Peculiar Court of Biggleswade • *RuralD/Chester* = Rural Dean of Chester
14	Sum sworn under	• Approximate value of estate.

Second set of column headings

Column	Heading	
1	Legacies	<ul><li>Description of items bequeathed in the will, including type and size. **Abbreviations used:**</li><li>*anny ch'd on R and P Est* = annuity charged on real and personal estate</li><li>*chgd* = charged</li><li>*3 P C Cons* = 3% Consols</li><li>*3 P C Red* = 3% Reduced Bank Annuities</li></ul>
2	Observations	<ul><li>Notes on the legacies or other information for the purposes of estimating duty payable.</li></ul>
3	To whom in trust	<ul><li>To whom estate is entrusted (e.g. the executors).</li><li>The date of codicils in which legacies are bequeathed. **Abbreviations used:**</li><li>*exors* = executors</li></ul>
4	For what purpose	<ul><li>What is to be done with the legacy.</li><li>Into how many portions it is to be divided.</li><li>Upon what conditions legatees are entitled to it.</li><li>Whether the legacies have to be converted into certain forms for payment, etc.</li></ul>
5	Legatee	<ul><li>To whom the legacies are due. **Abbreviations used:**</li><li>*Resy Legatee* = residuary legatee (i.e. the legatee who receives the remainder of the estate once the claims of the other legatees have been satisfied).</li></ul>
6	Consanguinity	<ul><li>Relationship of legatees to the deceased (for the purposes of calculating the rate of duty payable on the legacy). **Abbreviations used:** See table below.</li></ul>

7	Upon what contingency or, if in succession, of equal rate	• Upon what conditions the legacies are bequeathed and the procedure to be followed when the legatee dies (i.e. does the legacy pass to the legatee's heirs or to other defined persons?). **Abbreviations used:** See table below.
8	What deemed	• The form of the bequest. Whether an absolute gift or an annuity, and whether there are any contingency clauses to the bequest. **Abbreviations used:** • *abs* = absolute legacy (i.e. unconditional) • *abs & int* = absolute and interest • *abswp* = absolute legacy with a proviso (conditional grant) • *ann^y* = annuity • *ann^y wp* = annuity with a proviso (conditional annuity) • *dwp* = ditto (usually absolute) with a proviso • *in def^t of app^t eq^y am^g them* = in default of apportionment equally among them
9	Age of annuitant	• Age of the annuitant (given in some cases only).
10	Value of annuities and bequests	• Value of bequests received by legatees; or total value of annuities as computed for paying duty.
11	Rate of duty	• Percentage of bequest or annuity to be paid as duty, according to degree of consanguinity.
12	Date of payment	• Date when payments of duty were made.
13	Annuity instalments	• Value of instalments of duty paid on annuities (there were usually four such payments).
14	Total duty	• Total duty paid on legacy.

Note: Columns 9–14 sometimes contain no information, presumably because duty was never paid or because there were insufficient assets to pay for legacies. In place of such information, there is often a reference such as RA 767/46 1 LD, which refers to a residuary account (see 8.8). Most residuary accounts have been destroyed, although a few still survive in IR 19 and IR 59.

Abbreviations used in Column 6 of the second set of headings (Consanguinity)

BF	brother of a father (i.e. uncle)
BM	brother of a mother (i.e. uncle)
Child or Ch	child of deceased
DB	descendant of a brother (niece, nephew, etc.)
DS	descendant of a sister (niece, nephew, etc.)
DBF	descendant of a brother of a father (i.e. cousin)
DBM	descendant of a brother of a mother (i.e. cousin)
DSF	descendant of a sister of a father (i.e. cousin)
DSM	descendant of a sister of a mother (i.e. cousin)
DBGF	descendant of a brother of a grandfather
DBGM	descendant of a brother of a grandmother
DSGF	descendant of a sister of a grandfather
DSGM	descendant of a sister of a grandmother
G child	grandchild
GG child	great-grandchild
G daughter	granddaughter
G son	grandson
SF	sister of a father (i.e. aunt)
SM	sister of a mother (i.e. aunt)
Str or Stra or Strag	stranger in blood
Stra BL	stranger, brother-in-law
Stra DL	stranger, daughter-in-law
Stra NC	stranger, natural child (i.e. illegitimate)
Stra ND	stranger, natural daughter (i.e. illegitimate)
Stra NS	stranger, natural son (i.e. illegitimate)
Stra NC (of a daughter)	stranger, illegitimate child of a daughter
Stra NC (of a son)	stranger, illegitimate child of a son
Stra (sent)	stranger, servant of deceased
Stra SL	stranger, sister-in-law *or* stranger, son-in-law
Stra or 'son'	stranger, natural son (i.e. illegitimate)
Stra or 'daughter'	stranger, natural daughter (i.e. illegitimate)

Abbreviations used in Column 7 of the second set of headings (Contingency)

Amg	among
att^n	attain
contingency	condition of bequest
divid^{ds}	dividends
eq^y	equally
Est	estate
Int	interest
int dur^g min^y prin^l when 21	Interest on bequest payable during minority of legatee, and principal when legatee attains 21 years of age.
Pble	payable
P or *princ^l*	principal
reversion	Bequest reverts to another legatee upon a certain condition (e.g. upon the death of the first beneficiary).
Ring etc.	mourning ring and other bequests
SER or *suc of equal rate*	Succession of equal rate after death of legatee (i.e. equal division of the bequest among the heirs of the legatee).
until she att^{ns} 21 or marr	Legacy not operable until the beneficiary reaches the age of 21 or marries.
when 21 with accum^{ls}	Legatee to receive principal and accumulated interest when he/she attains 21 years of age.
with ben^t of surv^p	With benefit of survivorship (e.g. if a bequest is distributed between a group of legatees and one dies, the rest will be entitled to share out the legacy equally among themselves within six months).

Abbreviations found in various columns of the registers

de bonis non /15th Oct 1851/	date of later grant of administration.
in res^d	in residue
not liable	no duty payable (on bequests to relatives closely related to the deceased).
not subject to Duty	no duty payable (on legacies to be paid out of the profits from real estate sales, prior to 1805).
P E	personal estate
Qy	query
RA/1448–1837/	Residuary account RA 1448 1837. Reference to a residuary account (see 8.8). Most residuary accounts have now been destroyed, although a few remain in IR 19 and IR 59.
R E	real estate

8.8 Related records at the National Archives

8.8.1 Residuary accounts

Examples of residuary accounts (1796–1903) can be found in IR 19. Unfortunately, this series has been heavily weeded: so you may, for example, find that only accounts for surnames beginning with the letters A to G have been preserved for a particular year. However, copies of death duty accounts can sometimes be found among family papers. In IR 59 there are residuary accounts, ranging from 1805 to 1993, for famous people – including Jane Austen, Dickens, Friedrich Engels, Disraeli, Gladstone, Florence Nightingale and Shelley. The more modern accounts are closed for 75 years.

Residuary accounts are identified in death duty register entries by a reference number preceded by the initials RA (see 8.7). They supplement the death duty registers by providing a detailed breakdown of the residuary part of the estate. This is shown as listings with valuations – with one side of the account for assets (including cash, stocks and shares, and household furniture) and the other for liabilities, including debts. Most wealthy men left the major part of their fortunes as residuary estate. Sometimes letters from the executor or administrator and affidavits are attached to the accounts.

8.8.2 *Correspondence and reports on contentious cases*

Although the death duty registers contain numerous references to correspondence, most of it has not been preserved. Nevertheless, letters relating to
'contentious cases', 1812–36, survive in IR 6. This description is in fact misleading,
as all communications between the Legacy Duty Office and executors or
administrators were described as 'contentious'. Correspondence of this kind can
be revealing – for example, it may explain why there was a delay in the payment
of the duty by the executor or administrator. The IR 26 registers give the year and
number of the letter.

Further material on contentious cases can be found in the following series:

IR 49	Reports on contentious cases	1800–25
IR 50	Reports on contentious cases	1825–33
IR 67	Case books	1853–66

Unlike the letters in IR 6, these include only a small number of cases.

IR 62 contains Estate Duty Board Papers, 1869–1975. Among them are a number
of files relating to cases where exemption or postponement of Estate Duty was
claimed for paintings and manuscripts and other works of art. These files are
mostly closed for 75 years; others can be viewed at the National Archives in Kew,
but need to be ordered three working days in advance.

8.8.3 *Example of a death duty register entry and residuary account*

The novelist Jane Austen died in Winchester in 1817. The executor and chief
legatee of her will (reproduced on p. 19) was her sister Cassandra, who nursed
her through her final illness. Also mentioned in the will and in the death duty
register entry are Jane's brother Henry and his housekeeper, Mme Bigeon (spelt
Bidgeon in the register entry).

Jane Austen's death duty register entry, reproduced on p. 123, shows the layout
adopted in 1812. The top of the page gives the following information (reading
from left to right):

● name and address of the deceased
● date of will
● name and place of residence of the executor
● where and when proved
● value of personal estate

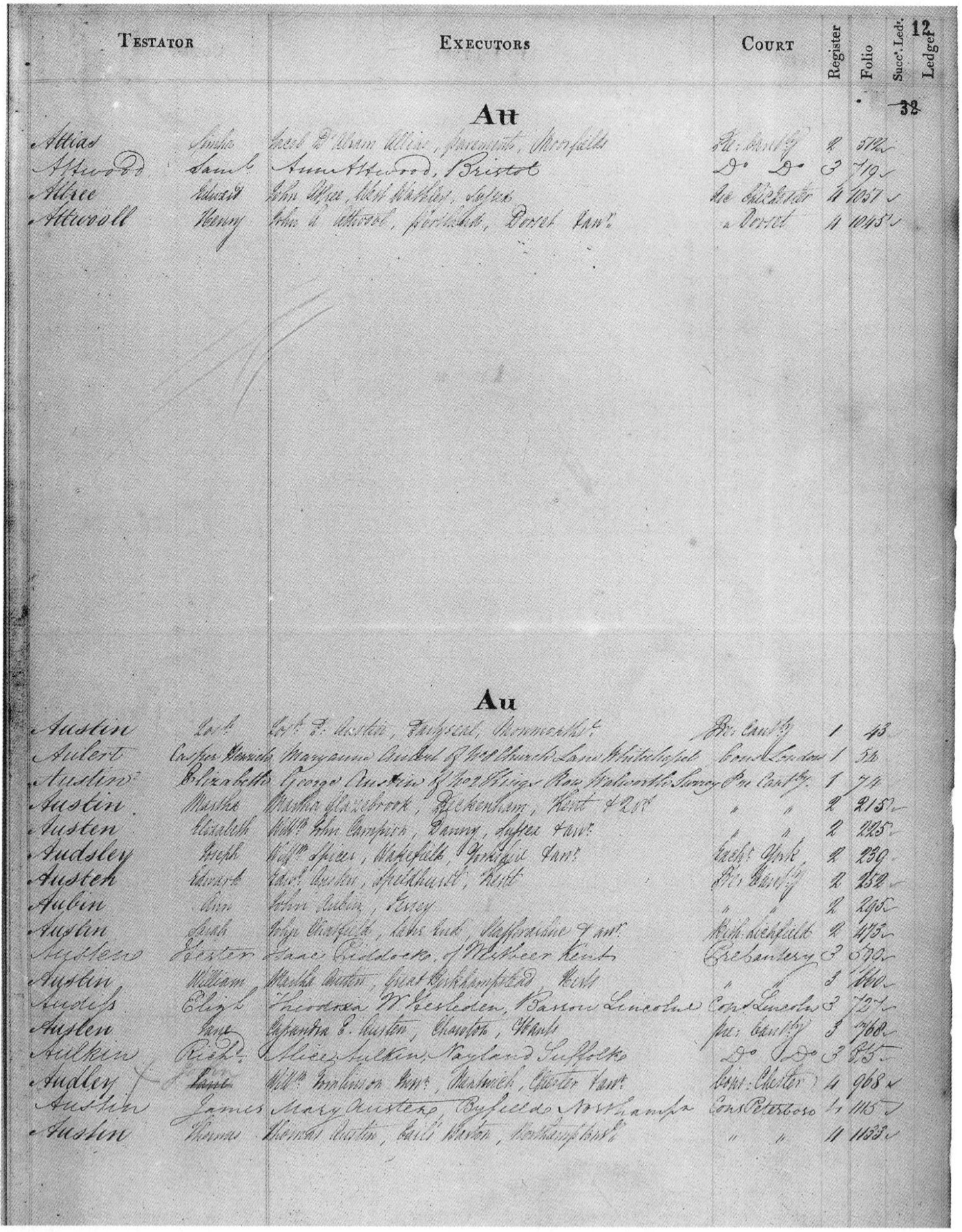

Figure 20 Death duty index page showing the entry (fifth from bottom) for Jane Austen. (IR 27/160)

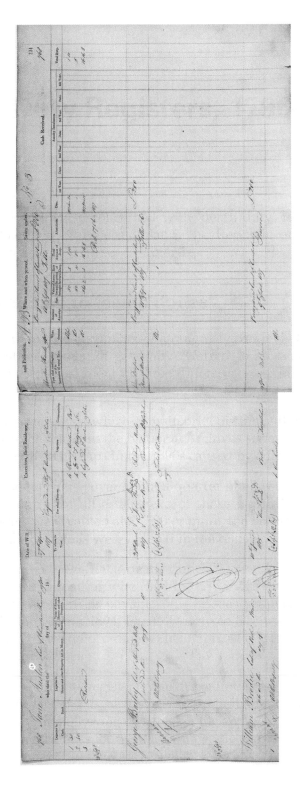

Figure 21 Death duty register entry for Jane Austen. (IR 26/698, f. 768)

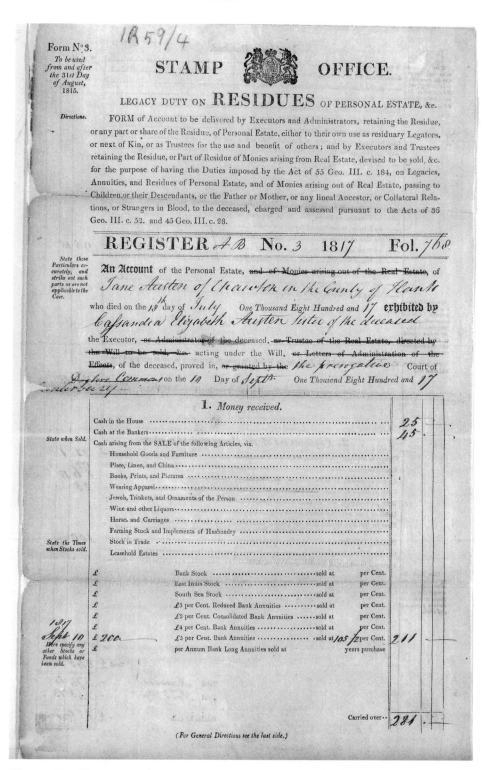

Figure 22 First page of the residuary account of Jane Austen. (IR 59/4)

At the very top of the page, 'A B' and 'no. 3' are of no consequence: they simply indicate that the register is the third one covering surnames beginning with the letters A and B.

The information given in the entry extends right across the two pages. For example, reading from left to right, under legacies in cash, £50 was left to Jane Austen's brother Henry, on which the rate of duty was 3% (note the higher rate of 10% for the non-relation, Mme Bigeon), the amount payable being £1 10 shillings. This is followed by the date of payment.

The lines drawn across the page below the entry for Jane Austen separate it from the entry for another person, George Bailey.

Other features to note include the following:

- The number 768 is the folio number given in the index.
- 'Consanguinity' indicates the relationship to the deceased. That the second named person, Mme Bigeon (Bidgeon), the housekeeper, is not a relation is confirmed by the abbreviation *Str* next to her name (short for 'stranger in blood').
- The abbreviation *abs* indicates that each legacy was absolute (i.e. unconditional).
- RA 1756 1817 is the residuary account number, 1817 being the year of the residuary account. Jane Austen's residuary account is reproduced on p. 124. For more about residuary accounts, see 8.8.2.
- In the entry for George Bailey, immediately below Jane Austen's, the dates given under 'Observations' refer to correspondence (in later registers there is a column headed 'Correspondence'). For more about correspondence, see 8.8.1 and 8.8.2.

9
Litigation

In the context of wills and administrations, litigation is regarded as including both non-contentious business (for example, when an executor wishes to renounce his or her role) and disputes over wills and administrations (sometimes referred to as contentious business).

This chapter describes the kinds of dispute brought before the church courts and the courts of common law and equity; the types of records generated, with special reference to the Prerogative Courts of Canterbury and York; and the appeal procedure in church courts. In addition, it looks at the appointment of guardians for minors in the church courts and covers the subject of dormant funds (commonly called 'money in chancery').

9.1 What was the difference between the types of dispute brought before church courts, equity courts and common-law courts?

The church courts mainly dealt with disputes regarding:

- the validity of a will
- the authenticity of a document produced as a will
- the mental capacity of the deceased when making a will
- rival claims to be next of kin in cases of intestacy
- the conduct of executors and administrators in distributing the deceased's estate

The equity courts, the most important of which was the Court of Chancery, dealt with cases relating to the interpretation of wills and matters arising out of their content. The records are held at the National Archives (see 9.13.2.1 and 9.13.2.4).

The common-law courts – the two largest being the Court of King's Bench and the Court of Common Pleas – dealt with disputes concerning freehold property and other issues that were heard under the common law. These included matters such as the deceased's state of mind (also dealt with by the church courts, under ecclesiastical law). The relevant records are held at the National Archives (see 9.13.2.3 and 9.13.2.4).

9.2 In which church courts were disputes heard?

Disputes were heard at all levels of the church courts, from the lowest (archdeaconry courts) to the highest (the Prerogative Courts of Canterbury and York). Sometimes disputes that would normally have been handled by the lower courts were heard by the Prerogative Courts – especially that of Canterbury, because of its prestige. The records of disputes are usually held in the same archives as the associated wills and administrations (see 3.2).

9.3 Types of records and their arrangement

The records of the Prerogative Courts of Canterbury and York are described in 9.11 and 9.15. Those of the lower courts tend to follow the same arrangement as the Prerogative Court of York – with individual files of case documents and act books, which recorded the daily business of the courts.

9.4 The language of the records

The pleadings, including allegations, answers and depositions (the written statements of witnesses), were mainly in English. However, before 1733 the records of the proceedings are in Latin – except for 1651–60 (see 2.2.2).

9.5 Possible difficulties in finding a case

You may find that a case relating to a will or administration commences a generation or more after the grant of probate or administration, especially in disputes over legacies or trusts affecting the children or grandchildren of the deceased. Also, when there is more than one case concerning a will or administration, the parties may be different.

9.6 Disputes over wills and intestates' estates – people at their worst, records at their best

The records relating to disputes over wills and the estates of people who failed to leave a will can be the most interesting of probate records, sometimes encompassing the records of both ecclesiastical and non-church courts. They represent only a small proportion of all testators and administrators, but certainly justify the effort involved in undertaking a search for a dispute. They also provide a high percentage of female litigants.

The depositions (see 9.11.3) provide wonderful details about families and communities. The animosity and greed of individuals are often cruelly exposed. Charles Dickens referred to this as 'hatred pursued beyond the grave'. There can sometimes be 20 or more witnesses in a case. Deponents (witnesses) had to give their age, occupation and address (the seventeenth-century and early-eighteenth-century depositions also record place of birth, annual income, and when the deponent last took the sacrament). Every character involved as a witness can therefore be quickly placed in context. These witnesses may be family members, who would need to state their relationship to the deceased; and often they were domestic servants, who might provide intimate details of what took place in a household.

There is information about illnesses and medical practices; about the strange behaviour of the deceased, since insanity of the deceased was often the grounds for questioning the legality of a will; and about drinking habits (as drunkenness was also frequently cited as the reason why the deceased was not in a fit state to make a will), together with vivid scenes from local public houses.

The varied nature of the types of cases brought before a church court can be illustrated by looking at just one year. In 1752, for example, one case at the Prerogative Court of Canterbury involved the violent conduct of the wife; in another case, a will was set aside on the grounds of fraud and failure of proof; and in another, forgery of a will failed to be established.

Intestacy cases produce much information about marriage customs. It was common for children or other close relatives to dispute the widow's claim to marriage, to try to prevent her gaining administration of the estate. Typically, they would attempt to blacken her name.

Disputes can be found in all levels of church courts. With the exception of the Prerogative Court of Canterbury, they were also dealing with the spiritual discipline of parishioners and their moral behaviour – including matters such as defamation, heresy, marriage and tithes.

9.7 How do you find references to a dispute?

9.7.1 Sentences in the Prerogative Court of Canterbury

If you find references to a 'sentence' in court records, this indicates that the judge delivered a final judgment in a disputed case. Until 1803 the sentences (judgments) of the Prerogative Court of Canterbury were filed in the probate registers (PROB 11), and they can now be found on DocumentsOnline (see 3.3.1). The published indexes to wills from 1383 to 1700 and those for later wills also contain references to sentences among the alphabetical listings of the registered copy wills (see 2.4.1).

The yearly indexes to wills and administrations (PROB 12) contain not only references to 'by sentence' (often abbreviated to 'by sent') but also annotations next to entries indicating that the judge had granted an 'Interlocutory Decree' (usually abbreviated to 'Int Dec' or simply to 'Decree'). This was less final than a sentence and commonly used in administration cases, where someone could appear after a judgment had been given and prove that they were the true next of kin, as a result of which the original decree would have to be revoked.

9.7.2 Card index to PCC allegations (PROB 18), inventories/exhibits (PROB 31) and exhibits indexes (PROB 33)

See 9.11.2 and 9.11.4.

9.7.3 PCC probate act books (PROB 8) and administration act books (PROB 6)

There will be a grant of probate or administration associated with the litigation. This will be shown as a marginal note against the grant indicating the existence of a sentence or a revoked administration.

9.7.4 PCC act of court books (PROB 29) and acts of court books (PROB 30)

See 9.11.5.

9.7.5 Online catalogues

You may find references to disputes over wills or administrations – including Court of Chancery cases – by searching the National Archives online catalogue by name. For example, if you search for the name Leonard Potter, you will find 'William Potter and Agnes Potter v Margaret Potter widow: personal estate of Leonard Potter, deceased, of Kendal, Westmorland 1648' given under the Chancery Proceedings document reference C 10/1/88.

Descriptions of many of the case files for the various bishop and archdeacon courts are given on the Access to Archives (A2A) database on the Internet (see 3.3.9). Some records can be searched by the name of the testator and/or parties. Others are described in more general terms – for example, for Worcestershire Record Office, within the Diocesan Central Registry records, one file of consistory court papers dating from the eighteenth and nineteenth centuries is described as consisting of 'papers relating to testamentary and miscellaneous causes'.

9.7.6 Death duty registers

Death duty register entries (see 8.3.1) may make reference to Court of Chancery cases and sometimes give the Chancery action number.

9.8 An indicator of a dispute or problem with probate

If you find that probate was granted more than a few months after death, the delay may indicate that there was a dispute. However, a more likely reason is that there was a procedural problem with probate (see 9.18).

9.9 Types of dispute

9.9.1 Authenticity and validity

One of the most frequent subjects of dispute was the question of whether a will was genuine. A church court could declare that a will was a forgery, or that it was invalid because the testator was drunk or insane when making the will.

9.9.2 Proof of pedigree

Proof of pedigree cases – or 'interest cases', as they were also known – arose when the legal interest of a person purporting to be the next of kin was denied on grounds of illegitimacy or lack of evidence supporting their claim. Such cases could be concerned with determining the right to administer the goods of someone who died without leaving a will. In cases involving a will, the main proceedings would be suspended until questions of pedigree had been resolved.

9.9.3 Inventory and account

Any person having an interest in an estate, whether as a legatee, beneficiary, creditor or next of kin, could ask the court to order the executor or administrator to produce an inventory and account (see 7.1.1 and 7.2.1 for a full explanation of these terms). This happened in the event of failure to pay a legacy or legacies, or where fraud was suspected. The church courts had no power to compel payment of legacies, but an action 'in inventory and account' did enable a beneficiary to determine the amount of assets in the estate before bringing a separate action to enforce payment in the Court of Chancery.

9.9.4 Subtraction of legacy

This is where the intended recipient of a legacy brought proceedings against an executor or administrator because payment of the legacy had been either deferred beyond the legal period or refused. The legatee would have first ascertained that there were sufficient assets to cover payment of the legacy – usually by forcing the executor or administrator to produce an inventory and account (see 9.9.3).

9.10 What is the difference between contentious and non-contentious business?

The contentious (contested) business of the courts – also called the testamentary business – comprised cases that involved disputes over wills or administration, as described in 9.9. They could involve simply one person against another, or more than one person or party on either side.

Non-contentious (non-contested) business involved procedures invoked where probate was not straightforward (typical situations are described in 9.18).

9.11 The litigation process and PCC records

9.11.1 Bringing a dispute before a church court

The main method of bringing an action before a church court was by a *citation* (summons). These documents contain the name of the judge, the plaintiff (sometimes referred to as the *promoter*) and the defendant (sometimes referred to as the *ministrant*), along with the cause of the action and time and place of appearance. The party cited might either appear in person or be represented by a *proctor* (attorney), who was appointed by an instrument called a *proxy*.

The process of litigation was sometimes commenced by the issuing of a *caveat*. This was a formal notice, usually entered by a proctor on behalf of a party that had an interest in the estate of the deceased, restraining the court from making a grant of probate or letters of administration without first giving notice to the issuer of the caveat. The proctor entering the caveat was then 'warned' by the party claiming representation as an executor or administrator – meaning that the proctor had to appear in court if he intended to continue with the case. Both parties were then 'assigned' by order of court to set out their respective claims. At this point the suit or action would commence to try the validity of the will or the right to administration, as appropriate, either under intestacy or with 'will annexed' (see 4.7).

9.11.2 Pleadings

The *pleadings* – the written case made by each side in a dispute – are also sometimes referred to as *proceedings*. They consist of a statement of the facts that the parties are relying on and propose to prove, the grounds of the action, and the defence. Both the first plea and subsequent pleas are called *allegations*. These are similar to *bills* and *answers* in the Court of Chancery. Each contains a statement of facts, but unlike Chancery bills and answers they are broken down into *articles* – the facts being arranged under separate heads, often numbered, according to subject matter or the order in which they occurred. In church courts, the defendant's responses to the allegations are called *answers*.

Relevant series at the National Archives

TNA series	Content and date range	Indexes
PROB 18	Allegations, 1661–1858	Card index arranged by name of testator/intestate and plaintiff.
PROB 25	Answers, 1664–1854	
PROB 28	Cause papers, 1642–1722	
PROB 37	Cause papers, 1783–1858	Index to testators and intestates.

9.11.3 Evidence

The next stage in the litigation process was the examination of witnesses. They were examined on written interrogatories – a series of questions submitted by the proctors, regarding any articles in an allegation that contained facts within their knowledge. (Confusingly, these interrogatories were also sometimes referred to as 'articles'.)

Either the witnesses were brought to London to be examined or, if it was inconvenient for them to attend, they were examined by commission – that is, a suitable person was commissioned to question them – near their place of residence. Witness statements taken in London were known as town depositions, those taken outside London as country depositions.

The town depositions were taken in private by examiners (before 1691 by a deputy registrar) of the court. The relevant allegation was delivered to the examiner, who after studying the contents of the document devised questions based on each article of the allegation, which were put to the witnesses.

The cross-examination, a series of questions put to the witnesses of the opposing side, was conducted by interrogatories. The witness was given a copy of the interrogatories, after they were sworn, so that he or she could study them before being examined.

The deponents (witnesses) were required to give their age, occupation, place of residence, and sometimes former places of residence and place of birth. Ages given are often imprecise (a common problem for genealogists).

Relevant series at the National Archives

Town depositions

TNA series	Date range	Indexes and search facilities
PROB 24	1657–1809	Paper catalogue index to deceased and to details of deceased and parties given (such details as yet not included in the online catalogue).
PROB 26	1826–58	Indexed by name of testator or intestate, plaintiff and parties to dispute.
PROB 37	1810–58	See 9.11.4.

Country depositions

TNA series	Date range	Indexes and search facilities
PROB 26	1826–58	Indexed by name of testator or intestate, plaintiff and parties to dispute.
PROB 28	1660–c.1722	Indexed by name of testator or intestate, plaintiff and parties to dispute.
PROB 31	1722–c.1780	See 9.11.4.
PROB 37	1783–1858	See 9.11.4.

9.11.4 Exhibits

These are documents produced in court as evidence. The range of exhibits is illustrated by PROB 31, which covers the years 1722 to 1858. These include inventories, declarations in lieu of inventory (which can be as detailed as inventories in listing the effects of the deceased; see 7.1.8), and accounts of executors and administrators. In addition, there are various copies of wills, including both 'authentic' and 'bogus' wills. The exhibits also include certificates of burial from parish registers, private diaries, account books, newspapers including death announcements, and bibles.

In one extreme case, that of 'Mad Mrs Morice', who left 17 wills, there is a painting showing coal kept on her sitting-room floor – a sure sign of madness – plus a book of fairly unfunny jokes and, of course, the 17 wills. The TNA's exhibits collection also includes illustrations made by the landscape artist Joseph Mallard Turner, whose will was the subject of a dispute.

Relevant series at the National Archives

Finding aids

TNA series	Date range	Indexes and search facilities
PROB 31	1722–1858	Card index. Also, the PROB 33 exhibits indexes, both in hard-copy form and on microfilm (see below).
PROB 32	1666–1717	Searchable on online catalogue, by name of deceased.
PROB 35	1529–86	No names given in series list.
PROB 36	1662–1720	Searchable on online catalogue, by name of deceased and names of parties.
PROB 37	1783–1858	Searchable on online catalogue, by names of parties.
PROB 49	1686–1849	Searchable on online catalogue, by name of deceased and names of parties.

In the reading rooms at the National Archives there is a card index for the exhibits series PROB 31, arranged by name of testator, names of plaintiffs and also by place, with separate sections for each English county, Wales, Scotland, Europe, Africa, Asia and America and for ships' names. This card index purports to be an index to inventories and executors' and administrators' accounts. However, it often includes references to related material such as declarations in lieu of inventory. PROB 37 references are included in the personal-name index, but omitted from the place-name index. The references provided in the card index are not full TNA references, so need to be converted. They are given in the form 1800/10, which can be translated into a TNA series reference by consulting the PROB 31 series list.

If you have found an entry or entries in the card index, this establishes that there were exhibits in a case and will have given you the names of the parties in the case. However, because of the limited scope of this card index, even if you do not find any relevant entries you should next consult the PROB 33 exhibits indexes, either in hard-copy form or on microfilm.

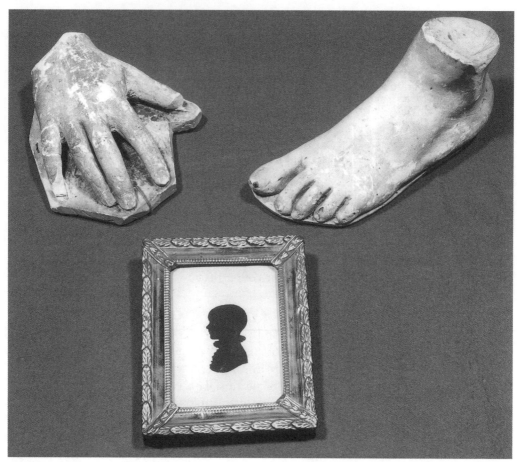

Figure 23   Plaster casts and a likeness in silhouette of J. B. Burgess (a boy) – exhibits from the case of *Wormsley* v. *Burgess*, 1818–20. (PROB 49 43/1–3)

9.11.5 The hearing

All the court papers in a case were delivered to the judge. The hearings took place in open court, and proceedings were opened by the counsel on both sides stating the points of law and fact on which they were basing their arguments. The evidence was then read in court, unless the judge indicated that he had already read it, though certain passages might be read again for clarification.

The case was then discussed and argued by counsel. Finally, the judgment was given by the judge in open court, including the reasons for the decision. The question of costs, claimed by the successful side in order to recover the amount spent on fighting the case, was mainly at the discretion of the judge. Reasons for granting or refusing costs were given when the judgment was delivered.

Court books and acts of court

The progress of a case can be traced through court books and similar records. These include the orders of the judge and petitions of the parties (requesting, for example, that a particular witness be examined). Up to 1733, apart from 1651–60 (see 2.2.2), the records are in Latin. At the National Archives these records are in two series: acts of court books (PROB 29) and bundled acts of court documents (PROB 30). These provide the only evidence relating to all disputed cases.

Some of the entries will resemble disputed cases but are in fact *Proofs in Solemn Form* – wills that were proved by witnesses (unlike the vast majority of wills, which are proved in *Common Form*). Nuncupative (oral) wills (see 1.5.2 and 6.1.3) were often proved in this way, because objections were frequently anticipated. This type of process also generated records similar to those you would normally find in a disputed case.

Relevant series at the National Archives

TNA series	Content and date range	Indexes
PROB 29	Acts of court books, 1536–1819	
PROB 30	Acts of court, 1740–1858	Many of the volumes are internally indexed.

9.11.6 Other PCC record series relating to disputes

There are a number of other series of PCC records which, although they generally give less information than the series already described, can fill gaps in the records of a case and supply details regarding the case's progress:

Caveat books 1666–1858 (PROB 40)
This series contains a sample of the entry books in which caveats (see 9.11.1) were recorded. They are all internally indexed by the name of the deceased. The first three volumes (1666, 1774 and 1776) give the name of the person entering the caveat, normally the plaintiff in the case. Thereafter the caveats are entered under the name John Thomas – a name (among a few others) often used in legal documents up to the nineteenth century, though more typically for fictitious disputes invented as a legal contrivance in order to transfer freehold land from one person to another.

Court caveat books 1678–1857 (PROB 41)
These record the next step after the entry of the caveat, the summoning of the party into court. These volumes are useful in covering for the paucity of caveat books (see above) and gaps in the act of court books (PROB 29).

Citatory mandates 1666–1857 (PROB 48)
This series consists of files and bundles of citatory mandates summoning the parties and witnesses to attend court. Often a brief outline of a case is given – usefully filling gaps in the act of court books (PROB 29).

Assignations 1665–1858 (PROB 43)
As well as assignation books, PROB 43 includes draft acts. The assignation books contain entries noting appointments for court hearings and give a brief summary of the proceedings in each case. The draft acts, which are usually on a single sheet of parchment, also provide a brief summary of the proceedings.

Muniment books 1611–1858 (PROB 16)
These books contain the registration of some exhibits produced in court and, before the nineteenth century, orders and decrees.

Instruments from other courts, Commonwealth to George III (PROB 44)
These include legal-process documents relating to Prerogative Court of Canterbury cases referred to the High Court of Delegates (see 9.12.4), plus a few injunctions from the common-law courts stopping proceedings in the PCC deemed prejudicial.

Supplementary wills, Series II 1623–1857 (PROB 22)
This series contains copy wills that were made for exhibiting in other courts.

9.12 Appeals

9.12.1 History and structure

The entering of an appeal automatically suspended the execution of the sentence (final judgment). There could be several levels of appeal, each one being referred to a higher court. There were different appeal paths for courts under the jurisdiction of the two Prerogative Courts. A case could start in an archdeacon's court, be appealed to the bishop's diocesan court, and then be appealed to the relevant archbishop's court. A case could be referred to the Court of Arches for the province of Canterbury, or the Chancery Court (not be confused with the non-ecclesiastical Court of Chancery in Westminster) for the province of York. Above them was the High Court of Delegates (see 9.12.4).

9.12.2 Court of Arches and equivalent courts

The records of the Court of Arches are held by Lambeth Palace Library (for address, see Useful Addresses, p. 211). For details of these records, consult *Index to the cases in the records of the Court of Arches at Lambeth Palace Library 1660–1913* (British Record Society, Index Library, Vol. 85, 1972). The records of the Chancery Court for the province of York (see 9.15) are held at the Borthwick Institute of Historical Research (for address, see Useful Addresses, p. 211).

At one time the provinces of Canterbury and York each had a Court of Audience, the status of which was similar to that of the Court of Arches. In 1660, the Court of Audience for the province of Canterbury merged with the Court of Arches. The records for the province of Canterbury are held by Lambeth Palace Library, those for the province of York by the Borthwick Institute. Few pre-1660 records survive for either of these courts.

9.12.3 Papal Court in Rome

Until 1533 the final appeal from church courts in England and Wales was to the Papal Court in Rome. There are published calendars giving translations of the Papal Registers, the originals of which are held by the Vatican Archives. Copies of the calendars can be seen at the National Archives.

One example of such an appeal, dating from 1450, is the petition of William Hipper, Joan Hipper and William Hardegate, executors of the will of John Hipper, who contended that the prioress of the Benedictine convent of Maryck (Marrick) in Yorkshire had falsely alleged that they had to give the convent a horse under the terms of the will. The decision of the court in York had gone against them, and when they failed to comply with the court's instructions they were excommunicated. The Pope – on this occasion presiding in the church of Santa Maria Maggiore, in Rome – absolved the executors.

9.12.4 High Court of Delegates

The High Court of Delegates developed from 1533 to take over the appeal function from the Papal Court (and from 1834 that of the Judicial Committee of the Privy Council). The delegates consisted of a number of judges, from different types of court, appointed by the Lord Chancellor. One case, *Franco* v. *Alverenza*, in 1753, started in the Consistory Court of Bangor, was appealed to the Court of Arches, then went to the High Court of Delegates, next to the Prerogative Court of Canterbury, and eventually back to the High Court of Delegates.

For details of the records of the High Court of Delegates, see 9.12.7.

9.12.5 Court of High Commission

In addition to the High Court of Delegates, until 1641 there was another ecclesiastical tribunal, called the Court of High Commission. This operated in the provinces of Canterbury and York and in the dioceses. In the province of York it was established in 1561. As with the High Court of Delegates, there was no right of appeal from the decision of the court, but a Commission of Review (see 9.12.6) could be applied for.

At the National Archives, among State Papers, Domestic, Charles I (SP 16) there is a short run (1634–6 and 1641) of minute books of the High Commission for

Ecclesiastical Causes for Canterbury. These calendars group together all the cases for a period, but none of them concern wills or administrations. Along with some other records among the State Papers, these are the only records pertaining to the High Commission for Ecclesiastical Causes for Canterbury to have survived the destruction ordered by Parliament during the English Civil War.

High Commission records for York are held by the Borthwick Institute (see 9.15). There are also a number of surviving records for the High Commission courts of the dioceses, held by the relevant local archives, some of which have been transcribed and published.

9.12.6 Commissions of Review

Although there was no appeal against a decision of the High Court of Delegates, very occasionally, if there was an error in law or fact, a petition could be made to the king or queen in council asking for the matter to be heard before judges under an instrument known as a Commission of Review. The petition was usually heard by the Lord Chancellor. Some of these documents survive among the records of the High Court of Delegates. In addition, petitions can be found among the State Papers (SP) and Privy Council (PC) records at the National Archives.

9.12.7 Records of the High Court of Delegates, 1536–1834

The records of the High Court of Delegates are to be found at the National Archives, in DEL 1 to DEL 11. They include:

TNA series	Content	Date range
DEL 1	Processes (copies of the proceedings) in the lower courts	1609–1834
DEL 2	Miscellaneous papers, including country depositions	c.1600–1834
DEL 3	Personal answers and London depositions	1564–1735
DEL 4	Act books	1539–1818
DEL 5	Sentences	1585–1802
DEL 7	Bound volumes of printed appeal cases (these copy documents, produced by the court from which appeal was made, provide a summary of the proceedings in the lower court)	1796–1834

There is a parliamentary paper (Sessional Papers, House of Commons, 1867–8, 199) listing all the appeals taken to the High Court of Delegates between 1533 and 1832. This is available under the reference DEL 11/11 and can also be consulted in the reference library. It does not include document references but is a useful point of departure – although many of the DEL series lists give the names of the parties and can therefore be searched on the TNA online catalogue.

A detailed analysis of the court's role and records is contained in G. I. O. Duncan's *High Court of Delegates* (Cambridge University Press, 1971).

9.12.8 Records of the Judicial Committee of the Privy Council, 1834–70

The records of the Judicial Committee of the Privy Council are in PCAP 1 to PCAP 5.

PCAP 1 contains processes (copies of proceedings) in the lower courts from 1834 to 1870, while PCAP 3 consists of printed appeal cases for the same period. PCAP 3 contains copies of many of the documents in PCAP 1 and, additionally, the case for both sides. References to PCAP 3 are provided in the series list and index for PCAP 1. Both series can be searched by the names of the parties and by testator or intestate.

9.13 Disputes heard in courts of equity and common law

9.13.1 Types of cases heard

Church courts dealt mostly with the *validity* of wills. Consequently disputes over the *interpretation* of a will often went to the courts of equity – typically to the Court of Chancery (especially from the eighteenth century), but also to the equity side of the Court of Exchequer. Moreover, equity courts were attractive to litigants because the judges were obliged to reach their judgments on the basis of 'fairness', and church courts had no real powers to call in the assets of an estate.

The majority of actions in the courts of equity related to claims for payment of legacies and the fulfilment of other provisions of wills – including complicated cases involving trusts or charitable bequests and actions brought to secure the assets of the deceased. Detailed studies of the equity courts can be found in Henry Horwitz's books *Chancery Equity Records and Proceedings 1600–1800* (PRO, 1998) and *Exchequer Equity Records and Proceedings 1649–1841* (PRO, 2001). Information leaflets about these records can be found on the National Archives website.

All disputed cases regarding issues of law ('law' is often used as shorthand for the unwritten common law of England) that concerned freehold property or questions such as whether the testator was of sound mind were heard by the common-law courts – namely the King's Bench, the Court of Common Pleas and the common-law side of the Court of Exchequer (sometimes referred to as the

Exchequer of Pleas). Such common-law cases were also heard outside London, in the assizes courts of the provincial towns of England and Wales. There were also the courts of the Palatinates of Chester, Durham and Lancaster and the Duchy of Lancaster, which may need to be searched for disputes over wills and administrations, too. The relevant records are mostly held by the National Archives.

Although an action over the validity of a will bequeathing personal property could be heard by a church court, it might be necessary to bring an action in Chancery to gain an order authorizing the hearing in a common-law court to decide whether, for example, the testator was of unsound mind. As a result, you may find the Prerogative Court of Canterbury, the Court of Chancery and the Court of King's Bench all hearing cases involving the same will or estate. Also, a frequent reason why more than one court would be involved was that only the common-law courts were able to hear disputes regarding freehold property (often referred to as cases of *ejectment*).

A multi-court dispute – an example of a long and expensive legal wrangle

One labyrinthine case involving a church court, a court of equity and a common-law court concerned Ann Millington, spinster, who died intestate in 1743. Claiming they were the deceased's only next of kin, being her cousins-german (first cousins) once removed, William Bouchier and his sisters applied to the Prerogative Court of Canterbury for letters of administration. But in the meantime caveats on behalf of Ursula Hanyold and Theresa Dutling and others, also claiming to be next of kin to Ann Millington, had been entered and a temporary grant of letters of administration was made *pendente lite* (pending litigation).

Then in 1746 Alice Merchant alleged that she was Ann Millington's next of kin, being the only surviving child of Francis Millington, the brother of Ann's father, Thomas Millington. Shortly after lodging her claim, Alice Merchant died – but a few days earlier she had made a will whereby she left all her real estate and the residue of her personal estate to George Taylor and his wife Hannah.

Once Alice Merchant's will had been proved, George Taylor entered an action to claim administration of Ann Millington's estate. At the subsequent hearing at the Prerogative Court of Canterbury, in 1754, William Bouchier was successful in proving that he was the next of kin, on the grounds that he was a cousin-german, and was granted administration. Taylor then entered an appeal in the High Court of Delegates, though in the end he decided not to pursue his claim in this higher court.

Also in 1754, the claim of Alice Merchant regarding the real estate of Ann Millington was heard before a jury at the Court of King's Bench, after an order from the Court of Chancery directed that the issue should be tried under common law.

In 1758, George Taylor and his wife filed a bill of complaint in the Court of Chancery asking that Bouchier should account for all the personal estate of Ann Millington. Also that Alice Merchant's will, including trusts, should be executed (i.e. its provisions carried out). The bill of complaint mentioned the death of Thomas Millington in 1630 and other details about the family. It also referred to the Prerogative Court of Canterbury hearing. Bouchier filed an answer in the Chancery case; and a number of pleadings were filed by both sides, each in response to the last pleading filed.

Eventually, in 1774, the Chancery judge ordered that the parties proceed to a trial at law in the Court of King's Bench on the issue of whether Francis Millington, father of Alice Merchant, was the brother of Sir Thomas Millington, physician to William III and Mary II. When the plaintiffs brought an appeal in Chancery, this was varied to the issue of whether Alice Merchant was the first cousin and next of kin of Ann Millington at the time of Ann Millington's death. The judge also ordered that the trial be before a jury, at 'the bar'.

However, in 1775, a final appeal in Chancery was brought by William Bouchier, and the judge, Lord Chancellor Bathurst, decided that the 1774 decree of the court should be reversed – giving victory to William Bouchier, confirming him as the administrator and enabling him to lawfully distribute Ann Millington's estate.

This was an extraordinary case. Litigation had spread over 33 years, due to the inordinate delays of the defendants in instigating proceedings and filing replies. And the costs must have been onerous. More than 100 witnesses were examined – just for the claim initiated by Alice Merchant in the Prerogative Court of Canterbury.

9.13.2 *Relevant records*

9.13.2.1 *Court of Chancery/Chancery Division*

The records of the Court of Chancery are mostly in English. They are also well indexed and contain much family, local and social history detail, especially among the depositions (witness statements). Some of the series of pleadings can be searched by name of plaintiff or defendant on the National Archives online catalogue. The Equity Proceedings Database (**www.records.pro.gov.uk/equity**) – also accessible via the main TNA website – includes some of the pleadings in the Chancery series C 6, dating from 1606 to 1722. It can be searched by names (including that of the testator in cases involving a will), places, and subject of dispute.

Indexes arranged by name of plaintiff are available on the open shelves in the reading rooms at the National Archives, including indexes to decrees and orders (C 33 and J 15). Also at the National Archives there are unpublished alphabetical indexes, mostly compiled by P. W. Coldham, to the pleadings in the personal-estate cases in C 5 to C 8 and in C10 (part of the Six Clerks Series), covering the period 1613–1714. These indexes are particularly useful because they are arranged by name of the deceased.

The masters' reports and certificates in C 38 for 1544–1875 and J 57 for 1876–1962 are worth mentioning as they often provide a rich source of information, especially for administration of estates, which was the responsibility of the masters. Judges frequently referred matters to masters – legally qualified officers of the court, subordinate to the judges – for further investigation, and their reports were often very detailed.

Many wills were deposited in Chancery as exhibits. There is a card index, arranged by name of testator, to wills found among the exhibits series C 103 to C 114. The names given on the index cards can also be searched on the National Archives online catalogue.

Exchequer depositions by commission in E 134 can be searched on the TNA online catalogue by names of parties and name of the deceased. The Bernau index held by the Society of Genealogists (for address, see Useful Addresses, p. 211) is an additional source for names of deponents in some of the Chancery and Exchequer depositions series.

9.13.2.2 Treasury Solicitor papers

A number of cases relating to wills, especially Chancery cases, were referred to the Treasury Solicitor (the government lawyer). Often the documents are merely court copies, but sometimes they include law officers' opinions. However, there is a straightforward route to these records, as they can be searched by names of parties and name of testator on the TNA online catalogue. Series that can be searched in this way are TS 11 (1584–1858), which is an especially good source, TS 18 (1517–1953) and TS 27 (1706–1996).

9.13.2.3 Common-law records

Compared with the records of the courts of equity, the common-law records are formulaic. Also, a lot of the records were destroyed and up to 1733, apart from 1651–60 (see 2.2.2), they are all written in Latin. For the detail of cases to 1875, consult the relevant plea rolls (King's Bench in KB 122, Common Pleas in CP 40, and Exchequer in E 13).

9.13.2.4 Main record series for will and intestate disputes in equity and common-law courts

Name(s) of court	Decrees and orders (decisions)	Pleas/ pleadings	Affidavits	Depositions	Exhibits
Court of Chancery Chancery Division	**C 33** (1544–1875) **J 15** (1876–1954)	**C 1–C 16** (c.1386–1875) **J 54** (1876–1945)	**C 31** (1611–1875) **J 4** (1876–1945)	**C 21** (Country) (1558–1649) **C 22** (Country) (1649–1714) **C 24** (Town) (1534–1867) **J 17** (1880–1925, 1960–91)	**C 103–C 114** (1180–1859) **C 171** (1350–c.1850) **J 90** (1700–1953)
Court of Exchequer, equity side (King's Remembrancer)	**E 123–E 131** (1559–1841)	**E 112** (1558–1841)	**E 207** (to 1774)	**E 133** Barons (Town) (1558–1841) **E 134** Commission (Country) (1558–1841)	**E 140** (1319–1842) **E 219** (1625–1841)
Court of King's/ Queen's Bench King's/Queen's Bench Division	**KB 122** (1702/ 3–1875) **KB 168** (1699–1875) **J 168** (1879–1937)	**KB 122** (1702/ 3–1875) **J 55** (1875–80) **J 54** (1880–1945, 1979–1985)	**KB 101** (1734–1874) **J 4** (1881–95)	**KB 144** (1792–1875) **J 16** (1871–80)	
Court of Common Pleas/ Common Pleas Division	**CP 40** (1273–1875)	**CP 40** (1273–1875) **J 55** (1875–80)	**CP 3** (1704–1876)	**CP 22** (1831–79)	
Court of Exchequer, common-law side (Exchequer of Pleas)/ Exchequer Division	**E 13** (1236–1875)	**E 13** (1236–1875) **J 55** (1875–80)	**E 1** (1830–81)	**E 20** (1853–67) **J 16** (1871–80)	

9.14 Other sources

9.14.1 Newspapers

Newspaper reports of trials usually provide a useful account of the proceedings, certainly from the eighteenth century onwards. The British Library's newspaper library in Colindale (for address, see Useful Addresses, p. 211) holds a large collection of national and local newspapers. The National Archives has *The Times* on microfiche, plus the yearly indexes to *The Times* known as Palmer's, both in hard-copy form and on CD-ROM. You can also search *The Times* online at the National Archives. The online version of the newspaper and the CD-ROM indexes have the advantage of enabling you to conduct a search easily when you are not sure of the date of a trial.

Newspaper reports are especially important for the period since 1858, when the Court of Probate was formed (see 5.1), as so few of the records have been preserved at the National Archives (see 9.16). An example is the case of *Broadbent* v. *Hughes*, relating to the will of Joseph Hugh Hughes, formerly a surgeon in the Royal Navy and a prisoner of war in Verdun for 10 years. Although the case papers have not survived, a detailed report of the trial, which lasted three days, appeared in *The Times* on 6 February 1860, including quotes from the depositions that were brought before the court.

9.14.2 Law reports

Some cases generated law reports, especially where they gave rise to legal precedents or new points of law. Before 1866 a high percentage of cases were reported; but from 1866, when law reporting became more structured, the percentage declined. Because law reports tend to be more concerned with legal points than with the facts surrounding a case, you need to treat details contained in them with caution, as they were often reported inaccurately and the spelling of names can be inconsistent. Where possible, you should therefore compare the information given in the reports with surviving original records. All the courts that heard will or intestate disputes generated law reports – including the church courts, though mainly those for London.

Examples of law reports that covered Prerogative Court of Canterbury cases are *Phillimore Ecclesiastical*, *Robertson Ecclesiastical* and *Haggard Ecclesiastical*. Known collectively as the *English Reports*, they are usually available in law libraries in that form. One significant series is the *Lee Reports* for 1752–8, which are especially valuable – not only because they were written by the presiding judge but also because they are concerned with the facts of the cases, report witness depositions in much detail, and provide the judge's full reasons for his judgments. They are included in *English Law Reports 1220–1865* (see below) on CD-ROM; and in *British Trials 1660–1900* (Chadwyck-Healy) on microfiche, a copy of which can be viewed at the National Archives. The latter mainly consists of contemporary pamphlet accounts of criminal cases but, as well as the *Lee Reports*, it includes a small collection of reports on equity and common-law disputes over wills, which record in detail what was said in court by counsel and witnesses – something that is rarely found in other sources.

Law reports held at the National Archives

The National Archives has an incomplete collection of law reports in hard-copy form up to 1865. However, it also holds *English Reports 1220–1865* (Juta Hart) and *Electronic Law Reports 1866–2004* (Justis) on CD-ROM. *English Reports 1220–1865* is especially useful as it not only enables searches by names of parties but also provides a keyword-search facility covering the whole text of each report, so you can search for other people involved in a case, including the testator or intestate. *Electronic Law Reports 1866–2004* searches by names of parties and the subject matter of the dispute. Both CD-ROMs enable you to conduct searches for very specific types of cases – for example, if you are interested in disputes that focused on the type of ink used by the testator in writing his or her will, you can use the keywords 'will' and 'ink' and enter a date range.

9.14.3 Family papers

Although most researchers seem to come across disputed cases almost by chance, sometimes family papers that they or a relative hold will contain legal documents and/or documents relating to a case. Such documents generally contain the names of the parties, a date and the name of the court – making it possible for you to locate other documents in the relevant archive. In addition, you may find that family papers have been deposited in local archives or libraries. The National Register of Archives database (**www.nra.nationalarchives.gov.uk/nra**) is the best place to search for the location of private papers, some of which are also catalogued on the Access to Archives (A2A) database (**www.a2a.org.uk**).

9.15 Records of the courts of York held by the Borthwick Institute

The records relating to the various courts of York (see 2.3) fall into two categories:

- Court books (the equivalent of the Prerogative Court of Canterbury acts of court books), containing the formal proceedings and cause papers, which bring together the pleadings of both parties.
- Similar individual documents (at present only partly indexed).

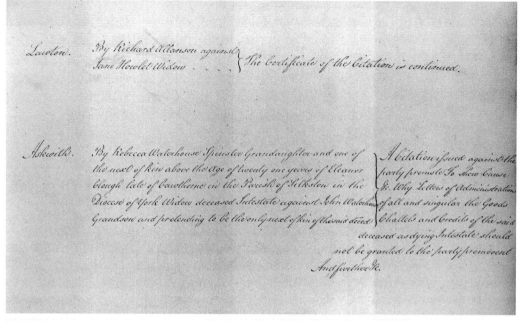

Figure 24   Page from Exchequer act book, Prerogative Court of York, showing entry for *Waterhouse* v. *Waterhouse*, concerning the administration of the estate of a person dying intestate. *Borthwick Institute of Historical Research: Exchequer act book 34, p. 56*

Unlike the records of the PCC, those of the Prerogative Court of York encompass all types of church-court disputes. Details of their arrangement and references can be found on the Borthwick Institute's website (**www.york.ac.uk/inst/bihr**). A brief summary of the records is given below:

Cause papers (early fourteenth to twentieth century)
These include a separate collection of cause papers for the Court of High Commission dating from the late sixteenth to the early seventeenth century. A project to catalogue the files of cause papers has begun. Two volumes have been indexed: *Ecclesiastical Cause Papers at York 1301–1399* by D. M. Smith (Borthwick Text and Calendar 14, 1988) and *Ecclesiastical Cause Papers at York: Files Transmitted on Appeal 1500–1883* by W. J. Sheils (Borthwick Text and Calendar 9, 1983).

Court books
Court of High Commission 1562–1641
Consistory Court 1417–1911
Chancery Court and Court of Audience 1525–1956
Exchequer Court and Prerogative Court 1548–1857

Deposition book 1676–8
This is the only PCY deposition book known to have survived.

Abstract books 1634–1948

These books, which cover all courts, are similar to court books.

Caveat books 1521–1859

These include notes of caveats, including those relating to probate matters.

Citations

Citation books 1611–92 (these generally cover all courts)
Citations 1595–1857 (these bundles derive from the Consistory, Chancery, Exchequer and Prerogative courts)
Citation notes (seventeenth to nineteenth centuries)

Commission books 1611–83

These record commissions issued to clergy out of all PCY courts (though mainly the Exchequer and Prerogative courts). They include commissions issued for granting probate and administration, as well as those issued for swearing executors, administrators and witnesses.

9.16 Litigation after 1858

From 1858 actions were brought before the new Court of Probate (see 5.1), which in 1873 became part of the Probate, Divorce, and Admiralty Division of the High Court. In 1970 this division was renamed the Family Division. Appeals were made to the House of Lords, whose records are held by the House of Lords Record Office (for address, see Useful Addresses, p. 211).

From 1858 onwards, very few records relating to contentious probate cases have been preserved at the National Archives – which is why newspaper reports and law reports are so valuable for the post-1858 period. Only 7% of the case files have been kept, in J 121, for the years 1858–1960 – although ironically the series does contain details of the dispute in 1905 concerning the will of the president and senior judge of the court responsible for hearing these cases, Sir Francis Henry Jeune, Baron St Helier (J 121/5754). There is also a small sample of exhibits in J 165, which covers the years 1854–1934. Both of these series can be searched on the TNA online catalogue by names of parties and name of testator. There is also a small run of minute books, covering the years 1858–66, in the series J 169. These include registrars' notes that provide details such as dates of the filing of documents, the reading of affidavits and wills, grants of administrations and the stopping of proceedings.

In the cause books in J 168, there are some entries regarding Probate Division cases. These commence in 1876 and end in 1937 and are arranged by initial letter of name of plaintiff. However, the few entries for the Probate Division tend to give the names of parties and representatives and date of appearance only, with no judgment details.

The Court of Chancery and, from 1876, the Chancery Division of the newly created Supreme Court continued to hear cases concerning the interpretation of wills. You will find the decrees and orders for the Chancery Division (1876–1955) in J 15 and pleadings (1876–1942) in J 54. The reports and certificates of the Supreme Court masters (see 9.13.2.1) from 1876 to 1962 are in J 57. For other series, see 9.13.2.4. There is also a small sample of case files, mainly from 1968, in J 83 and J 84. Many of these files are still closed, but they can be searched on the TNA online catalogue. For requests to see or obtain copies from closed files, or for files that have yet to be transferred to the National Archives, contact:

Department of Constitutional Affairs
Departmental Record Officer (Court Side)
1st Floor
Clive House
70 Petty France
London SWIH 9HD

9.17 Criminal trials for fraud over wills and administrations

Sometimes there was sufficient evidence to bring a criminal prosecution for fraud over wills and administrations. Such cases can be found among the records of the assize courts, the Old Bailey (Central Criminal Court) and the criminal side of the Court of King's Bench. Many examples of such trials, especially those concerning wills and administrations of Royal Navy seamen, can be found among the published Old Bailey session papers, which run from 1674 to 1913. These often give a verbatim account of what was said in court.

An example of such a trial was that of Leah Wilkinson in 1727. It was said in court that she was one of those 'vile persons' who make a practice of drawing up 'false powers' (of attorney) and letters of administration to defraud the widows of seamen who die while at sea. She had forged a will in the name of William Bar, a seaman on board HMS *Mary*, and filed it in the Prerogative Court of Canterbury. She was found guilty both of this act of fraud and of persuading Margaret Smith to impersonate and take the name of Anne Bar in order to claim the outstanding wages of William Bar. Leah Wilkinson was sentenced to being put in the pillory and imprisoned, though details of the sentences are not given.

The records of the assize courts are mainly held by the National Archives – except for the Old Bailey records up to 1834, which are held by the Corporation of

London Records Office and the London Metropolitan Archives (for addresses, see Useful Addresses, p. 211).

Published accounts of the proceedings of the Old Bailey are already partially available online on **www.oldbaileyonline.org**. These will be fully available for the years up to 1834 by the end of 2004. The text of the entries can be fully searched.

9.18 Non-contentious business

Non-contentious (non-contested) business was where there was no dispute but there was some complication or variation in the process of probate or administration. If you find there was a long interval between the dates of death and probate, then that may have been because of one of the circumstances described below.

Sections 9.18.1 to 9.18.3 list the main types of non-contentious business that went through the courts.

9.18.1 Special or limited grants of probate

A grant of probate normally gives the testator powers to deal with the whole estate. But sometimes, for various reasons, a grant of probate or administration is limited to a particular part of the deceased's estate or to a specified period of time (see also 4.6).

Lost or mislaid will
When an original will was lost or mislaid but a true copy had been made, the executor might receive a limited grant of probate, conditional on either the original or an authentic copy being brought into the registry. Under certain circumstances, from the nineteenth century, the executor had to advertise for recovery of the lost will, usually in two newspapers. If the will was lost outside London, its loss was advertised in a local newspaper; if it was lost in London, then the advertisement had to be placed in *The Times* and one other London paper.

Limited probate of an authentic copy of a will
Similar to the above. When the executor could not obtain the original will but an authentic copy was available, probate was limited until the appearance of the original will.

Probate of a married woman's will
Until 1882 a married woman – in legal terminology referred to as a 'feme covert' – could only bequeath part of her goods (see 1.5.1). A grant of probate might therefore be made to her husband limited to what she could legally dispose of.

Probate limited to 'assign a term'
This happened when a testator held all his goods in one diocese (see 2.1.4) except for the lease of a property in another diocese for a term of years. In these circumstances probate was normally granted in the court of the diocese, and the Prerogative Court would assign a person to take over the lease.

Probate limited to goods in Great Britain
When someone left goods both at home and abroad, the Prerogative Courts would deal only with the goods in Great Britain. Any part of the estate abroad would be dealt with in the foreign country.

For limited or special administrations, see 4.6. For administrations granted as part of the probate process see 4.7.

9.18.2 Double probates

These are separate grants made to two or more executors who were unable to apply for probate together – for example, because one of them was abroad.

9.18.3 TNA records relating to non-contentious business

You will find that many of the entries in PROB 29 (acts of court books) and PROB 30 (acts of court) are concerned with non-contentious business, providing an account of the formal proceedings leading to the final order of the court.

Renunciations of rights of executors and next of kin can be found among the proxy records (see 9.19).

9.19 Children and the appointment of guardians

The church courts had the power to appoint guardians for orphaned minors. Sometimes the term used was 'curator' or 'tutor', instead of 'guardian'. A *tutor* was a guardian of a minor – under the age of 15 for a boy and 13 for a girl. A *curator* was a guardian for boys over the age of 14 and under 21, or for girls over 12 and under 21. Additionally, the term *tuition* is used in the Prerogative Court of York – but not in the Prerogative Court of Canterbury – to describe the testamentary guardianship of minors.

In the Prerogative Court of Canterbury a minor could choose his or her guardian from the age of seven. Regarding legacies left to children, many 'subtraction of legacy' cases (see 9.9.4) were brought by minors. At the National Archives, there are many records of appointment of guardians. These are to be found among the records of proxies – documents appointing proctors to act on behalf of parties (see 9.11.1) – in PROB 19 for the years 1674–1714, PROB 36/17–21 for 1654–1713, and PROB 31 (see 9.11.4) for 1722–1858.

The Court of Chancery also dealt with guardianship matters. To find documents relating to guardianship, you may therefore also need to search the Court of Chancery records (see 9.13.2.1 and 9.13.2.4).

9.20 Dormant funds (money in chancery)

There is a popular story handed down within many families that a large unclaimed pot of money has been gathering interest for generations because one or more legatees entitled to inherit it could not be found.

Such monies are variously referred to as dormant funds, funds in court, estates in chancery, or money in chancery. Where necessary, the central courts of law would take responsibility for money and property on behalf of people who could not be traced, or could not look after it themselves due to a disability or for other reasons. The traditional court for this role was the Court of Chancery, though the Court of Exchequer and the King's/Queen's Bench were also sometimes involved.

The normal practice was to sell the property and for the Crown to administer the residue, which was lodged with the appropriate court. Provided you have the necessary documentary evidence to prove your descent from the individual concerned, it is possible to claim this money back. After a fixed period of inactivity (set by the legislation under which the residue is lodged), accounts are classed as dormant funds and no longer attract interest. Most often, their value is less than £150.

9.20.1 Finding a dormant fund

The Court Funds Office – which receives, deals with and disposes of funds as directed by the civil courts of England and Wales – has an index to dormant funds in England and Wales. This can be consulted in person or by writing to:

The Court Funds Office
22 Kingsway
London WC2B 6LE

If you write to the Court Funds Office, you should provide as much detail about the case as possible. Helpful information includes:

- the name of the court
- the title of the court proceedings
- the name(s) of the person(s) who lodged the money with the court
- the name(s) of the person(s) for whose benefit the money was lodged
- relevant dates
- evidence of beneficial interest (i.e. the alleged link between you and any of the persons who lodged the money with the court or for whose benefit the money was lodged)

The Court Funds Office requests that no original documents, such as birth, marriage or death certificates, are sent. At this stage, photocopies are acceptable.

You will be notified of the result of the search, but should be aware that:

- Records concerning dormant funds are confidential and will not be disclosed to anyone who cannot produce evidence of beneficial interest.
- Fees are payable – and you are strongly advised to obtain details of these before initiating an investigation, as it is always possible that the value of the funds may turn out to be less than the fees charged.
- The Court Funds Office does not hold any original court documents.
- The Court Funds Office cannot answer any questions regarding entitlement by descent or relationship, or about legal procedures or selection of legal advisors.

9.20.2 Proving a line of descent

If you find a relevant entry in the dormant funds index, before any money is paid out you will have to prove to the satisfaction of the originating court that you are related to the individual whose money is lodged with it. The main sources for proving descent are the same as those used when tracing a family tree, namely:

- birth, marriage and death registers
- wills, grants of probate and letters of administration
- census returns
- orders of the High Court

9.21 A disputed will in the Prerogative Court of Canterbury (case study)

The mid-eighteenth century case of *Jordan and George* v. *Bostock and others* is a typical example of a dispute over a will involving relatives. The plaintiffs, Jordan and George, were the executors of the will of Jane Johnson. Hannah Bostock was the sister of Jane Johnson; the other defendants in the case were Jane's nephews and nieces and her half-blood sisters.

Jane Johnson wrote two wills, one in 1746 and the other, on her deathbed, in 1747. According to the defendants, the second will was written in suspicious circumstances. They claimed that, without their knowledge, Jane summoned some people to her house and a new will was written.

The plaintiffs claimed that the testator had cancelled the first will by tearing the seal from it. This will had favoured the Bostock family – the copyhold estate being left to the daughter of Hannah Bostock, whereas in the second will it was left to John Robinson, a wig maker.

Two wills were exhibited in court, the 1747 will (Exhibit A) and the 1746 will (Exhibit B), which included the signature and seal of the testator, Jane Johnson. The judge ruled in favour of the plaintiffs, and the 1747 will (Exhibit A) was proved and is now lodged among the original wills in PROB 10. Exhibit B was then filed with the other court papers, among the court exhibits.

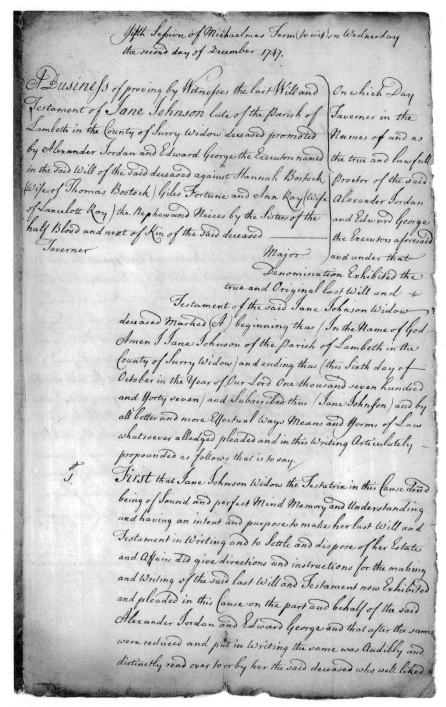

Figure 25 Documents relating to the case of *Jordan and George* v. *Bostock and others*, concerning the will of Jane Johnson (see 9.21).

(a) Allegation of the plaintiffs, Jordan and George. (PROB 18/9, no. 8)

(b) Interrogatories. The third group of questions is shown here. (PROB 18/9, no. 8)

(c) Depositions. The beginning of the deposition (witness statement) from Jonathan Ford, gingerbread baker. (PROB 24/73, f. 892)

(d) Depositions. The response to the third Interrogatory. (PROB 24/73, f. 893)

(f) Minutes of proceedings from act of court book, 1748.
(PROB 29/152, f. 68)

(e) Personal answer of Hannah Bostock (PROB 25/15, f. 5)

Sentence for the validity of the Will of Jane Johnson Widow deceased

In the Name of God Amen

We John Bettesworth doctor of Laws Master Keeper or su...

declare for the fforce and validity of the said Will of the said Will of the said deceased be marked A and do decree a probate thereof to Issue under Seal of this Court to the said Alexander Jordan and Edward George the Executors therein named by this our Definitive Sentence or final decree which we read and promulge by these presents

Geo: Lee
Ed: Simpson

J: Bettesworth

This Definitive Sentence was read given and promulged for the validity of the said Will of the said deceased by the Right Worshipful John Bettesworth doctor of Laws Master Keeper or Commissary of the Prerogative Court of Canterbury lawfully constituted on the ffourth day of May in the year of our Lord One thousand seven hundred and forty eight in the common Hall of Doctors Commons situate in the parish of Saint Benedict near Pauls Wharfe London in presence of the Witnesses mentioned and specified in the Acts of Court thereupon had and used./

(g) The sentence (final judgment) in the case of *Jordan and George* v. *Bostock and others*. (PROB 11/764, ff. 364–5)

10
Other Probate Records

In addition to the main record series described in the previous chapters, wills and related records can be found in a variety of series at the National Archives and elsewhere. This chapter examines some of these sources.

Many wills held by the National Archives can be found by using a surname search on the online catalogue along with an appropriate search term such as 'will', 'administration' or 'probate'. However, catalogues of some series are not available online, in which case it will be necessary to search the original documents, with the help of supplementary finding aids.

10.1 Military wills and powers of attorney

10.1.1 Royal Navy wills

The Royal Navy actively encouraged ratings to leave wills, so their families would be taken care of in the event of death. From 1796, the office of Inspector of Wills was established in order to prevent alleged next of kin making fraudulent claims for prize money and unpaid wages.

1786–1861

During this time, naval wills were usually written on preprinted forms. These records are in the National Archives series ADM 48/1–105, with surname indexes in ADM 142/1–14. There is also a card index for surnames A–H. The registers in ADM 142 provide the following information:

- name
- date of will
- name of ship
- man's number in the ship's muster
- current residence
- name, address and occupation of executor
- name(s) of the beneficiary or beneficiaries

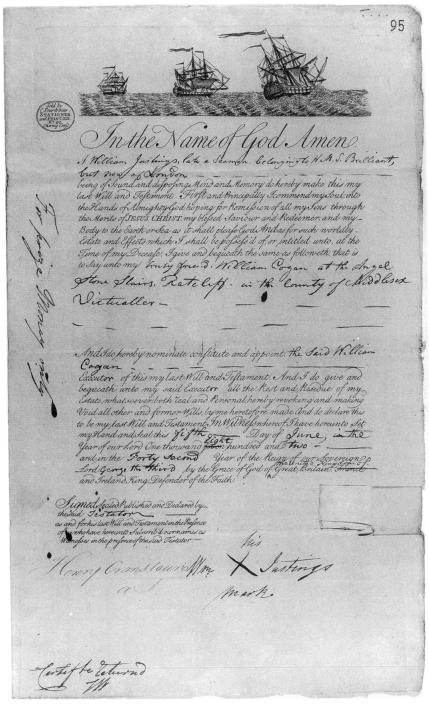

Figure 26 The will of William Justings, formerly of *HMS* Brilliant, 1802. (ADM 48/48)

Applications (1830–60) by next of kin for unpaid wages or pensions due to deceased Royal Navy and Royal Marines officers, or their widows, and to civilian employees of the navy will be found in ADM 45. Some applications are supported by birth or marriage certificates or wills. A surname card index to ADM 45/1–39 is available in the Microfilm Reading Room at the National Archives.

Applications from the next of kin of deceased Royal Navy ratings and Royal Marines other ranks for unpaid wages (1800–60) are in ADM 44. Some are supported by birth or marriage certificates or wills. The letter included in the piece number is the initial letter of the surname of the seaman or marine, and there is a range of certificate numbers for each letter of the alphabet.

Indexes to ADM 44 will be found in ADM 141, which uses an unusual system of alphabetization. You have to take the first letter of the surname you are looking for and add to it the next vowel (Y is treated as a vowel) followed by the first consonant after the initial letter (regardless of whether it precedes or follows the vowel): for example, Pritchard will be found under PIR, Evans under EAV, and Whyte under WYH. Cross-references are given for variant spellings (e.g. Towel/Tole). You should end up with the three letters that appear at the top of the relevant page in ADM 141. Having made a note of the registered number given in the third column of the entry in ADM 141, the next step is to look it up in the ADM 44 catalogue, where you will find the relevant document reference. The annotations in ADM 44 are more difficult to read than the ADM 141 register entries, so note down as much as you can from the register.

Registers of wills made at the Naval Hospital, Gibraltar (1809–15) are in ADM 105/40 and are searchable by name on the National Archives' online catalogue. The wills in this register (which occupy only 12 pages) provide the following information:

- name of ship
- name of testator
- date of will
- in whose favour drawn (a brief abstract of the will)
- when sent to the Inspector of Wills
- witnesses' names
- by whom filled in
- name of physician or surgeon who certified the sanity of the patient

1862–1901

In 1862 the Royal Navy began a new system of recording wills, which were registered after the death of the testator. The records are in ADM 48/106–107 (1862–82) and ADM 142/15–19 (1862–1901). A name index is included in *A List of*

Wills, Administrations etc. in the Public Record Office, 12th–19th Century (Baltimore, 1968), which is available at the National Archives. The series contains original wills which the Admiralty accepted as valid; those not declared valid appear to have been returned to the executors. The registers provide:

- name
- ship
- date of registering the will
- date of death

The survival rate for these wills is quite poor, but entries for those proved in or after 1868 should be found in the National Probate Calendar (see 5.2). Information in ADM 154 (Registers of Men Discharged Dead, 1859–78) may also be useful.

For more detailed information about naval wills, administrations, effects papers and associated records, see section 5.3 of *Tracing Your Naval Ancestors* by Bruno Pappalardo (PRO, 2003).

10.1.2 *Royal Navy powers of attorney*

Miscellaneous power of attorney for the Royal Navy can be found in the following series:

TNA reference	Content	Date range
PMG 50	Miscellaneous registers of probates and administrations	1836–1915
PMG 51	Registers of miscellaneous powers of attorney	1800–99

10.1.3 *Royal Marines*

See also 10.1.1.

There is a collection of copies of Royal Marines wills and administrations (1740–64), extracted from probate registries, in ADM 96/524, which is searchable by name using the National Archives' online catalogue. These were presumably obtained to settle questions relating to arrears of pay of officers and other ranks in the Marines. Later, after the establishment of the Inspector of Wills in 1796 (see 10.1.1), Royal Marines other ranks were encouraged to deposit wills in the Navy Pay Office. There is a register of probates affecting the payment of pensions (1836–1915) in PMG 50.

10.1.4 Army wills

Before 1858, for soldiers who died abroad leaving assets over a certain amount, grants of probate or administration were issued by the Prerogative Court of Canterbury (see 2.4). Also useful are the casualty returns in WO 25/1359–2407 (1809–55). These sometimes include wills, or copies of wills, of deceased soldiers and inventories of their effects. They are arranged by regiment.

Application papers for widows' pensions and dependents' allowances (1755–1908) which include wills are in WO 42.

10.1.5 Army letters and powers of attorney

Registers or entry books of letters and powers of attorney for army officers can be found in several series:

TNA reference	Content	Date range
WO 30/1	Registers of letters of attorney	1755–83
PMG 14/142–164	Registers of letters of attorney	1756–1827
PMG 14/104–125	Entry books of powers of attorney	1759–1816
PMG 14/165–167	Registers of letters of attorney granted by officers' widows	1802–21
PMG 14/126–137	Alphabetical entry books	1811–14
PMG 51	Registers of letters of attorney (includes Ordnance Officers from 1858)	1836–99
WO 54/494–510	Indexed registers of attorney Royal Artillery and Royal Engineers (officers, civilians and creditors)	1699–1857

See also WO 54/494–510, which are indexed registers of letters of attorney for Ordnance (Royal Artillery and Royal Engineers) officers, civilian staff and creditors, 1699–1857.

10.2 Deeds

These series relate mainly to records of conveyances and other deeds of title, but they also contain references to wills and grants of probate and administration. Most of the deeds in these series were probably lodged with the particular court either for enrolment or as evidence in legal proceedings. Some of these series are searchable, either wholly or in part, on TNA's online catalogue.

TNA reference	Name of series	Date range
C 146	Ancient Deeds Series C	1100–1695
E 40	Ancient Deeds Series A	c. 1100–1603
E 41	Ancient Deeds Series AA	c. 1100–1642
E 42	Ancient Deeds Series AS	c. 1100–1590
E 44	Modern Deeds series A	1504–1764
E 210	(King's Remembrancer) Ancient Deeds Series D	c. 1120–1609
E 211	Ancient Deeds Series DD (bundle 10)	c. 1101–1645
E 214	Modern Deeds	c. 1603–1851
E 326	Ancient Deeds Series B	c. 1200–1592
E 327	Ancient Deeds Series Maddox	c. 1100–1543
E 329	Ancient Deeds Series BS	1148–1560
LR 14	Ancient Deeds Series E	1223–1730
WALE 29	Ancient Deeds Series F	1265–1602

10.3 The royal household

10.3.1 Lord Chamberlain's Department

LC 5/104–106 (1748–84)
These are entry books of wills, letters and assignments of household servants that affected payment of salaries or pensions due to officials of the royal household. A name index is available in *A List of Wills, Administrations etc. in the Public Record Office, 12th–19th Century*.

10.3.2 Lord Steward's Department

LS 13/195 (1712–26)
Similarly, these are entry books of assignments of board wages in the Office of the Clerk of the Kitchen, together with letters of administration and probates of wills.

10.4 Overseas probate courts

The probate records of the British Consular Court at Smyrna, Turkey (1820–1929) and of the Shanghai Supreme Court (1857–1941) are to be found in FO 626 and FO 917 respectively. Other wills of Britons in China (1837–1951) are in FO 678/2729–2931. Wills from the British Consulate in Russia are in FO 184/14 (1817–66), while wills and private papers from Tunis are in FO 335/164 (1866–85). A name index is available in *A List of Wills, Administrations etc. in the Public Record Office, 12th–19th Century.*

10.5 Royal wills and other probate records

The National Archives has an impressive collection of royal wills and other probate records (see table below). Others are held by the Royal Archives, Lambeth Palace Library and the British Library.

Date	Member of royal family	TNA reference
1189	Henry II	E 164/12, f. 1 (illuminated) T 48/23 (copy)
1199	Richard I	TS 18/249 (copy) Includes a history of the wills of reigning sovereigns from the Norman Conquest to George I.
1327	Edward II	TS 18/249 (copy) Includes a history of the wills of reigning sovereigns from the Norman Conquest to George I.
1399	Richard II	E 23/1/1 T 48/23 (copy)
1422	Henry V	C 65/87, m. 3 E 23/2
1509	Henry VII	E 23/3 T 48/23 (copy) TS 18/249 (report)
1547	Henry VIII	PROB 11/31, q. 32 (no probate clause) E 315/469 (contemporary transcript) E 23/4/1, E 23/4/2 and SP 1/227, f. 217–229 (drafts) T 48/23 (copy)
1548	Catherine Parr (wife of Henry VIII)	PROB 11/32, f. 142-143 (no original will)

Date	Member of royal family	TNA reference
1557	Anne of Cleves (wife of Henry VIII)	PROB 11/39, f. 261 (no original will)
1669	Henrietta Maria (wife of Charles I)	PROB 6/44, f. 114 (19 October 1669) T 27/2, p. 116
1702	William III	TS 18/249
1705	Catherine of Braganza (wife of Charles II)	PROB 1/56 PROB 11/487, f. 274-278
1708	George of Denmark (consort of Queen Anne)	PROB 6/85, f. 89–90 PROB 16/6, f. 133–148 (papers concerning the distribution of his estate)
1714	Anne, Queen of England	PC 1/2/260 (incomplete draft) T 48/23 SP 44/116
1760	George II	TS 18/249 (extracts and comments)
1818	Charlotte Sophia (wife of George III)	PROB 1/97 PROB 11/1612, q. 37
1820	George III	TS 18/249 (extracts and comments)
1821	Caroline Amelia Elizabeth (wife of George IV)	PROB 1/98 PROB 11/1653, q. 97
1850	Adelaide of Saxe-Coburg-Meiningen (wife of William IV)	PROB 1/99 PROB 31/1526/1482–1485 There was some doubt about this will, due to erasures.

In the table above: f. = folio
m. = membrane
p. = page
q. = quire

See 5.6 for details of royal wills from 1858.

10.6 Enrolled wills

C 54 (Close Rolls, 1591–1810)

'Letters closed' conveyed orders and instructions to royal officers and others and were therefore of a confidential nature. They are known as such because, before being dispatched, they were folded and then closed by the Great Seal. They were enrolled on the Close Rolls to create a permanent and authoritative record. Following a statute introduced in 1717, during the reign of George I, some Roman Catholic wills were enrolled on the Close Rolls.

Lists of wills enrolled on the Close Rolls (from 13 William III to 5 George IV) can be found in *The Genealogist*, Vol. 1, p. 267 (1877) and Vol. II, pp. 59 and 279 (1878); and also in *A List of Wills, Administrations etc. in the Public Record Office, 12th–19th Century*.

CP 43 (Recovery Rolls, 1583–1837)
These contain enrolments of transfer of property and include Roman Catholic deeds and wills. A list of CP 43 wills appears in *The Genealogist*, New Series Vol. III, pp. 122, 185 and 220 (1886).

Also see 6.1.7.2.

10.7 Miscellaneous series at the National Archives

Wills, probates and other associated testamentary records occur in a variety of 'miscellaneous' series at the National Archives. The main ones are listed below.

10.7.1 Chancery Miscellanea

C 47 (1324–1577)
Among the various items in this series are a number of ecclesiastical documents that relate to testamentary matters, including transcripts of wills, probates and administrations. They are indexed in *A List of Wills, Administrations etc. in the Public Record Office, 12th–19th Century*.

10.7.2 Exchequer: Miscellaneous Books

E 135/7 (1325–1628)
This series contains the transcripts of proceedings in various courts relating to ecclesiastical and monastic matters concerning the possession of church lands and tithes, rights of presentation, taxation and indulgences. Wills also feature among the collection, which does not have a name index. The origin of these wills is unknown, but it is assumed that they were sent to the Exchequer for financial or judicial reasons. They are indexed in *A List of Wills, Administrations etc. in the Public Record Office, 12th–19th Century*.

10.7.3 Exchequer: Miscellaneous Ecclesiastical Documents

E 315/31–54 (c. 1100 to c. 1800)
The main contents of this series are private grants to monastic houses and grants relating to property acquired by the monastic houses. They are indexed in *A List of Wills, Administrations etc. in the Public Record Office, 12th–19th Century*.

E 315/483 (1648–59)
This series contains copies of wills, grants of probate and letters of administration extracted from the Registers of the Prerogative Court of Canterbury during the Commonwealth. They relate mostly to individuals who served during the Commonwealth, either in the army or otherwise. Copies were presumably taken for the purposes of settling arrears of pay. They are indexed in *A List of Wills, Administrations etc. in the Public Record Office, 12th–19th Century*.

10.7.4 Exchequer: Issue Rolls and Registers

E 403/2372–2378 (1681–1718)
Documents contained in these volumes include copies of wills, grants of probate and letters of administration taken from the various courts of probate, though they mainly relate to the Prerogative Court of Canterbury. The entered documents were those which affected annuities and other payments from the Exchequer. There is a name index in each volume.

10.7.5 Exchequer: Assignments and Exchequer Bills

E 406/27–44 (1677–1704)
These books include brief entries concerning wills, copies of probates and letters of administration that affected assignments made as a result of the settlement between Charles II and the London goldsmiths in 1677.

E 406/45–80 (1622–1834)
Among the items in this series are deeds of assignment whereby pensions, annuities and other payments from the Exchequer were sold in whole or in part. It also contains letters of attorney, letters of administration and probates of wills, along with other documents recorded in the Auditors' Assignment Books. There is a name index in each volume.

10.7.6 Office of Land Revenue Records and Enrolments

LRRO 13/91 (1900–3)
Includes probates of wills.

10.7.7 National Debt Office

NDO 1/4 (1746–67)
Consists of entry books of assignments and wills relating to life annuities granted in 1745, 1746 and 1757.

10.7.8 Treasury

T 16/1–13 (1857–87)
Contains letters relating to intestates' estates.

T 64/292–293 (1792–4)
These registers of wills proved in the Consistory Court of London were presumably compiled for Legacy Duty purposes, as they list the value under which the will was proved. They are indexed in *A List of Wills, Administrations etc. in the Public Record Office, 12th–19th Century* and provide the following information:

- total amount (or proportion) of the whole estate bequeathed
- name of widow
- relationship of legatees to the testator

10.7.9 Treasury Solicitor

TS 8 (1804–15), TS 9 (1815–44)
The letter books in these series include details of wills and intestates' estates. See also 4.8.

10.8 Probate records at the British Library

The Oriental and India Office Collections (OIOC) at the British Library include records of estates and wills of 'home and overseas servants' of the East India Company and India Office and their dependants who died in the UK and Europe while in receipt of salary, leave pay or pension, and of members of the Indian civil and military services who died in India. The records, which give the name and address of the deceased, names of beneficiaries and sometimes of relatives, details of bequests and names of executors, cover the following:

1704–80	Court proceedings
1727–74	Bengal Mayor's Court proceedings
1774–79	Supreme Court proceedings
Up to 1783	Bombay Mayor's Court proceedings

These are indexed by:

Up to 1783	Alphabetical index of wills, on the OIOC Reading Room shelves
1780–1909	Indexes available in the OIOC Reading Room
1909 onwards	General card index of wills and a typescript version (in progress) in the OIOC Reading Room

In addition, these indexes act as an index to grants of probate, grants of administration and inventories. See also the *Guide to Wills, Probates, Administrations and Inventories in the India Office Records* on the shelves in the OIOC Reading Room.

Further information about the probate records at the British Library can be found on **www.bl.uk/collections/oiocfamilyhistory/familywills.html**.

10.8.1 Grants of administration (1774–1948)

These records provide:

- name of deceased
- date of death
- name of the High Court of the Presidency where the administration was registered
- name and address of the person granted administration of the estate

10.8.2 Grants of probate (1865–1938)

These include administrations as well as probates granted by District Courts in India and by High Courts and Chief Courts established since 1865, except for those in Calcutta, Madras and Bombay. They are indexed for the years 1865–1910.

10.8.3 Inventories of deceased estates and copies of estate accounts (1780–1938)

These give the name of the deceased and a list of his or her possessions at the time of death.

10.8.4 Military estate papers (1849–1937)

These comprise estate accounts, inventories and wills for European officers and other ranks of the East India Company and the Indian Army. There are no indexes as such, but they can be approached via the indexes to Treasury Deposits 1849–1919.

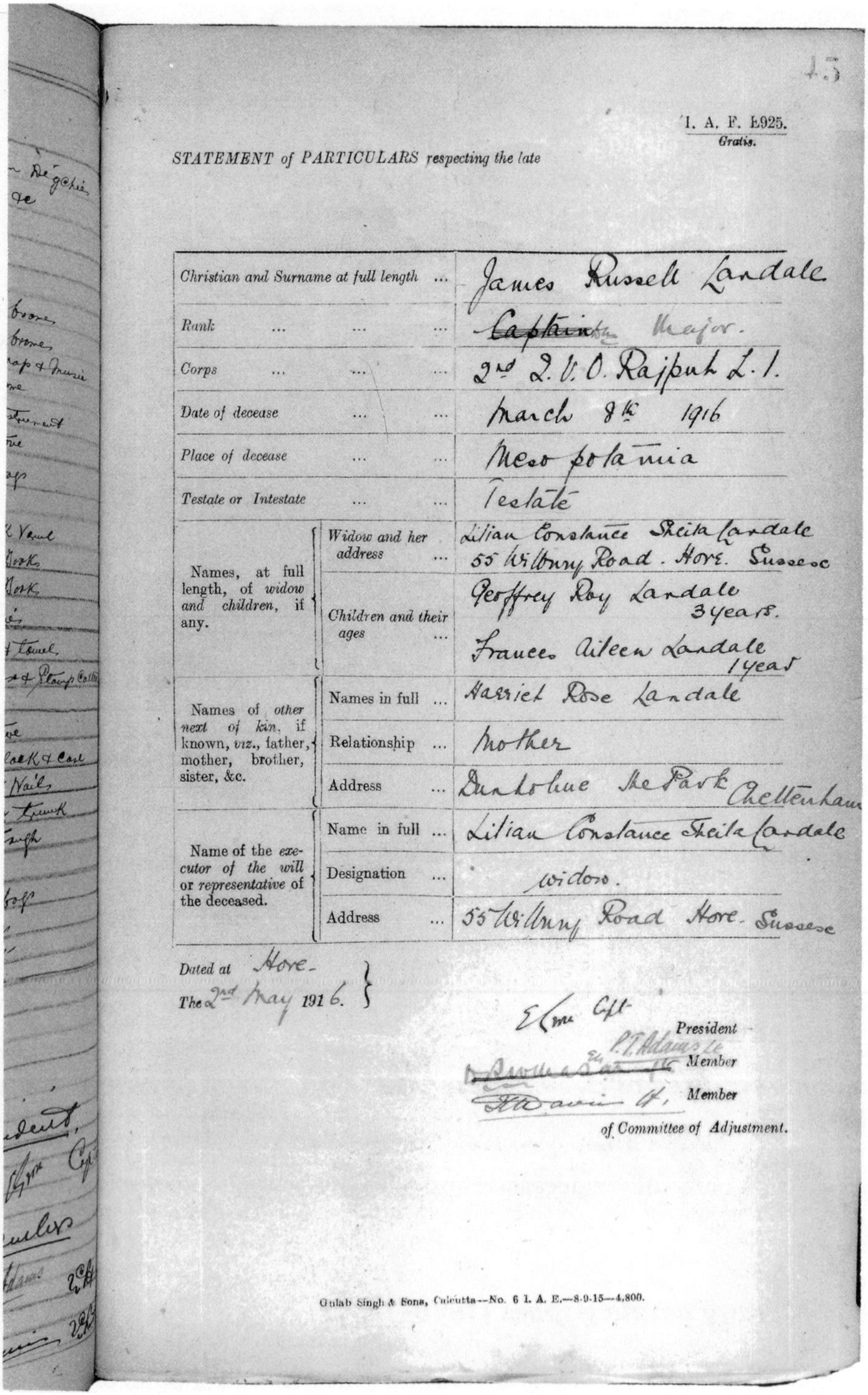

45

I. A. F. B925.
Gratis.

STATEMENT of PARTICULARS respecting the late

Christian and Surname at full length ...		James Russell Landale
Rank		~~Captain~~ Major.
Corps		2nd Q. V. O. Rajput L. I.
Date of decease		March 8th 1916
Place of decease		Meso potamia
Testate or Intestate		Testate
Names, at full length, of *widow and children*, if any.	*Widow and her address* ...	Lilian Constance Sheila Landale 55 Wilbury Road. Hove. Sussex
	Children and their ages ...	Geoffrey Roy Landale 3 years. Frances Aileen Landale 1 year
Names of *other next of kin*, if known, *viz.*, father, mother, brother, sister, &c.	Names in full ...	Harriet Rose Landale
	Relationship ...	Mother
	Address ...	Dunlolue The Park Cheltenham
Name of the *executor of the will* or *representative* of the deceased.	Name in full ...	Lilian Constance Sheila Landale
	Designation ...	widow.
	Address ...	55 Wilbury Road Hove. Sussex

Dated at Hove.
The 2nd May 1916.

President
Member
Member
of Committee of Adjustment.

Gulab Singh & Sons, Calcutta—No. 6 I. A. E.—8-9-15—4,800.

Figure 27 Military estate paper of James Russell Landale, 1916.
British Library: L/AG/34/40/82, f. 45

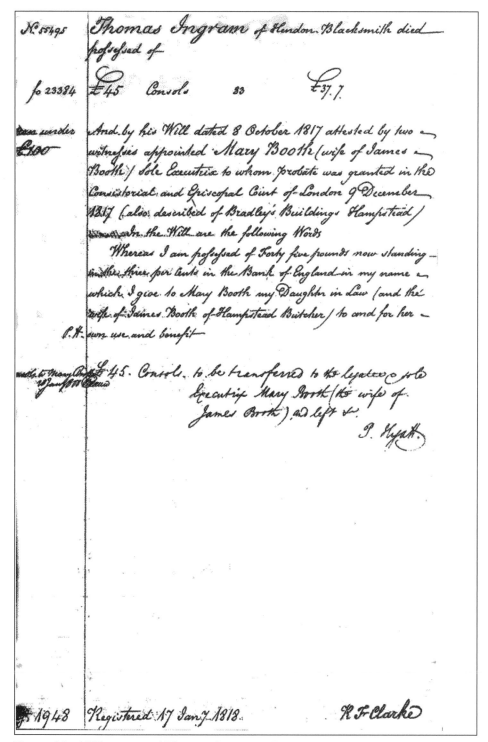

Figure 28 Will extract of Thomas Ingram, 1815.

Bank of England: Book 5 A–I Register 1041

10.9 Probate records at the Bank of England (1717–1845)

These records consist of extracts of wills of people who died with monies in public funds, as well as abstracts of orders made for stockholders who went bankrupt or were declared lunatic. They extend from 1717 to 1845, when the process of recording bequests of stock ceased. In 1812 the Bank ruled that, from then on, it would accept grants of probate from the Prerogative Court of Canterbury only.

Since the Bank of England holds extracts only, for the full text of a will you need to consult the records of the court that proved it. However, although the extracts do not include all the information contained in the original wills, they often identify members of the deceased's family as beneficiaries.

Indexes to Bank of England extracts can be searched, for a fee, on the English Origins website (**www.englishorigins.com**). Hard copies of extracts can be ordered via the English Origins website. Access to the Bank of England's archives is restricted, but applications can be made, in writing only, to:

The Bank of England
Archive Section HO-M
Threadneedle Street
London EC2R 8AH

10.9.1 Other material in the Bank of England extracts

10.9.1.1 Burial extracts

In some cases, the Bank of England appears to have considered records of probate insufficient. Occasionally burial extracts were recorded, presumably as evidence that a stockholder had died.

10.9.1.2 Records of lunatics

The Bank of England also kept records of the stocks, consols and annuities held by people declared lunatic. In these cases, instead of a will extract, the register records the order of the court that declared the lunacy, such as the Court of Chancery.

11

Scotland, Ireland, the Isle of Man and the Channel Islands

11.1 Introduction

This chapter deals with the differences between Scottish and English rules for wills and inheritance. It also explains how to find wills in Scotland, Northern Ireland and the Republic of Ireland, the Isle of Man and the Channel Islands. Included here, too, are death duty records and *bona vacantia* (estates without next of kin) in Scotland and Ireland.

11.2 Scottish wills

England, Wales and Scotland still maintain separate legal systems and have historically different legal structures for wills. In Scotland, from 1804 property was divided into 'heritable, and 'moveable'. *Heritable property* is what is known in England as freehold property or real estate. *Moveable property* is what is called personal estate in England. Before 1804, in Scotland, testaments (see 11.2.1) dealt with moveable property only. After this date heritable property was transferred via other types of legal documents, such as settlements, but it was not until the Heritable Jurisdictions Act of 1868 that heritable property figured on a regular basis in wills and inventories.

It is interesting to compare the practices concerning wills, intestates and inheritance in Scotland with those in England and Wales. In Scotland anyone over the age of 16 can make a will, whereas in England and Wales the age is 18. An old will is not invalidated when someone north of the border gets married, legally separated or divorced. Widowed spouses, children and other descendants in Scotland are entitled to a fixed share of moveable or personal property, regardless of what is expressed in a will. And when someone dies without leaving a will, the rules of intestate succession are different.

11.2.1 *Terminology*

The Scottish system of probate differs slightly from the practice in England and Wales. In Scotland *testament* is a collective term used to describe documents relating to the estate of a deceased person. Testaments may include:

- an inventory (of varying length) of the testator's property
- a will (occasionally) detailing how the testator wished his or her goods to be divided.

In Scottish legal terminology a will is called a *testament testamentar*, and the equivalent of letters of administration is a *testament dative*.

As is the case with England and Wales (see 1.1.1), it is difficult to estimate what proportion of Scottish people left wills.

Although the form and process of probate differs from the system in England and Wales, the type of information that can be obtained from Scottish wills is similar to that described in 6.2

11.2.2 *Scottish court structure*

From 1515 to 1823 the secular commissary courts were responsible for the probate of wills. These were based on the same administrative areas as the medieval dioceses (the authority of the bishops being abolished in 1560). Between 1824 and 1875 all but one of the commissary courts were abolished and replaced with sheriff's courts (the sheriff being the chief judge of a county or district). The one exception was the Edinburgh commissary court, which continued until 1830. The courts also held jurisdiction for non-residents dying in Scotland; and residents dying outside Scotland could have their wills registered there.

The records of all these courts are held by:

National Archives of Scotland
HM General Register House
Edinburgh EH1 3YY
Telephone: 0131 535 1334
Website: **www.nas.gov.uk**

11.2.3 *Where to find the records*

1513–1901
Scottish wills from 1513 to 1901 have been digitally imaged by the Scottish Archive Network and can be found on their website (**www.scottishdocuments. com**). All of these wills can now be searched on this site, although the digital images of some wills are not yet available. The index (which covers testaments and inventories, too) is free to search, but there is a small charge for downloading the image of a will. This excellent website also has information on reading old handwriting, weights and measures, and occupations.

1876–91
From 1876 there are annual indexes of testaments, known as the Calendar of Confirmations, which can be found at the National Archives of Scotland, large Scottish libraries and local archives. From 1876 to 1959 they are in the form of printed or typed volumes; from 1960 to 1984 they take the form of microfiche cards.

These indexes give:

- name of deceased
- place of death
- date of death
- date testament was recorded

1992 onwards
Records from 1992 to the present day are held by:

The Commissary Department
Edinburgh Sheriff Court
27 Chambers Street
Edinburgh EH1 1LB

11.2.4 *Inheritance rules*

Before 1868, Scottish wills could transfer moveable property (see 11.2) only. Heritable property (real estate) could be inherited by two methods. One was by *retour* (also known as *services of heirs*), which was part of the Scottish feudal land system. Local landowners would decide whether an individual was the rightful heir. Their decision was communicated by a retour (return) to the Scottish Chancery, who would then give full title to the lands. These Chancery records are held at the National Archives of Scotland. The other method was by trust deposition and settlement (*testamentary deed*), which would be recorded in the relevant registry of deeds. These records are also held at the National Archives of Scotland.

From 1868 Scottish wills could transfer both moveable and heritable property, and from 1964 the formal abolition of the retour procedure began. However, for a few properties, this method is still used even today.

11.3 Irish wills

Before 1858 wills were proved and administrations granted by the courts of the Church of Ireland, which consisted of the Prerogative Court of Ireland and 28 diocesan consistory courts (note that the boundaries of the dioceses do not coincide with county boundaries). There are separate indexes for each of these courts.

After 1858, grants of probate and administration were made in the Principal Registry and district registries of the Probate Court up to 1877; and from 1877 in those of the High Court.

Wills proved up to 1903 held in the Four Courts building in Dublin were destroyed by a fire during the troubles of 1922. No original wills survive from the Principal Registry in Dublin, nor for the counties of Dublin, Kildare, Meath and Wicklow.

However, the National Archives of Ireland holds the following records:

- Original wills and administration papers for the Principal Registry from 1904; and for most district registries since 1900.
- Will books, containing copies of most wills proved in district registries since 1858; and, for a few years, some of the wills proved in the Principal Registry.
- Grant books containing copies of grants of wills and administrations made in the Principal Registry from 1922 and also for a few earlier years; and most grants made in the district registries since 1858.
- The Calendars of the Grants of Probate and Letters of Administration made in the Principal Registry and the district registries from 1858. These were produced annually and give basic details, including occupation and address of deceased, date of death, name and address of executor, and value of estate. Sets also survive in the Public Record Office of Northern Ireland and at the district registries. There are indexes for some years.
- There are also Betham's abstracts of wills before 1827; Inland Revenue registers of wills and administrations 1829–39 (indexes cover 1829–79); and Charitable Donations and Bequests will extract books 1800–1961 (there is a separate card index for 1800–58). And there are other copies of wills and administrations, too.

The Society of Genealogists, in London, holds abstracts of Irish wills from 1569 to 1909.

There is now an *Index of Irish Wills, 1484–1858* on CD-ROM (Eneclann, Dublin, 2000), which covers the wills held at the National Archives of Ireland, including miscellaneous collections of wills or will abstracts. This is available at the National Archives of Ireland in Dublin and in the library of the National Archives at Kew. There are also a number of published indexes in book form. These include *Index to Prerogative Wills, 1536–1810*, edited by Arthur Vicars (Dublin, 1897), which is available at the National Archives of Ireland and in the library of the National Archives at Kew.

Contact details for the National Archives of Ireland are as follows:

The National Archives of Ireland
Bishop Street
Dublin 8
Republic of Ireland
Telephone: 00 353 1 407 2300
Website: **www.nationalarchives.ie**

Republic of Ireland grants of probate and administration for the last 20 years, as well as the original wills, schedules of assets and associated documents, are available for public inspection at:

Probate Office, High Court
First Floor
15/24 Phoenix Street North
Smithfield
Dublin 7
Republic of Ireland
Telephone: 00 353 1 888 6174
Website: **www.courts.ie**

11.3.1 *Northern Ireland wills*

For wills and administrations up to the last five years, contact:

Public Record Office Northern Ireland
66 Balmoral Avenue
Belfast BT9 6NY
Telephone: 028 9025 5905
Website: **www.proni.gov.uk**

Wills and administrations for the last five years (only the last two years are held on site), contact:

The Probate and Matrimonial Office
Royal Courts of Justice
Chichester Street
Belfast BT1 3JF
Telephone: 028 9072 4683
Website: **www.courtsni.gov.uk**

Before 1858, because wills were probated and administrations granted by the diocesan bishops of the Established Church (see 11.3), the probate records are arranged by diocese, namely:

Diocese of Armagh
Diocese of Clogher
Diocese of Connor
Diocese of Derry and Raphoe
Diocese of Down
Diocese of Dromore

1900 onwards
From 1900 all probated wills and grants of administrations and associated documents are available, filed in a separate envelope for each testator. There are bound indexes to wills from 1858 to 1984, arranged by date of probate.

Before 1900
All original wills prior to 1900 were destroyed in the fire in Dublin mentioned above (see 11.3). But before sending an original will to Dublin the local registry copied it into a register, and these copies have now been put onto microfilm.

Also, printed and manuscript indexes to pre-1858 wills, administrations and administration bonds exist. These records are of value to the genealogist because, although the wills themselves have not survived, the indexes make it possible to determine whether there was a will.

11.4 *Isle of Man wills*

The Isle of Man was in the diocese of Sodor and Man – which included the Consistory Court of Sodor and Man and the Archdeaconry of the Isle of Man – and came within the jurisdiction of the province of York (see 2.3). Consequently, a will or administration for someone who resided in the Isle of Man may be held at the Borthwick Institute of Historical Research. From 1874 the consistory court had sole jurisdiction on the island, then in 1885 the civil High Court of Justice took over jurisdiction for the probate of wills and grants of administrations.

The Manx National Heritage Library holds wills proved by the two consistory courts from around 1600 to 1910; and on microfilm up to 1916. The majority of the wills have been indexed. These records are held at:

Manx National Heritage
Douglas
Isle of Man IM1 3LY
Telephone: 01624 648000
Website: **www.gov.im/mnh/National_Library.asp**

Wills and administrations for 1912–39 are held at:

Isle of Man Public Record Office
Unit 40a Spring Valley Industrial Estate
Douglas
Isle of Man IM2 2QS
Telephone: 01624 693569
Website: **www.gov.im/registries/publicrecords**

Those for 1940 to the present day are held at:

Deeds and Probate Registry
Registries Building
Deemster's Walk
Bucks Road
Douglas
Isle of Man IM1 3AR
Website: **www.gov.im/registries/courts/probate**

11.5 Channel Island wills

11.5.1 *Jersey*

The church court, that of the Dean of Jersey, had responsibility for the probate of wills and granting of administrations up to 1949. Jersey Archive has a searchable online catalogue (**http://jerseyheritagetrust.jeron.je/**). The archive's address is:

Jersey Archive
Clarence Road
St Helier
Channel Islands JE2 4JY
Telephone: 01534 833333
Website: **www.jerseyheritagetrust.org**

From 1851, as well as the wills of personalty, there are also wills of realty. These are in French and are held by the Jersey land registry at:

The Judicial Greffe
Royal Court House
Royal Square
St Helier
Jersey JE1 1JG
Telephone: 01534 502300
Website: **www.judicialgreffe.gov.je**

11.5.2 Guernsey

Wills and administrations were, and still are, proved or granted in the Ecclesiastical Court of the Bailiwick of Guernsey, including those for Alderney, Sark, Herm and Jethou. Wills in Guernsey are split between wills of personalty and wills of realty, and there are separate indexes for these two types of wills. Enquiries should be made to:

States of Guernsey
Island Archive Service
29 Victoria Road
St Peter Port
Guernsey GY1 IHU
Telephone: 01481 724512
Website: **http://user.itl.net/~glen/archgsy.html**

11.6 Estates without next of kin *(bona vacantia)*

For an explanation of the term *bona vacantia*, see 4.8. See also 9.20, regarding dormant funds.

11.6.1 Scotland

Enquiries concerning Scottish estates that have fallen to the Crown in default of heirs, should be made to:

The Queen's and Lord Treasurer's Remembrancer
Crown Office
5/7 Regent Road
Edinburgh EH7 5BL

Funds lodged in the Court of Session and other unclaimed sums resulting from situations such as company liquidations, bankruptcies and judicial factories (the placing of the affairs of a person under the control of someone appointed by the court) are held for seven years from the date of consignation (lodgement) by:

The Accountant of Court
Parliament House
Parliament Square
Edinburgh EH1 1RQ

After seven years, they are transferred to the Queen's and Lord Treasurer's Remembrancer at the address above.

Other enquiries may be made to:

The Keeper of the Records of Scotland
National Archives of Scotland
HM General Register House
Edinburgh EH1 3YY

11.6.2 Northern Ireland

For funds lodged in court in Northern Ireland since 1921, write to:

The Court Funds Office
Third Floor
Bedford House
16–22 Bedford Street
Belfast BT2 7FD

For records prior to the institution of the Supreme Court in Northern Ireland in 1921, contact the Accountant of the Courts of Justice in Dublin (for address, see 11.6.3).

11.6.3 Republic of Ireland

For funds under the control of the Supreme Court and High Court of Justice in Ireland, write to:

Accountant of the Courts of Justice
The Courts Service
15–24 Phoenix Street North
Smithfield
Dublin 7
Telephone: 00 353 1 888 6214

11.7 Death duty records

11.7.1 Scotland

The National Archives of Scotland hold Estate Duty records commencing in 1804, among the records of the Inland Revenue in Scotland. However, these records may not contain more genealogical information than can be found in the commissary and sheriff court records.

Death duty records held at the National Archives of Scotland comprise:

- Personal legacy registers, 1804–29.
- Return ledgers for Inventory Duty, 1831–92.
- Residue Duty account books and legacy receipt books, 1819–38.
- Register of inventories received from commissary offices, 1824–76; indexes, 1863–84.
- Testate register and indexes, 1828–79.
- Intestate register and indexes, 1829–79.
- Succession Duty register and indexes, 1853–68.
- General registers and separate indexes to the last three series in the list above, 1829–79.

At the National Archives, Kew, in series IR 7, there is a small amount of correspondence concerning contentious cases relating to Scotland for the years 1839–41.

11.7.2 Ireland

The only identified sources relating to death duties are the Inland Revenue registers of wills and administrations for 1828–39, with indexes for 1828–79. These are held at the National Archives of Ireland. No other records appear to have survived.

Appendix 1

The National Archives' Prerogative Court of Canterbury (PROB) Series

PROB 1	**Wills of selected famous people (1552–1854)** The original wills of famous people removed from PROB 10, including the wills of Shakespeare, Drake and Nelson.
PROB 2	**Inventories compiled before 1661 (1417–1668)** These are the small number of pre-1661 inventories that have survived. A few of the inventories are accompanied by executors' or administrators' accounts.
PROB 3	**Filed engrossed 18th-century inventories and associated documents (1701–82)** Engrossed copies of inventories preserved in their original filing arrangement. A few of the inventories are accompanied by executors' or administrators' accounts.
PROB 4	**Engrossed inventories exhibited from 1660 (1660–c.1720)** Engrossed copies of inventories. Some of them are copies of those in PROB 5 and PROB 32. A few of the inventories are accompanied by executors' or administrators' accounts.
PROB 5	**Miscellaneous inventories, accounts and associated documents (1643–1836)** Inventories, executors' and administrators' accounts and associated documents, including commissions to appraisers to make or receive inventories and accounts.
PROB 6	**Administration act books (1559–1858)** These books record letters of administration. They include limited grants to 1809.
PROB 7	**Limited administration act books (1810–58)** These books record limited grants of administration.
PROB 8	**Probate act books (1526–1858)** These books record both probate acts and letters of administration with will annexed. They also record limited grants of probate for 1780, 1782–99, 1801 and 1805.

PROB 9	**Limited probate act books (1781–1858)** These books record limited grants of probates for 1781, 1800, 1802–4 and 1806–58.
PROB 10	**Original wills and sentences (1484–1858)** The majority of the documents are original wills signed and sealed by testators and attested by witnesses. However, many of the pre-1600 wills are merely copies.
PROB 11	**Will registers (1383–1858)** These are the will registers into which the court clerks copied the text of the wills. Most of the PCC wills were registered and can therefore be found in PROB 11.
PROB 12	**Indexes of wills and administrations grants (1383–1858)** This is the main series of original indexes to PROB 6–PROB 11.
PROB 13	**Original calendars and indexes of wills and administrations (1384–1800)** These are original indexes to PROB 6 and PROB 8–PROB 11. Many of them were transcribed to produce the indexes in PROB 12 and PROB 15.
PROB 14	**Warrants (1657–1858)** These warrants were used to authorize the issue of a grant of administration or probate.
PROB 15	**Original calendars and indexes of wills and administrations (1655–1858)** These consist of several series of original indexes to PROB 6–PROB 11.
PROB 16	**Muniment books (1611–1858)** These volumes contain registration of exhibits, orders and decrees, and appointments of officers of the court.
PROB 17	**Commission books (1678–1857)** These books document the issue of commissions and requisitions to swear executors and administrators.
PROB 18	**Allegations (1661–1858)** The allegations (plaintiffs' pleas) are arranged in bundles.
PROB 19	**Bundles of proxies (1674–1718)** Documents appointing proctors to act on behalf of persons involved in litigation or in non-contested business. The most common are those relating to the renunciation of executors or of next of kin in the case of administrations.
PROB 20	**Supplementary wills, Series I (1623–1838)** Mostly wills rejected by the court on the grounds that they were not the latest will of the deceased.

PROB 21	**Supplementary wills, Series II (1623–1857)** Court copies of wills made when the original was to be removed from the registry for exhibition in another court of law. There are also affidavits setting out reasons why the original document was required.
PROB 22	**Supplementary wills, Series III (1782–1851)** Wills lodged for safekeeping.
PROB 23	**Supplementary wills, Series IV (1629–1827)** Mostly court copies of wills originally proved in lower church courts.
PROB 24	**Depositions (1657–1809)** Statements of witnesses given in court during litigation cases. Also referred to as town depositions.
PROB 25	**Answers (1664–1854)** These bound volumes contain the response (known as the answer) made by the opposing party to the plaintiff's plea (the allegation).
PROB 26	**Bound volumes of depositions (1826–58)** These volumes contain statements of witnesses produced in evidence during litigation cases.
PROB 27	**Sentences** Not available. Unsorted and uncatalogued.
PROB 28	**Cause papers taken by commission (1641–1722)** Answers sworn by commission and depositions taken by commission. Sometimes known as country depositions, to distinguish them from those taken at the court in London.
PROB 29	**Acts of court books (1536–1819)** These volumes contain the minutes of the proceedings of the court. They summarize each stage of the proceedings and the judgment reached. They record information concerning disputed wills and administrations, along with non-contested business such as renunciations by executors and the appointment of guardians.
PROB 30	**Acts of court (1740–1858)** These contain the same information as PROB 29, but take the form of individual documents bound into bundles.
PROB 31	**Exhibits, main series (1722–1858)** This is the main series of exhibits brought into the registry of the court – including affidavits, depositions, inventories, accounts, draft wills, and personal items such as account books and diaries.
PROB 32	**Files of exhibits (1658–1723)** These files contain exhibits from the period preceding the establishment of PROB 31.

PROB 33	**Indexes to exhibits (1722–c.1900)** These yearly indexes were compiled at the same time as the registration of the exhibits. They mainly index PROB 31, but also provide an index to PROB 37, PROB 26 and PROB 49.
PROB 34	**Special jurisdiction miscellanea (1536–1698)** These consist of volumes and loose documents that were found among the Prerogative Court of Canterbury records but did not originate from that court.
PROB 35	**Original files, 16th century: exhibits (1529–86)** This small collection contains at least one example of almost every type of exhibit.
PROB 36	**Miscellaneous exhibits, pre-1722 (1653–1721)** Exhibits for the period preceding the establishment of PROB 31.
PROB 37	**Cause papers, later series (1783–1858)** These papers include allegations, answers, depositions, draft wills, inventories, and personal items such as account books and diaries.
PROB 38	**Orders of court books (1817–57)** These are volumes containing entries of various orders made by the court subsequent to grants of probate or administration. The orders are duplicated in PROB 30.
PROB 39	**Correspondence and papers of officials (1659–1857)** Miscellaneous correspondence and papers of officers of the Prerogative Court of Canterbury (mainly registrars, record keepers, clerks and proctors).
PROB 40	**Caveat books (1666–1858)** Entry books of caveats (notices or warnings) preventing the issue of grants of probate and administration.
PROB 41	**Court caveat books (1678–1857)** Court caveat books record the next stage in litigation after the issue of a caveat.
PROB 42	**Supplementary exhibits (16th–19th centuries)** Not available. Unsorted and uncatalogued.
PROB 43	**Assignations (1665–1858)** These include assignation books and draft acts recording appointments for court hearings concerning disputes over wills or administrations.
PROB 44	**Instruments from other courts (Commonwealth to George III)** Various documents directed to the Prerogative Court of Canterbury,

	by the King's Bench or other common-law courts or by the High Court of Delegates, to suspend an action in the PCC while a related case was taking place in one of these courts.
PROB 45	**Miscellaneous registers, lists and indexes (17th–19th centuries)** Not available. Unsorted and uncatalogued.
PROB 46	**Files and bundles of administration bonds (1713–1858)** These are bonds entered into by administrators and by administrators with will annexed. They include name and place of residence of sureties and give the approximate value of the estate.
PROB 47	**Unpublished evidence and miscellaneous depositions (17th–19th centuries)** Not available. Unsorted and uncatalogued.
PROB 48	**Files and bundles of citatory mandates (1666–1857)** This is the main series of citatory mandates summoning parties and witnesses to appear in court for disputed will or administration cases.
PROB 49	**Exhibits (volumes) (1686–1849)** These are exhibits in volume form.
PROB 50	**Bills of court** Not available. Unsorted and uncatalogued.
PROB 51	**Administration bonds before 1601 (1541–65)** These are bonds entered into by administrators and by administrators with will annexed. They include name and place of residence of sureties and give the approximate value of the estate. This series has only been partially sorted and catalogued. The majority of the bonds are therefore unavailable.
PROB 52	**Files of commissions and requisitions for wills (1796–1857)** These files contain commissions authorizing local officials to administer an oath to executors unable to visit the court in London.
PROB 53	**Early proceedings** Not available. Unsorted and uncatalogued.
PROB 54	**Administration bonds (1601–1713)** Not available. Unsorted and uncatalogued.
PROB 55	**Proxies (16th century)** Not available. Unsorted and uncatalogued.
PROB 56	**Files of commissions and requisitions for wills before 1796 (16th–18th centuries)** Not available. Unsorted and uncatalogued.
PROB 57	**Accounts and papers of record keepers and other officials (1676–1857)** This series of records gives details of Prerogative Court of Canterbury staff and the administrative mechanisms of the court.

Appendix 2

Published indexes to Prerogative Courts of Canterbury and York Wills and Administrations

Prerogative Court of Canterbury

	Date range	TNA references	Published indexes
1	1383–1558	PROB 11/1–41	*Index of wills proved in the Prerogative Court of Canterbury* (Vol. I: A–J, Vol. II: K–Z), ed. J. Challenor and C. Smith, Index Library, X–XI (London, British Record Society, 1893–5).
2	1558–83	PROB 11/42A–66	*Index of wills proved in the Prerogative Court of Canterbury*, Vol. III, ed. S. A. Smith and L. L. Duncan, Index Library, XVIII (London, British Record Society, 1898).
3	1584–1604	PROB 11/66–104	*Index of wills proved in the Prerogative Court of Canterbury*, Vol. IV, ed. S. A. Smith and E. A. Fry, Index Library, XXV (London, British Record Society, 1901).
4	1605–19	PROB 11/105–134	*Index of wills proved in the Prerogative Court of Canterbury*, Vol. V, ed. E. Stokes, Index Library, XLIII (London, British Record Society, 1912).
5	1620	PROB 11/135–136	J. H. Lea, *Abstract of wills in the Prerogative Court of Canterbury: Register Soame 1620* (Boston, Mass., 1904). Abstracts of all wills registered. A copy can be seen at the FRC but not at TNA, Kew.
6	1620–9	PROB 11/135–156	*Index of wills proved in the Prerogative Court of Canterbury*, Vol. VI, ed. R. H. E. Hill, Index Library, XLIV (London, British Record Society, 1912). See also 7 below.

7	1620–4	PROB 11/135–144	*Year book of probates: Abstracts of probates and sentences in the Prerogative Court of Canterbury*, ed. J. Matthews and G. F. Matthews (London, 1914). This index contains some references not in 6 above. The abbreviations it uses are explained in 9.1 below (on p. 5 of that volume). It does not have a place name index, but there is one in 6.
8	1630	PROB 11/157–158	J. H. Morrison, *Prerogative Court of Canterbury: Register Scroope (1630)* (London, 1934). Abstracts of all wills registered. A copy can be seen at the FRC but not at TNA, Kew.
9	1630–55	PROB 11/157–251	*Year books of probates (from 1630): Abstracts of probate acts in the Prerogative Court of Canterbury*, ed. J. Matthews and G. F. Matthews (London, 1902–27).
9.1	1630–4	PROB 11/157–166	Vol. I (1902).
9.2	1635–9	PROB 11/167–181	Vol. II (1903).
9.3	1630–9	PROB 11/157–181	*Sentences and complete index nominum (probates and sentences)*, extra volume (1907). This volume indexes sentences 1630–9, and all surnames in it and in 9.1–2.
9.4	1640–4	PROB 11/182–192	Vol. III (1905). See also 13 below.
9.5	1645–9	PROB 11/192–210	Vol. IV (1906). See also 13 below. Tracing probate acts and wills 1643–6 is subject to particular difficulties. Further information is supplied in the appendix to the introductory note to PROB 10.
9.6	1650–1	PROB 11/211–219	Vol. V (1909). See also 10 and 13 below.
9.7	1652–3	PROB 11/220–232	Vol. VI (1911). See also 10 and 13 below.
9.8	1654	PROB 11/233–242	Vol. VII (1914). See also 10 and 13 below.
9.9	1655	PROB 11/243–251	Vol. VIII (1927), surnames A–Musgrave only. See also 10 and 13 below. Although 9.8–9.9 do not have place-name indexes, there is one in 10 covering the same period.
10	1653–6	PROB 11/225–260	*Index of wills proved in the Prerogative Court of Canterbury*, Vol. VII, ed. T. M. Blagg and J. Skeate Moir, Index Library, LIV (London, British Record Society, 1925). See also 13 below.

11	1657–60	PROB 11/261–302	*Index of wills proved in the Prerogative Court of Canterbury*, Vol. VIII, ed. T. M. Blagg, Index Library, LXI (London, British Record Society, 1936). See also 13 below.
12	1658	PROB 11/272–285	W. Brigg, *Genealogical abstracts of wills proved in the Prerogative Court of Canterbury: Register Wootton 1658*, 7 vols (Leeds, 1894–1914). Abstracts of all wills registered. A copy can be seen at the FRC but not at TNA, Kew.
13	1640–60	PROB 11/182–302	Sentences registered in PROB 11/182–302 are indexed in *Index to administrations in the Prerogative Court of Canterbury*, Vol. VI, ed. M. Fitch, Index Library, C (London, British Record Society, 1986).
14	1661–70	PROB 11/303–334	*Prerogative Court of Canterbury: Wills, sentences and probate acts*, ed. J. H. Morrison (London, 1935).
15	1671–5	PROB 11/335–349	*Index of wills proved in the Prerogative Court of Canterbury*, Vol. IX, ed. J. Ainsworth, Index Library, LXVII (London, British Record Society, 1942).
16	1676–85	PROB 11/350–381	*Index of wills proved in the Prerogative Court of Canterbury*, Vol. X, ed. C. H. Ridge, Index Library, LXXI (London, British Record Society, 1948).
17	1686–93	PROB 11/382–417	*Index of wills proved in the Prerogative Court of Canterbury*, Vol. XI, ed. C. H. Ridge, Index Library, LXXVII (London, British Record Society, 1958).
18	1694–1700	PROB 11/418–458	*Index of wills proved in the Prerogative Court of Canterbury*, Vol. XII, ed. M. Fitch, Index Library, LXXX (London, British Record Society, 1960).
19	1701–49	PROB 11/459–775	Friends of The National Archives [formerly, Friends of the Public Record Office], *Index to PCC wills and administrations* (London, 1998, microfiche). The index has been compiled from PROB 12/71–119. Where entries in PROB 12/71–119 appear to be defective, they have been checked against the administration act books (PROB 6), the

			probate act books (PROB 8) and the registered wills (PROB 11).
20	1750	PROB 11/776–784	G. Sherwood, *A list of persons named in the PCC wills proved in the year 1750: Register Greenly* (London, privately published, 1918). Lists 40,320 persons named in 4,382 wills, arranged topographically in eight groups. There is a copy in the library of the Society of Genealogists, but not at TNA or the FRC.
21	1750–1800	PROB 11/776–1351	*An index to wills proved in the Prerogative Court of Canterbury 1750–1800*, ed. A. J. Camp, 6 vols (London, Society of Genealogists, 1976–1992). Compiled from PROB 13/186–242, checked (not systematically) against PROB 12/120–176.
22	1801–52	PROB 11/1352–2164	PROB 12/177–271
23	1853–8	PROB 11/2165–2263	PROB 12/272–288: *Calendar of the grants of probate and letters of administration made in the Prerogative Court of Canterbury, 1853–1857, 1858*, 16 vols (London, undated). Locations of copies of this index outside TNA are listed in Gibson, *Probate jurisdictions: where to look for wills*. It has also been published on microfiche by Hampshire Record Office, together with the calendars of grants of probate and administration for 1858–1935.

Wills of American testators

24	1610–1857	PROB 11/115–2262	P. W. Coldham, *American wills proved in London, 1611–1775* (Baltimore, 1992). This work, which supersedes Coldham's earlier works on the same subject, can be used to advantage in conjunction with his *American wills and administrations in the Prerogative Court of Canterbury, 1610–1857* (Baltimore, 1989).

Administrations

The index to PCC wills on DocumentsOnline (**www.documentsonline.nationalarchives.gov.uk**) does not include administrations. You will therefore need to use the indexes listed below.

25	1559–71	PROB 6/1	*Administrations in the Prerogative Court of Canterbury*, Vol. I, ed. R. M. Glencross (Exeter, 1912).

26	1572–80	PROB 6/2	*Administrations in the Prerogative Court of Canterbury*, Vol. II (Exeter, 1917).
27	1559–80	PROB 6/1–2	B. Lloyd, Preliminary addenda and corrigenda to Mr R. M. Glencross's *Letters of administration granted by the Prerogative Court of Canterbury, 1559–80* (typescript, 1979).
28	1581–95	PROB 6/3–5	*Index to administrations in the Prerogative Court of Canterbury*, Vol. III, ed. C. H. Ridge, Index Library, LXXVI (London, British Record Society, 1954).
29	1596–1608	PROB 6/5–7	*Index to administrations in the Prerogative Court of Canterbury*, Vol. IV, ed. M. Fitch, Index Library, LXXXI (London, British Record Society, 1964).
30	1609–19	PROB 6/7–10	*Index to administrations in the Prerogative Court of Canterbury*, Vol. V, ed. M. Fitch, Index Library, LXXXIII (London, British Record Society, 1968).
31	1620–30	PROB 6/10–13	*Prerogative Court of Canterbury: Letters of administration*, ed. J. H. Morrison (London, 1935).
32	1631–48	PROB 6/14A–23	*Index to administrations in the Prerogative Court of Canterbury*, Vol. VI, ed. M. Fitch, Index Library, C (London, British Record Society, 1986). This index also includes sentences registered from 1640 to 1660 in PROB 11/182–302.
33	1643–4	PROB 6/234	Grants made by the Prerogative Court of Canterbury at Oxford were omitted from 32 above. PROB 6/234 contains a contemporary index, which has been reproduced and is available on the open shelves. (This reproduction was formerly PROB 12/23B.)
34	1649–54	PROB 6/24–30	*Index to administrations in the Prerogative Court of Canterbury*, Vol. I, ed. J. Ainsworth, Index Library, LXVIII (London, British Record Society, 1944). For further information on tracing administration acts 1653–4, see Appendix 2 to the introductory note to PROB 6.

35	1655–60	PROB 6/31–36	*Index to administrations in the Prerogative Court of Canterbury*, Vol. II, ed. C. H. Ridge, 3 vols, Index Library, LXXII (A–F), LXXIV (G–Q), LXXV (R–Z) (London, British Record Society, 1949–1953).
36	1661	PROB 6/37	Surnames A–Sweetinge: typescript index.
37	1661	PROB 6/37	Surnames other than A–Sweetinge: PROB 12/38.
38	1662		The administration act book for 1662 has not survived. Use PROB 12/39; see also PROB 13/96–97 and PROB 15/72.
39	1663–4	PROB 6/38–39	Typescript index.
40	1665–1700	PROB 6/40–76	PROB 12/41–69.
41	1701–49	PROB 6/77–125	Friends of the Public Record Office, *Index to PCC wills and administrations* (London, 1998, microfiche). This index has been compiled from PROB 12/71–119. Where entries in PROB 12/71–119 appear to be defective, they have been checked against the administration act books (PROB 6), probate act books (PROB 8) and registered wills (PROB 11).
42	1750–1800	PROB 12/126–176	There is a card index to these administrations acts (largely compiled from PROB 13/186–236) at the FRC and the Society of Genealogists, which the Society will search for a fee.
43	1801–52	PROB 6/177–228	PROB 12/177–271.
44	1853–8	PROB 6/229–233	PROB 12/272–288: *Calendar of the grants of probate and letters of administration made in the Prerogative Court of Canterbury, 1853–1857, 1858*, 16 vols (London, undated). Locations of copies of this index outside TNA are listed in Gibson, *Probate jurisdictions: where to look for wills*, 12. It has also been published on microfiche by Hampshire Record Office, together with the calendars of grants of probate and administration for 1858–1935.

Administration acts relating to estates of American intestates			
45	1610–1857	PROB 6/7–233	P. W. Coldham, *American wills and administrations in the Prerogative Court of Canterbury, 1610–1857* (Baltimore, 1989). This work supersedes Coldham's earlier works on the same subject.

Prerogative Court of York

Date range	Published indexes
Indexes to wills proved in the Exchequer and Prerogative courts	
1389–1514	*York Archaeological Society Record Series*, Vol. 6.
1514–53	*York Archaeological Society Record Series*, Vol. 11.
1554–68	*York Archaeological Society Record Series*, Vol. 14.
1568–85	*York Archaeological Society Record Series*, Vol. 19.
1585–94	*York Archaeological Society Record Series*, Vol. 22.
1594–1602	*York Archaeological Society Record Series*, Vol. 24.
1603–11	*York Archaeological Society Record Series*, Vol. 26.
1612–19	*York Archaeological Society Record Series*, Vol. 28.
1620–7	*York Archaeological Society Record Series*, Vol. 32.
1627–36	*York Archaeological Society Record Series*, Vol. 35 (includes administrations 1627–52).
1636–52	*York Archaeological Society Record Series*, Vol. 4.
1660–5	*York Archaeological Society Record Series*, Vol. 49.
1666–72	*York Archaeological Society Record Series*, Vol. 60.
1673–80	*York Archaeological Society Record Series*, Vol. 68.
1681–8	*York Archaeological Society Record Series*, Vol. 89.
Many of the above volumes contain appendixes (mostly indexes to administrations).	
Chancery Court	
1427–1658	*York Archaeological Society Record Series*, Vol. 73. Incorrectly referred to as Consistory Court in this volume. Original wills (including what are now found to be Exchequer Court wills, 1427–1534).
1316–1822	*York Archaeological Society Record Series*, Vol. 93. Index to registered copies of Chancery notes.
1825–58	*Borthwick Institute Bulletin*, Vol. I, no. 1, pp. 39–42.
Dean and Chapter's Court	
1524–1724	*York Archaeological Society Record Series*, Vol. 78. Partial index of original wills and administrations 1321–1638. Also index to probate registers 1559–1636 and probate act books 1559–1636.

Glossary of Legal Terms

TERM	DEFINITION	ABBREVIATION
Account	Details of the executor's or administrator's expenditure in settling the deceased's personal estate (see **Charge** and **Discharge**).	Acc
Ad litem	For the purpose of the suit – for example, a guardian appointed pending the settlement of a lawsuit.	
Administration	A grant made by the court to an administrator in order to settle the deceased's estate in accordance with the rules of intestacy.	A, admon, ad
Administration bond	Bond entered into by the administrator, with one or more sureties, to guarantee the proper administration of the deceased's estate.	
Administratio cum testamento annexo	See **Administration with will annexed**.	Ad cum testo
Administratio cum testamento annexo de bonis non administratis	See **Administration with will annexed of goods not administered**.	Admon dbn, de bo non
Administratio de bonis non administratis	See **Administration of goods not administered**.	
Administration of goods not administered	Grant made following the death or renunciation of the initial administrator, in order to complete the administration of the estate.	AW
Administration with will annexed	Grant authorizing the implementation of a will when the	

	testator has failed to name an executor or when the named executor renounces his or her right to execute the will or is incapacitated in some way, or fails to respond to the summons asking him to prove the will.	
Administration with will annexed of goods not administered	Grant made when the named executor dies after probate has been granted but the estate has not been completely administered.	
Administrator (m. or f.), administratrix (f.)	Person appointed by the court to administer an estate following the death of an intestate, or to administer the estate of a testator where an executor has not been appointed or an appointed executor fails to act.	
Advocate	In church courts, the equivalent of a barrister.	
Affidavit	A written statement supported by the swearing of an oath or by affirmation.	Aff
Affirmation	Declaration by a witness who has no religious belief that the evidence he or she is giving is the truth.	
Allegation	The pleading of the plaintiff in a lawsuit.	
Amita	Father's sister.	
Amita uxoris	Wife's father's sister.	
Annuity	A sum paid annually.	
Answer	The defendant's response to the plaintiff's case, or to interrogatories.	
Appeal	Application to a higher court for review of a court's decision.	
Archdeaconry court	The lowest ecclesiastical court.	
Arches, Court of	The court of the Archbishop of Canterbury, which also acted as a court of appeal within the province of Canterbury.	

Archidiaconus	Archdeacon.	
Archiepiscopus	Archbishop.	
Assizes	Regional civil and criminal common-law courts – see **Common Pleas, Exchequer** (common-law side) and **King's Bench** for types of cases heard.	
Attestatio	See **Affidavit**.	
Avia	Grandmother.	
Avunculus	Mother's brother (or, sometimes, father's brother).	
Avus	Grandfather.	
Avus relicta	Grandfather's widow.	
Beneficiary	Someone entitled to benefit under a will or trust.	
Bequeath	To leave personal property by will.	
Bequest	A gift of personal property by will.	
Bona	Goods.	
Bona notabilia	'Noteworthy goods'. Refers to the requirement of the Prerogative Court of Canterbury that only estates valued at £5 or more in more than one diocese should come within its jurisdiction.	
Bona paraphernalia	Personal items belonging to a widow, such as her clothes, jewels and ornaments.	
Bona vacantia	An unclaimed estate, where no person entitled to inherit the estate is known.	
Breve	Writ.	
Canon law	The law of the Church of England. Unless canons (ecclesiastical decrees) received parliamentary endorsement, they were binding only on those holding ecclesiastical office.	
Catalla	Chattels.	
Cause	Case or lawsuit.	

Caveat	A notice that effectively prevents action by another party without first notifying the party entering the caveat.	
Cessate	A grant of limited duration that has come to an end. Usually applied to a child coming of age.	
Chancery, Court of	Equity court hearing cases such as those concerning wills, lands, inheritance, trusts or debt.	
Charge	The assets of the deceased's personal estate. Usually takes the form of a citation of the valuation given in the inventory.	
Chattels	A person's moveable goods and belongings.	Cat
Citation	A mandate (summons), obtained by a proctor at the request of a party to a lawsuit, ordering the attendance of another party so the case could be heard.	
Codicil	A properly executed (signed and witnessed) addendum to a will, amending, revising or revoking something in the will or making additional provisions.	
Comitatus	County.	Com
Commissary	An official deputizing for a bishop.	
Commissary court	Bishop's court. Large dioceses might be divided into smaller areas, each covered by a commissary court. See also **Consistory court**.	
Commission	A document appointing a person to a specific task. Such a document was used when executors and administrators were unable to attend court personally and were 'sworn by commission', usually by a local clergyman. Inventories and the examination of witnesses and could also be undertaken by commission. See also **Requisition**.	Com

Common form	The straightforward proving of a will by oath of executor.	
Common law	Law established by precedent, based on custom and judicial decisions.	
Common Pleas, Court of	Common-law court that heard cases such as those concerning chattels, freehold, debt or damages.	
Compos mentis	'Of sound mind' – used to describe a person judged fit to leave a will or act as an executor or administrator, or to participate in other legal matters.	
Compulsory	A strongly worded decree requiring a witness to attend court after repeated failure to comply with an order to do so.	
Consanguinity	Blood relationship.	
Consistory court	Bishop's court, covering the whole of the diocese. See also **Commissary court**.	
Contra	Can mean before, against or contrary to.	
Coparcener	A person who has jointly inherited a property.	
Court for the Probate of Wills and the Granting of Administrations	Court that exercised probate jurisdiction throughout England and Wales from 1653 to 1659.	
Coverture	The status of a wife during marriage.	
Curator	Guardian appointed by the court for boys over the age of 14 and under 21, or girls over 12 and under 21.	
Curation	A form of guardianship. See **Curator**.	
Custantia	Costs.	
Death duties	Collective name for Estate Duty, Legacy Duty and Succession Duty, payable by beneficiaries from 1796.	
De bonis non administratis	See **Administration of goods not administered**.	Admon dbn, de bo non

Declaration in lieu of inventory	Declaration submitted by some executors or administrators in place of an inventory, usually after the elapse of a considerable period of time since the death of the deceased.	
Decree	Sentence (final judgment). Can also mean an interlocutory decree. See **Sentence** and **Interlocutory decree**.	Dec
De facto	As a matter of fact.	
Defendant	Person defending a legal action.	
Denarius	Penny.	d
Deposition	A statement of evidence supported by the swearing of an oath or by affirmation.	
Desperate debt	A debt unlikely to be recovered.	
Devise	To leave real estate by will.	
Diocesan courts	See **Consistory court** and **Commissary court**.	
Discharge	The disbursements made by the executor or administrator, which may include medical and funeral expenses, legal fees for probate or administration, payment of legacies, settling the deceased's debts, and expenses incurred in the maintenance of dependants.	
Doctors' Commons	The building where the London ecclesiastical courts and the High Court of Admiralty court were formerly situated.	
Dominus	Sir or lord.	Dnus, dns
Domus	House.	Dom
Double probate	Separate grants made by the court to two or more executors who could not be sworn at the same time (e.g. because one was a child or abroad).	
Episcopus	Bishop.	

Equity	Law based on principles of fairness and natural justice.	
Estate	A deceased person's estate encompasses all his or her assets, including both personal estate and real estate.	
Examination	The putting of questions to someone giving evidence.	
Exchequer, Court of	The equity side of the Court of Exchequer heard cases concerning matters such as wills, land, inheritance, trusts and debt. The common-law side (Exchequer of Pleas) heard cases concerning matters such as chattels, freehold, debt or damages.	
Executor (m. or f.), executrix (f.)	A person appointed to carry out the provisions of a will – whose duties include burying the deceased, proving the will, paying debts and legacies, and distributing the residue.	Exec
Exhibit	Item or document referred to in an affidavit or used as evidence during a court hearing.	
Feme covert	A married woman.	
Feme sole	An unmarried woman.	
Filius	Son.	
Folio	A leaf of a document or book, numbered only on its front (recto). A page is one side of a folio.	F, f
Frater	Brother.	Frat
Freehold	See **Real estate**.	
Generosus	Gentleman.	Gen
Grant of administration	See **Administration**.	
Guardian	A person appointed to safeguard, protect or manage the interests of a child or of a person legally incapacitated due to mental disability. See also **Curator** and **Tutor**.	

Heres	Heir.	
Heresy	The ecclesiastical offence of holding opinions contrary to the tenets of the church.	
High Court of Delegates	The court of appeal from the Prerogative Court of Canterbury (1534–1834).	
Holograph	Will written entirely in the hand of the testator.	
Imperpetuum	For ever, in perpetuity.	
In partibus transmarinis	Died abroad.	Partibus, ptibus, parts, pts,
In servitio regis/ reginae	In the service of the Crown (King/Queen).	
Instance cases	Cases heard by ecclesiastical courts concerning disputes over matters such as probate, defamation, breach of promise, adultery or fornication, separation and divorce.	
Inter alia	'Among other things' – often used to indicate that the details given are only an extract from the whole.	
Interlocutory decree	A judgment that can be revoked (often used in administration cases where someone might subsequently appear and prove they were the true next of kin).	
Interrogatory	A formal question prepared by a litigant and put to a witness.	
Intestate	A person who has died without leaving a will, or leaving a will declared invalid by a court.	
Intimation	A decree including a clause warning a party who had failed to respond to an earlier summons that he would be liable to censure or excommunication, or that the case would be heard in his absence if he persisted in his contumacy.	
Intra vires	'Within the power of'' – indicates that	

	an act falls within the jurisdiction of the court.
Inventory	List of the deceased's personal estate and its appraised value.
Judex	Judge.
Judgment	Final decision of a court.
Judicial Committee of the Privy Council	The court of appeal for the Prerogative Court of Canterbury (1834–58).
Jurat	A statement at the end of an affidavit that gives the name of the person making the affidavit and states before whom and where the oath or affirmation was taken.
Jurisdiction	The area and matters over which a court has authority.
King's Bench, Court of	Common-law court hearing cases concerning matters such as chattels, freehold, debt or damages. Criminal court (Crown side) hearing cases concerning matters such as breach of the peace, forgery, deceit or high treason.
King's warrant	Royal warrant for a grant of administration to revert the deceased's estate to the Crown.
Leasehold property	Land or tenement conveyed by the owner to a tenant for a term (specified period of time).
Legacy	Gift of personal property by will.
Legantia, Legantio	Legacy.
Legatee	Person to whom personal estate is given by will.
Legatorius	Legatee.
Lego	'I bequeath'.
Letters of administration	Legal document, issued by a relevant court, authorizing an appropriate person to administer the estate when no valid will has been left by the

	deceased. The letters allow the administrator to carry out duties similar to those of an executor.	
Liberi	Children.	
Libra	Pound.	L, li
Limited administration	A grant of administration limited to a specified period of time or to a particular part of the estate.	Ad limit
Limited probate	A grant of probate limited to a specified period of time or to a particular part of the estate.	
Maritus	Husband.	
Mater, matris	Mother.	
Matertera	Aunt, mother's sister.	
Medietas	Half or moiety.	
Messuagium	Messuage.	
Ministrant	Another word for defendant.	
Moiety	A half share.	
Monition	A form of decree normally used only when the court required both a person and some evidence to be brought before it – for example, when a party was required to bring in testamentary scripts, or when the registrar of a lower court was ordered to bring in all relevant papers in a case that had been transferred to a superior court.	
Nepos	Grandson, nephew, descendant.	
Neptis	Niece.	
Non compos mentis	'Not of sound mind' – used to describe a person judged unfit to leave a will or act as an executor or administrator, or to participate in other legal matters.	
Nuncupative will	Spoken will – often from the deathbed.	Nunc
Nuncupativus	Nuncupative. See **Nuncupative will**.	Nunc
Nuper	Can mean either the late or lately or recently deceased.	

Nurus	Daughter-in-law.	
Oath	A promise to tell the truth sworn, usually on the Bible, by a person with religious beliefs.	
Obsequia	Funeral, funeral rites.	
Paraphernalia	See **Bona paraphernalia**.	
Para rationabilis	A reasonable portion.	
Parochia	Parish.	Par
Party	Any of the participants in a lawsuit or in other legal proceedings.	
Pater	Father.	
Patruelis	Cousin on father's side.	
Patruus	Paternal uncle, father's brother.	
Peculiar court	An ecclesiastical court exempt from the authority of the local archdeacon, and sometimes from the authority of the bishop.	
Personal estate, personal property, personalty	Possessions such as chattels (moveable goods), cash, credits and leasehold property.	
Plaintiff	Person bringing a legal action.	
Pratum	Meadow.	
Prerogative courts	The courts of the archbishops of Canterbury and York.	
Primogenitus	First-born.	
Privigna	Stepdaughter.	
Privignus	Stepson.	
Proavus	Forefather, great-grandfather.	
Probate	The legal recognition of the validity of a will.	
Probatio	See **Probate**.	
Probo	'I prove'.	
Proctor	In ecclesiastical courts, the duties of a proctor were similar to those of solicitors in other courts.	

Promoter	In ecclesiastical courts, another word for plaintiff.	
Province	The jurisdiction of an archbishop.	
Proxy	Document appointing a proctor to act on behalf of a person involved in litigation or in non-contested business.	·
Pur autre vie	For/during the lifetime of another person.	
Quire	In the Prerogative Court of Canterbury, a section of 16 pages in the series of registered wills (PROB 11).	
Real estate, real property, realty	Immoveable property, such as land and buildings held on a freehold basis.	
Relict	The person remaining after the death of a spouse. Widow.	Rel
Requisition	In the Prerogative Court of Canterbury, a commission outside the jurisdiction of the court was known as a requisition. See **Commission**.	
Residuary devisee	A person who takes the residue of the real property after the payment of all debts and legacies charged on the deceased's real estate.	
Residuary legatee	A person who takes the residue of the deceased's personal property after the payment of all debts and legacies.	
Residuum	Residue, remainder.	
Reversion	See **Reversionary interest**.	
Reversionary interest	An interest in property that reverts to its grantor or the grantor's heirs at the end of a specified period of time (e.g. the life of the grantee).	
Seat	From 1719 the Prerogative Court of Canterbury's probate and administration business was divided into five administrative divisions based on geographical areas. Each	

	of these divisions was called a seat (also known as 'walk').	
Sentence, definitive sentence	The final judgment in a cause.	Sent, S
Solemn form	Procedure for proving a will by witnesses before a judge.	
Solidus	Shilling.	Sol, S
Sororius	Sister's husband or son or wife's brother.	
Special administration	See **Limited administration**.	
Special probate	See **Limited probate**.	
Sperate debt	Debt thought likely to be recovered.	
Sponsa	Wife.	
Sponsus	Husband.	
Spurius	Illegitimate.	
Surrogate	In church courts, a deputy judge – an official deputizing for the archbishop, bishop or archdeacon.	
Susceptores	Godparents.	
Terra	Land.	
Testament	Originally the term 'testament' referred to personal estate only; but from the sixteenth century it has been used interchangeably with 'will', referring to both personal and real estate.	
Testamentum	See **Testament**.	
Testator (m. or f.), testatrix (f.)	A person who makes a will.	
Trust	The conveying of property (e.g. by will or by drawing up a trust) to a trustee or trustees with instructions to hold or administer it for the benefit of a beneficiary or beneficiaries.	
Trustee	A person who holds or administers property in trust for another or others.	

Tuition	Guardianship of a minor. See **Tutor**.	
Tutor	Guardian of a minor (a boy under the age of 15 or a girl under 13).	
Ultra vires	'Beyond the power of' – indicates that an act falls outside the jurisdiction of the court.	
Uxor	Wife.	
Uxoratus	Married, married man.	
Vacatur	Void.	Vacat, vac
Walk	See **Seat**.	
Warrant	Document issued by a church court authorizing a commission or requisition to swear an executor or administrator unable to come to court.	
Will	From the sixteenth century 'will' has been used to refer to both personal and real estate (originally 'testament' was used for personal estate).	
Writ	A document, issued under seal, conveying either a royal command or an order from a court of law.	

Useful Addresses

ENGLAND

Bank of England (*archive information and appointments*), The Archivist, Archive Section HO-SV, The Bank of England, Threadneedle Street, London EC2R 8AH (telephone: 020 7601 4889/5096, website: **bankofengland.co.uk/archive.htm**)

Borthwick Institute of Historical Research, University of York, Heslington, York YO10 5DD (telephone: 01904 642315, *appointments and archive enquiries* telephone: 01904 321166, website: **www.york.ac.uk/inst/bihr**) (**NOTE:** closed until mid October 2004)

British Library, 96 Euston Road, London NW1 2DB (reader enquiries telephone: 020 7412 7676, switchboard telephone: 0870 444 1500, website: **www.bl.uk**)

British Library, Newspapers, Colindale Avenue, London NW9 5HE (telephone: 020 7412 7353, website: **www.bl.uk/collections/newspapers.html**)

British Library, Oriental and India Office Collections, 96 Euston Road, London NW1 2DB (telephone: 020 7412 7873, website: **www.bl.uk/collections/orientaloffice.html**)

Catholic Central Library, Lancing Street, London NW1 1ND (telephone: 020 7383 4333, website: **www.catholic-library.org.uk**)

Corporation of London Records Office, PO Box 270, Guildhall, London EC2P 2EJ (telephone: 020 7332 1251, website: **www.corpoflondon.gov.uk**)

Court Funds Office, 22 Kingsway, London WC2B 6LE (website: **www.courtservice.gov.uk**)

Department of Constitutional Affairs, Departmental Records Officer (Court Side), 1st Floor, Clive House, 70 Petty France, London SWIH 9HD

The Family Records Centre, 1 Myddelton Street, London EC1R 1UW (telephone: 020 8392 5300, website: **www.familyrecords.gov.uk/frc**)

Federation of Family History Societies, The FFHS Administrator, PO Box 2425, Coventry CV5 6YX (website: **www.ffhs.org.uk**)

Guild of One-Name Studies, Box G, c/o 14 Charterhouse Buildings, Goswell Road, London EC1M 7BA (website: **www.one-name.org**)

Guildhall Library, Aldermanbury, London EC2P 2EJ (telephone: 020 7332 1862/3, website: **www.history.ac.uk/gh**)

House of Lords Record Office, The Clerk of the Records, Parliamentary Archives, London SWIA 0PW (telephone: 020 7219 3074, website: **www.parliament.uk**)

Lambeth Palace Library, Lambeth Palace Road, London SE1 7JU (telephone: 020 7898 1400, website: **www.lambethpalacelibrary.org**)

London Metropolitan Archives, 40 Northampton Road, London EC1R 0HB (telephone: 020 7332 3820, website: **www.corpoflondon.gov.uk/lma**)

The National Archives, Kew, Richmond, Surrey TW9 4DU (telephone: 020 8392 5200, website: **www.nationalarchives.gov.uk**)

Postal Searches & Copies Department, York Probate Sub-Registry, 1st Floor, Castle Chambers, Clifford Street, York YO1 9RG (telephone: 01904 6667777, website: **www.courtservice.gov.uk**)

Probate Searchroom, Principal Registry of the Family Division, First Avenue House, 42–49 High Holborn, London WC1V 6NP (telephone: 020 7947 7000, website: **www.courtservice. gov.uk**)

Royal Archives, Windsor Castle, Windsor, Berkshire SL4 1NJ (telephone: 01753 831118, ext. 260)

Society of Genealogists, 14 Charterhouse Buildings, Goswell Road, London EC1M 7BA (telephone: 020 7251 8799, website: **www.sog.org.uk**)

CHANNEL ISLANDS

Channel Islands Family History Society, PO Box 507, St Helier, Jersey JE4 5TN (website: **http://user.itl.net/~glen/AbouttheChannelIslandsFHS.html**)

Jersey Archive, Clarence Road, St Helier, Jersey JE2 4JY (telephone: 01534 833333, website: **www.jerseyheritagetrust.org**)

Judicial Greffe (Jersey), Royal Court House, Royal Square, St Helier, Jersey JE1 1JG (telephone: 01534 502300, website: **www.judicialgreffe.gov.je**)

Société Guernesiase, Candie Gardens, St Peter Port, Guernsey GY1 1UG (telephone: 01481 725093, website: **www.societe.org.gg**)

Société Jersiase, Lord Countanche Library, 7 Pier Road, St Helier, Jersey JE2 4XW (telephone: 01534 730538, website: **www.societe-jersiaise.org**)

States of Guernsey, Island Archive Service, 29 Victoria Road, St Peter Port, Guernsey GY1 1HU (telephone: 01481 724512, website: **http://user.itl.net/~glen/archgsy.html**)

IRELAND

Irish Genealogical Research Society, Stratford Avenue, Rainham, Kent ME8 0EP (website: **www.igrsoc.org**)

National Archives of Ireland, Bishop Street, Dublin 8, Republic of Ireland (telephone: 00 353 1 407 2300, website: **www.nationalarchives.ie**)

Probate Office, High Court, First Floor, 15/24 Phoenix Street North, Smithfield, Dublin 7, Republic of Ireland (telephone: 00 353 1 888 6174, website: **www.courts.ie**)

Public Record Office of Northern Ireland, 66 Balmoral Avenue, Belfast BT9 6NY (telephone: 028 9025 5905, website: **www.proni.nics.gov.uk**)

ISLE OF MAN

Deeds and Probate Registry, Registries Building, Deemster's Walk, Bucks Road, Douglas, Isle of Man IM1 3AR (website: **www.gov.im/registries/courts/probate**)

Isle of Man Public Record Office, Unit 40a Spring Valley Industrial Estate, Douglas, Isle of Man IM2 2QR (telephone: 01624 693569, website: **www.gov.im/registries/publicrecords**)

Manx National Heritage, Douglas, Isle of Man IM1 3LY (telephone: 01624 648000, website: **www.gov.im/mnh/National_Library.asp**)

SCOTLAND

Association of Scottish Genealogists and Record Agents, 51/3 Mortonhall Road, Edinburgh EH9 2HN (website: **www.asgra.co.uk**)

National Archives of Scotland, HM General Register House, Edinburgh EH1 3YY (telephone: 0131 535 1334, website: **www.nas.gov.uk**)

National Library of Scotland, George IV Bridge, Edinburgh EH1 1EW (telephone: 0131 226 4531, website: **www.nls.uk**)

Scots Ancestry Research Society, 8 York Road, Edinburgh EH5 3EH (telephone: 0131 552 2058, website: **www.royalmile.com/scotsancestry**)

WALES

National Library of Wales, Aberystwyth, Dyfed SY23 3BU (telephone: 01970 632800, website: **www.llgc.org.uk**)

Further Reading

FFHS = Federation of Family History Societies; PRO = Public Record Office; TNA = The National Archives

John Addy, *Death, Money and the Vultures: Inheritance and Avarice, 1660–1750* (Leopard's Head Press, 1992)

Tom Arkell, Nesta Evans and Nigel Goose (eds), *When Death Do Us Part: Understanding and Interpreting the Probate Records of Early Modern England* (Leopard's Head Press, 2000)

J. H. Baker, *An Introduction to English Legal History* (Butterworths, 3rd edn 1990)

John Barrett and David Iredale, *Discovering Old Handwriting* (Shire Publications, 1995)

Amanda Bevan, *Tracing Your Ancestors in the Public Record Office* (PRO, 6th edn 2002)

Joy Bristow, *Local Historian's Glossary of Words and Terms* (Countryside Books, 2001)

W. S. B. Buck, *Examples of Handwriting 1550–1650* (Society of Genealogists, 1985)

Richard Burn, *The Ecclesiastical Law* (S. Sweet, 4 vols, 1842)

Anthony Camp, *Wills and their Whereabouts* (Anthony J. Camp, 1974)

Colin R. Chapman, *Ecclesiastical Courts, Officials and Records: Sin, Sex and Probate* (Lochin, 1997)

Colin R. Chapman, *Ecclesiastical Courts, their Officials and their Records* (Lochin, 1992)

Peter Christian, *The Genealogist's Internet* (TNA, 2nd edn 2003)

P. W. Coldham, *American Wills and Administrations in the Prerogative Court of Canterbury, 1610–1857* (Baltimore, 1989)

Michael Collinge, 'Probate Valuations and the Death Duty Registers: Some Comments' (*Bulletin of the Institute of Historical Research*, Vol. LX, 1987, pp. 240–45)

Audrey Collins, *Wills After 1858* (FFHS, 1998)

Stella Colwell, *Family Roots* (Weidenfeld & Nicolson, 1991)

Stella Colwell, *The Family Records Centre: A User's Guide* (PRO, 2002)

Henry Charles Coote, *The Common Form Practice of The High Court of Justice in Granting Probates and Administrations* (Butterworths, 7th edn 1876)

Henry Charles Coote, *The Practice of the Ecclesiastical Courts With Forms and Tables of Costs* (H. Butterworth, 1847)

Jane Cox, *Affection Defying the Power of Death: Wills, Probate and Death Duty Records* (FFHS, 1993)

Jane Cox, *Hatred Pursued Beyond the Grave* (HMSO, 1993)

Jane Cox, *Wills, Inventories and Death Duties: A Provisional Guide* (PRO, 1988)

D. F. De L'Hoste, Ranking and others, *Executorship Law and Accounts* (Isaac Pitman, 1933)

G. I. O. Duncan, *The High Court of Delegates* (Cambridge University Press, 1971)

Mary Ellis, *Using Manorial Records* (PRO, 1997)

Barbara English, 'Probate Valuations and the Death Duty Registers' (*Bulletin of the Institute of Historical Research*, Vol. LVII, 1984, pp. 80–91)

Barbara English, 'Wealth at Death in the nineteenth century: The Death Duty Registers' (*Bulletin of the Institute of Historical Research*, Vol. LX, 1987, pp. 246–9)

Peter Franklin, *Some Medieval Records for Family Historians* (FFHS, 1994)

Jeremy Gibson and Else Churchill, *Probate Jurisdictions: Where to Look for Wills* (FFHS, 5th edn 2002)

Karen Grannum, *Using Wills* (PRO, 2001)

John Grenham, *Tracing Your Irish Ancestors: The complete guide* (Gill & Macmillan, 2nd edn 1999)

P. E. H. Hair and J. D. Alsop, *English Seamen and Traders in Guinea, 1553–1565: The New Evidence of Their Wills* (Edwin Mellen Press, 1992)

Felicity Heal, *Of Prelates and Princes: A Study of the Economic and Social Position of the Tudor Episcopate* (Cambridge University Press, 1980)

R. H. Helmholz, *Canon Law and English Common Law* (Selden Society, 1983)

R. H. Helmholtz, *Canon Law and the Law of England* (Hambledon Press, 1987)

Paul Hindle, *Latin for Family Historians* (Phillimore, 2000)

Sir William Holdsworth, *A History of English Law* (Methuen, 17 vols, 1903–72)

Henry Horwitz, *Chancery Equity Proceedings 1600–1800* (PRO, 1998)

Henry Horwitz, *Exchequer Equity Records and Proceedings* (PRO, 2001)

Jane Houston (ed.), *Index of Cases in the Records of the Court of Arches at Lambeth Palace Library 1660–1913* (British Record Society, Index Library, Vol. 85, 1972)

P. A. Howell, *Judicial Committee of the Privy Council, 1833–1876, its origins, structure and development* (Cambridge University Press, 1979)

Martin Ingram, *Church Courts, Sex and Marriage in England 1570–1640* (Cambridge University Press, 1987)

Alf Ison, *A Secretary Hand ABC Book* (Berkshire FHS, 3rd edn 2000)

Alwyn James, *Scottish Roots: The Step by Step Guide to Tracing Your Scottish Ancestors* (Luath Press, reprinted 2003)

Christopher Kitching, 'Probate during the Civil War and Interregnum. Part 1: The survival of the Prerogative Court in the 1640s' (*Journal of the Society of Archivists*, Vol. 5, No. 5, April 1976) pp. 283–93

Christopher Kitching, 'Probate during the Civil War and Interregnum. Part 2: The Court of Probate, 1653–1660' (*Journal of the Society of Archivists*, Vol. 5, No. 6, October 1976), pp. 346–56

Christopher Kitching, 'The Prerogative Court of Canterbury from Warham to Whitgift' (Chapter 8 of *Continuity and Change: Personnel and Administration of the Church of England, 1500–1642*, edited by Rosemary O'Day and Felicity Heal, Leicester University Press, 1976)

George Lawton, *A Brief Treatise of Bona Notabilia: Together, with an Account of the Archiepiscopal Courts of Probate, Within the Province of York* (J. Butterworth & Son and others, 1825)

Eve McLaughlin, *Reading Old Handwriting* (FFHS, 1987)

Eve McLaughlin, *Simple Latin for Family Historians* (FFHS, 1999)

Eve McLaughlin, *Wills before 1858* (FFHS, 1994)

Eve McLaughlin, *Wills from 1858* (FFHS, 1995)

Ronald A. Marchant, *The Church Under Law: Justice, Administration and Discipline in the Diocese of York 1560–1640* (Cambridge University Press, 1969)

Ronald A. Marchant, *The Puritans and the Church Courts in the Diocese of York 1560–1642* (Longman, 1960)

G. W. Marshall, *A Handbook to the Ancient Courts of Probate and Depositories of Wills* (Horace Cox, 1895)

G. H. Martin and Peter Spufford, *The Records of the Nation* (Boydell & Brewer, 1990)

R. Milward, *A Glossary of Household, Farming and Trade Terms From Probate Inventories* (Derbyshire Record Society, Occasional Paper No. 1, 3rd edn 1993)

Janet Morris, *A Latin Glossary for Family and Local Historians* (FFHS, 1989)

Lionel Munby, Steve Hobbs and Alan Crosby, *Reading Tudor and Stuart Handwriting* (British Association for Local History, 2002)

Nicholas Newington-Irving, *Will Indexes and Other Probate Material in the Library of the Society of Genealogists* (Society of Genealogists, 1996)

John Nichols, *A collection of all the wills, now known to be extant, of the kings and queens of England, princes and princesses of Wales, and every branch of the blood royal, from the reign of William Conqueror to that of Henry the Seventh exclusive* (London, 1780)

Bruno Pappalardo, *Tracing Your Naval Ancestors* (TNA, 2003)

Caroline Peacock, *Good Web Guide to Genealogy* (Good Web Guide, 2003)

Sir Robert Joseph Phillimore, *The Ecclesiastical Law of the Church of England* (Henry Sweet, 1873)

J. S. Purvis, *An Introduction to Ecclesiastical Records* (St Anthony's Press, 1953)

Stuart A. Raymond, *Words from Wills and Other Probate Records 1500–1800, A Glossary* (Federation of Family History Societies, 2004)

Ann Rycraft, *Sixteenth and Seventeenth Century Wills, Inventories and Other Probate Documents* (Borthwick Institute of Historical Research, 1973)

Miriam Scott, *Prerogative Court of Canterbury Wills and Other Probate Records* (PRO, 1997)

Michael M. Sheehan, *The Will in Medieval England* (Pontifical Institute of Mediaeval Studies, Toronto, Studies and Texts No. 6, 1963)

Cecil Sinclair, *Tracing your Scottish Ancestors: A Guide to Ancestry Research in the Scottish Record Office* (The Stationery Office, revised edn 1997)

M. Doreen Slatter, 'The Records of the Court of Arches' (*Journal of Ecclesiastical History*, Vol. IV, 1953, pp. 139–53)

Peter Spufford (ed.), *Index to the Probate Accounts of England and Wales*, Part I: A–J, Part II: K–Z (British Record Society, 1999)

G. D. Squibb, *Doctors' Commons* (Clarendon Press, 1977)

Henry Swinburne, *A Brief Treatise of Testaments and Last Willes* (Companie of Stationers, 1611)

Anne Tarver, *Church Court Records: An Introduction for Family and Local Historians* (Phillimore, 1995)

W. E. Tate, *The Parish Chest* (Phillimore, 1983)

David Thomas, *Shakespeare in the Public Records* (HMSO, 1985)

Gerald Warner, *Being of Sound Mind: A Book of Eccentric Wills* (Elm Tree Books, 1980)

Colin Waters, *A Dictionary of Old Trades, Titles and Occupations* (Countryside Books, 2002)

C. C. Webb, *A Guide to Genealogical Sources in the Borthwick Institute of Historical Research* (University of York, 1981)

Dorothy Whitelock, *Anglo-Saxon Wills* (Cambridge University Press, 1930)

H. A. R. J. Wilson, *Executorship Law and Accounts* (Sir Isaac Pitman & Sons, 11th edn 1933)

Index